Dan and Noel winsomely invite us to cultivate a habit of believing the gospel. That means looking constantly to Christ Jesus alone for acceptance, assurance, and even adoption as the Father's sons. Our old habits of self-salvation die hard, but Dan and Noel make great spiritual wrestling coaches. Keep this book by your "prayer chair." Follow daily these 24 engaging encounters with Galatians and see how a *habit of Christ* will grow joyfully through you. Chock full of great quotes from both the old and the new masters of spiritual insight, *Live in Liberty* flows with a fresh writing style, knitting us in mind and heart to two companions along the way of grace.

Rev. Dr. Gerrit Dawson
senior pastor, First Presbyterian Church, Baton Rouge, Louisiana;
author, *The Blessing Life: A Journey to Unexpected Joy* and
Jesus Ascended: The Meaning of Christ's Continuing Incarnation

St. Paul's passionate defense and explanation of the new life and freedom that we have in Christ is the heart of his Letter to the Galatians. In this book Daniel Bush and Noel Due reignite this message—affirming that Christ brings to humans hearts and lives freedom, life, hope, and peace. This book will inform and inspire readers who delight in the gospel.

Rev. Noel Noack
bishop, Lutheran Church of Australia, Queensland District

Adopting a reading of Galatians from the traditional perspective of Luther's "law and gospel" dialectics, the authors bring refreshing significance of the central message of justification by faith to the modern readers. Through the exposition of the epistle, they direct us to look beyond ourselves, pointing constantly to the gracious God who calls us to freedom, to the loving Christ who was crucified for us and to the enabling Spirit who transforms us.

Rev. Dr. Luke Cheung
vice-president and professor of New Testament,
China Graduate School of Theology, Hong Kong;
author, *The Genre, Composition and Hermeneutics of James*

In twenty-four well-written, easily digestible chapters, Daniel and Noel unpack for us the deep truths of Paul's words in Galatians that we may apply it to our minds and souls. I trust you will be as blessed reading this as I was and through it discover the key to joy and peace with God in Galatians as Luther had.

Rev. Dr. Terry Kee Buck Hwa
bishop, Lutheran Church in Singapore;
former missionary to Thailand;
former pastor, Bedok Lutheran Church

If you are tired of doing church or have quit church-going because you've been hurt once too often, if you have lost your early Christian joy or simply feel dirty in your sin, this is a must-read for you. In a fresh and engaging way, and writing out of their own rich experience of God's grace, the authors help to bring the message of Galatians alive to a modern audience as they highlight the centrality and transforming power of the grace of God manifest in the all-sufficiency of Christ for cleansing, salvation, renewal, and the whole of life—the Christ in and through whom we are brought into the loving embrace of the Father and by whose Spirit we are able to exult forever in the knowledge of "Abba," our Father who loves us with the same love he has always had for his eternal Son!

Rev. Hector Morrison
principal and lecturer in Old Testament, Highland Theological College,
Inverness, Scotland;
former pastor, Barvas Church of Scotland, Isle of Lewis

Dan and Noel take us on a joy-filled journey through the Letter to the Galatians, drenching us with God's grace and gospel freedom along the way. Their compass is the total love of God in Jesus, his all-fulfilling death and resurrection, and the Spirit-filled life of faith. Exploring the collected witness of generations of believers, they help us reengage with the message of the God who loves us unconditionally. Readable, accessible, and digestible, *Live in Liberty* is a great companion for any reader who wants to dive deeper into the message of this most vital biblical letter.

Rev. John Henderson
national bishop, Lutheran Church of Australia (LCA) and New Zealand (LCNZ);
former principal, Australian Lutheran College;
former general secretary, National Council of Churches in Australia

If you hear "gospel" and think "old news," if you hear "grace" and feel boredom, if your Christian walk is more duty than delight, you need a fresh treatment of Paul's passionate, powerful letter to the churches of Galatia. Daniel Bush and Noel Due's *Live in Liberty* preaches, vividly and soundly, to our all-too-self-reliant hearts the liberating truth of Christ's cross and righteousness and the transformative power of Christ's Holy Spirit. In contrast to legalists' suspicions and antinomians' preferences, Bush and Due show that the freedom that Jesus gives from the law's conditions and condemnation does not foster self-indulgence, but rather promotes genuine, hearty love for God and others. I am pleased to recommend this fresh, pastoral exposition of Galatians.

Rev. Dr. Dennis E. Johnson
professor of practical theology, Westminster Seminary California;
associate pastor, New Life Presbyterian Church, Escondido, California;
author, *Him We Proclaim: Preaching Christ from All the Scriptures*

I keep having to leave behind the self-justifying flesh and rest by faith in the righteousness. There's never a day without a battle not to dispense with faith-in-Christ as the only way to live with God and stay sane. I am not alone in this! Those whom I pastor and to whom I preach, along with me, constantly face the "Galatian Problem" of becoming bewitched by the non-gospel of religion. In fact it's the keenest and most committed people in my church who face it the most! Its like we've created a whole culture of "ministry" and "service," of virtue and apparent maturity, that is in fact a carefully ordered and cherished system for dispensing with faith in Christ and replacing it with faith in our religious works. And you can have an apparently successful church on this system—amazing! Horrendous!! We need Dan Bush and Noel Due's careful, lively, and richly layered book. Searching and thorough exegesis of the text of Galatians is coupled with deeply reflective awareness of the life of the Christian in the church. Read this, and you'll find yourself constantly drawn to worship God and fortified in your faith by the sheer wonder of the gospel.

Rev. Dominic Smart
senior pastor, Gilcomston Church, Aberdeen, Scotland;
visiting lecturer, Highland Theological College;
author, *When We Get It Wrong: Peter, Christ and Our Path Through Failure* and
Grace, Faith, and Glory: Freedom in Christ

Daniel and Noel present insights and an inspiring message on the Letter to the Galatians. They provide biblically sound, quality scholarship in understandable language, communicating clearly the Scripture's thrust to God's people today. The book will hold the interest of common readers and provide pastors and Bible teachers with much material. I highly recommend it! May God bless many through these pages in the days to come.

Dr. Suresh Vemulapalli
director, India Village Ministries, Andhra Pradesh, India

You have in your hands a book written in love about an epistle that Luther described as having been written with "a pen dipped in fire." Whilst not a technical commentary, it does what all commentaries should do: It clearly and faithfully expounds the meaning and implications of the Word of God in Scripture. Moreover, it does so in a way that is heart-warming as well as being accessible to both pastors and their people. *Live in Liberty* will not only help readers to come to grips with the truth and grace of the gospel, but will, I am confident, send them on their way rejoicing.

Rev. Rob Smith
lecturer in theology, Sydney Missionary & Bible College, Sydney;
minister at St Andrew's Cathedral, Sydney;
author of *Justification and Eschatology: A Dialogue with "The New Perspective on Paul"*

Every Christian needs to grasp what was at stake when Paul wrote his Letter to the Galatians because what was at stake was the gospel of God's saving grace to sinners in Christ and its implications. Daniel Bush and Noel Due address the issues with the clear understanding of theologians, with the clarity and simplicity of preachers, and with the passion of pastors who are concerned for the well-being of their flock. In clear, readable prose, Bush and Due lead the reader through this rather daunting letter with a light touch. The attentive reader will finish the book in no doubt about what the gospel is and with a heart full of praise to God for his great salvation by grace.

Rev. Dr. Alistair Wilson
principal and professor, Dumisani Theological Institute, King William's Town, South Africa;
associate professor of New Testament, North-West University, Potchefstroom;
editor, The Scottish Bulletin of Evangelical Theology;
author, *The God of Covenant: Biblical, Theological and Contemporary Perspectives*

Most Christians live their lives as if their justification depends on their sanctification: If I do and become all that I must do and become, God will love me and accept me. The message of Galatians is that God's love for sinners like you and me is one way—it is not dependent on what we do, but on what Jesus has done for us. Church should be the one place in all of society where the weary and heavy laden should be able to go and find rest. But all too often they get to-do lists. This needs to change. We need a new reformation. And that's why I love *Live in Liberty*. Thank you Noel and Dan for reminding me that "it is finished." I keep forgetting.

Rev. Tullian Tchividjian
director of ministry development, Willow Creek Presbyterian Church, Winter Springs, Florida

This spiritual commentary on Galatians by Dan Bush and Noel Due is filled with a passionate love for the gospel of Jesus Christ. While focusing primarily on the reality of justification by God's grace alone received by faith alone, Bush and Due also explore sanctification and the spiritual life, arguing that this too is to be experienced by God's grace through faith. In every case, the authors' love for Christ pours out, and their passion for life lived by faith in the crucified and risen Christ is evidenced on every page. Like Paul with the Galatians, Bush and Due fear that many evangelicals have left the gospel and have become enslaved again to law and legalism. Their goal of the full freedom of grace is urgently needed. This book promises to be a great help to many who need to drink deeply of the grace of God once again.

Dr. Steven C. Roy
associate professor of pastoral theology, Trinity Evangelical Divinity School;
author, *What God Thinks When We Fail: Finding Grace* and *True Success*

Dan Bush and Noel Due present a zealous defense of Galatians' emphasis on the preeminence of God's abounding grace. While grace is virtually always asserted in our preaching on entering into relationship with Christ, in some occasions that clarity becomes more clouded when emphasizing our life journey with Christ. What God does tragically morphs into an emphasis on what we should do. Bush and Due are unswerving in their encouragement that we recalibrate and fix the trajectory of our thinking on God's magnificent grace.

This volume offers a useful pastoral preaching resource, as well as a very usable teaching guide for lay-led study groups. I wish that it would have been available a year ago while preparing a series of messages for our congregation that focused on this letter of the Apostle Paul. I could easily see myself using this book as a text for a study on Galatians.

Seldom giving a review or reference do I have the privilege of being very autobiographical. However, several times while reading through these pages and assimilating the truth presented, I had flashbacks to when one of the authors—Dan Bush—was an elementary-age boy, who in worship on Sundays, would come forward and sit on the chancel steps for the children's message and, to the chagrin of his mother and the delight of his father, would pose questions that inevitably put me on the spot. For me, one of the great joys of reading this book was to have this articulate proclaimer of the Gospel remind one of his earliest pastors of "the marvelous grace of a loving Lord that exceeds our sin and guilt ... a grace that will pardon and cleanse within." May God be praised for what Dan and Noel have given us.

Dr. James E. Tuttle
senior pastor, First United Methodist Church of Saline, Michigan

Dan Bush and Noel Due provide us with a work that marvelously blends together solid biblical interpretation, sound theological grounding, and helpful practical application for Christian living. Without skimping on faithful exposition of Paul's Letter to the Galatians, the authors artfully integrate wisdom from a wide range of secondary sources to drive home the apostle's message. As a pastor who preaches to a local congregation on a weekly basis, I gladly will take up and read Bush and Due when preparing to proclaim the good news from Galatians to listeners. *Live in Liberty* is a welcome contribution to bringing the Word of God alive to the people of God.

Rev. Dr. Timothy Janiszewski
lead pastor, Mt. Lebanon Evangelical Presbyterian Church,
Mt. Lebanon, Pennsylvania

In our time, when truth is taken as relative and authentic faith is, once again, centered on personal experience, St. Paul's Letter to the Galatians provides important theological insight into our personal quest for holiness. Cowriters Dan Bush and Noel Due bring to light the complete and total freedom of the gospel and the centrality of salvation by grace alone in Christ alone. Everyday Christians will benefit from this book's rigorous and rich study of Paul's letter, as each page leads the reader into a deeper understanding of the gospel and its application to everyday life.

Rev. Brenton Fiedler
pastor, Good Shepherd Lutheran Church,
Toowoomba, Queensland, Australia

Dan and Noel take us on a joy-filled journey through the Letter to the Galatians, drenching us with God's grace and gospel freedom along the way. Their compass is the total love of God in Jesus, his all-fulfilling death and resurrection, and the Spirit-filled life of faith. Exploring the collected witness of generations of believers, they help us reengage with the message of the God who loves us unconditionally. Readable, accessible, and digestible, *Live in Liberty* is a great companion for any reader who wants to dive deeper into the message of this most vital biblical letter.

Rev. John Henderson
national bishop, Lutheran Church of Australia (LCA) and New Zealand (LCNZ);
former principal, Australian Lutheran College;
former general secretary, National Council of Churches in Australia

There is arguably no clearer presentation of the gospel in the New Testament than that provided by Paul's Letter to the Galatians—but commentaries on that gospel are still needed for each new generation and context where circumcision and dietary laws are not issues, but legalism in its other forms is well and truly alive. *Live in Liberty* is such a commentary which can awaken twenty-first century readers of Galatians to an even clearer understanding of the gospel than the letter alone might deliver.

Rev. Andrew Jaensch
Lutheran studies coordinator, Australian Catholic University;
lecturer of educational theology, Australian Lutheran College

This skillful exposition of Paul's Epistle to the Galatians oscillates between two terms: "reformation" and "self-reformation." It is an ancient tension, and it is still with us. Relief is found in Christ and his cross. In every generation, the church threatens to lose the good news. This gripping book helps readers rediscover it. It deserves to find wide use among earnest seekers, study groups and college classrooms.

Rev. Dr. Robert W. Yarbrough
professor of New Testament, Covenant Theological Seminary, St. Louis, Missouri;
author, *1, 2, and 3 John* (Baker Exegetical Commentary on the New Testament)

I never set out purposefully to change the gospel. When I first came to Christ with my sin and stupidity, what I found in the gospel humbled and amazed me. I found that because Jesus loved me, he paid the price for all of my sin; he wrapped me in his own righteousness; he reconciled me to God and gives me his Spirit to keep me close. So when I came to him, I was filled with a joy that surged through my life and swept fears and sins aside in its wake. Over years in the church, though, my joy ebbed. It seemed that the harder I tried, the more sermons I heard and preached, the faster I ran, the further I found myself from that first love. Never meaning to, I had somehow changed what I first heard while trying to do everything right. What a paradox!

Noel and Dan in this wonderful book reminded me again of what I already knew in my heart. The struggle to keep the gospel fresh in my heart is daily. The grace of God in Jesus is what brings new life, the love of God, new obedience, true liberty and joy. As they unfold the central message of joy in their commentary on Galatians, *Live in Liberty*, I found my heart encouraged to believe the gospel again today, even as a longtime believer. Since I am so prone to change the gospel in subtle ways, I need to hear it fresh everyday for each day's new moments of unbelief and self-righteousness. Thank you for the wonderful reminder of the power of the gospel when I put no trust in the flesh and instead trust Christ alone.

Rev. Josiah Bancroft
director of mission, Serge | World Harvest Mission;
former co-pastor, Grace Community Church,
Asheville, North Carolina

Also by Daniel Bush and Noel Due:

Embracing God as Father: Christian Identity in the Family of God

LIVE IN
LIBERTY

THE SPIRITUAL MESSAGE
OF GALATIANS

LIVE IN
LIBERTY

THE SPIRITUAL MESSAGE
OF GALATIANS

DANIEL BUSH & NOEL DUE

Foreword by Steve Brown

LEXHAM PRESS

Live in Liberty: The Spiritual Message of Galatians

Copyright 2016 Daniel Bush and Noel Due

Lexham Press, 1313 Commercial St., Bellingham, WA 98225
LexhamPress.com

Print ISBN 9781577996293
Digital ISBN 9871577996296
Study Guide Digital ISBN 9781577996989

Lexham Editorial Team: Lynnea Fraser, Abigail Stocker
Cover Design: Christine Gerhart
Typesetting: ProjectLuz.com

For
Kioni
&
Isaiah, Haruto, Flossie, Ellia, and Nelson

"If the Son sets you free, you will be free indeed."

(John 8:36)

"The Epistle to the Galatians is my epistle.
To it I am as it were in wedlock.
It is my Katherine."

—Martin Luther

CONTENTS

ACKNOWLEDGMENTS

God is the giver of all good things, not least good friends. This book would have been impossible without them.

No piece of writing falls complete from the sky. However much we might wish a first draft were the final edition, it refuses to be so. We're singularly grateful for friends who have taken the time to review our stammering and stuttering words and to suggest changes so they may be more easily understood.

We extend our most sincere appreciation and thanks to Kay Carney, who spent countless hours painstakingly proofreading each chapter and became an expert in the Chicago Manual of Style in the process. Thank you for your patience, exactitude, and invariably helpful suggestions. As one who has believed in this book and whose desire to see it in print has been as strong as ours, we hope that it lives up to your expectations.

To Hector Morrison, who has read each chapter, adorned the work by selecting the sidebars, commented on the text, and been eagle-eyed proofer to boot—thank you. Your heartfelt encouragement has blessed us throughout the project.

Lee Beckham, you have read so as to understand deeply, and then framed questions so as to aid others in following; yours has been a massive task that makes this book ever more useful than it might have been. We're indebted to you and so thankful that you chose to embark on this journey with us.

Steve Brown: a pastor, mentor, and friend. What can we say, except that God loves you, but don't let it go to your head!

FOREWORD

P aul Zahl wrote, "In life there are two governing principles that are at war with one another. The first is law; the second is grace. So powerful are these two principles, so virile and unquenchable, so captivating and irresistible, that all relationships, all human operations, simply lie down before them. The law crushes the human spirit; grace lifts it. The story of the Bible is the story of this perpetual war between law and grace."[1]

It really is a war and I've fought in that war most of my life. There is a degree of comfort in the realization that I'm not the first and I'm not alone. Not only that, there is even more comfort in the knowledge that God gave clear instructions to those of us who are in the battle. This book is about those instructions.

The battle is, of course, a personal one for me and for all of us. One time a man who attended a Bible conference where I was teaching came up to me after the last session and said, "Steve, all my life I've been hearing preachers and missionaries say they are sinners. Just wanted you to know that you're the first one I ever believed."

I really thought I would be better than I am. It's not that I haven't tried. You probably don't know anyone who wants to please God more than I do ... or anyone who fails at that effort more often. As my friend's grandson said, "Granddaddy, I can be good. I just can't be good enough long enough." When Paul wrote that he didn't understand his own sinful actions, he was speaking the universal language of all of us who fight in the battle. And when he spoke the truth that where sin abounded, grace abounded all the more and there was no condemnation for those who were in Christ, my heart leapt up and sang the "Hallelujah Chorus."

It's sometimes easy to forget. There are so many voices telling me I've failed, I've betrayed the name of Christ and I'm probably not even a Christian, that it's easy to want to run away or to fake it. Thus the battle. Luther's admonishment to us that we must "preach the gospel" to one another to prevent discouragement isn't a nice suggestion. It's an absolute necessity. Paul wrote to the Galatians, "For freedom Christ has set us free; stand firm therefore, and do not submit again to a yoke of slavery" (5:1).

But the battle isn't just a personal battle. The battle is a corporate battle. It's a battle that has a tendency to define the church and who we are. It's the place where standards (i.e., the law) are used to manipulate, control, and acquire power. I've been there, done that and wince when I think of it. I told people that I was concerned with the peace, unity and purity of the church and I was—at least in the beginning. But the heart is deceitful and my motives got confused.

I'll never forget the words of a note from a young woman who left the church I pastored years ago. "Steve," she wrote, "I'm leaving and I didn't want you to hear it from someone else. I just can't do it anymore. I've tried but I'm not good enough."

I tried to call but her phone line was disconnected. I never heard from her again but I think about her a lot. And when I think of her, I think of so many others who have remained in the church bathed in guilt and condemnation they can't share with anyone and those many others who simply gave up and left. If the battle between law and grace is lost in the church, the church will become just another religious, self-righteous institution trying to sell goods that nobody can use.

When Paul wrote in Galatians that he couldn't believe the people there had been "bewitched" (3:1) and when he expressed his fear that they had "fallen away from grace" (5:4), he was speaking from a pastor's heart and concerned about the battle taking place in the family.

The battle isn't just a personal and church battle either. It's a battle that has to do with the world. We're here for them. If the message is unclear and the gospel compromised, we have nothing of import to speak to anybody. Everybody preaches the law whether it's in a corporate employees' manual, from a platform at a political rally, or our mothers trying to urge us to be good. If our voice is no different except for the use of God words, we're just another voice calling those who are already burdened down by guilt, shame and condemnation to try harder and work more. The church isn't a moral improvement society and insofar as we become that, we have nothing to say to anybody that can be defined as good news.

Paul was a missionary called from his nice, religious, and law-saturated heritage to a world that desperately needed to hear the truth of God's unconditional grace and mercy. His call to "go to the Gentiles" (2:9) was nothing less than a call to go to the whole world with the only message he had—a message where "there is neither Jew nor Greek, there is neither slave nor free, there is neither male or female ... [but] heirs according to promise" (3:28–29).

The spiritual commentary you hold in your hands isn't just a nice religious book. Of the making of those books there is no end. It is, rather, a call to a battle.

Someone told me the other day about a woman who worked for an orthopedic surgeon. They were moving the office to a new location and she was charged with moving a number of office items, including a display skeleton used in the practice. She put the skeleton in the front seat of her car and draped the bony arm across her seat. When she stopped at a traffic light, she noticed the man next to her staring. She felt constrained to offer an explanation.

"I'm delivering him to my doctor's office."

"I hate to tell you this, lady," he replied, "but I think it's way too late."

Sometimes I think it's too late. I see so many falling prey to the modern Pharisees who (maybe even from good motives) preach "another gospel" than the one Paul preached in Galatians. That's the reason this book is so essential. It is a "before it's too late" commentary about principles of engagement in the most important battle of our time.

I pray to "Abba" (Gal 4:6) that what you read here will call you to rejoice in the gospel and then to determine in your heart to never shilly-shally in the battle.

Steve W. Brown
Orlando, Florida

PREFACE

Confederate cadets stationed near Charleston, South Carolina, fired across the bow of the *Star of the West*, a merchant steamship chartered by the US War Department to resupply a garrison at Fort Sumter, on January 9, 1861. Receiving the message loud and clear, the steamer turned about, only to be hit three more times by what were effectively the first shots of the American Civil War. The consequences of this short, one-sided scrimmage would prove to be enormous.

Such is also the case with what is likely the Apostle Paul's first letter, the Epistle to the Galatians. It's a short book, but the consequences of its teaching have been, and remain, truly enormous. And as the American Civil War would ultimately culminate in the preservation of the Union and the abolition of slavery, so Paul's letter secures both Christian freedom and the preservation of the Church's unity in the gospel.

His message of "grace alone through faith alone in Christ alone" remains essential. Not only is it the touchstone of Christian liberty, it's the lens through which we come to understand Paul's wider work and the engine which powers his teaching on the Christian life.

The church habitually loses the gospel. It's not a new problem—the many revivals and reformations sprinkled across church history speak to the problem loud and clear. Today, the gospel is taken for many things: God making us feel better, or his making us prosperous. Some equate it with a political program, while others confine it to merely substitutionary atonement—which is admittedly the hinge of the gospel, but not the whole door. Still others equate the gospel with laws for virtuous living; in fact, this confusion is so widespread that many look upon Christianity as a patrolman with a blackjack, come to put an end to all fun. All such perceptions paralyze the mission of the church: finding truly abundant and joyful life in Christ. Martin Luther saw this, and in his *Lectures on Galatians* (1535) he wrote, "For they suppose that the function of the Law is to justify. And that is the general opinion of human reason. ... Reason will not permit this extremely dangerous opinion to be taken away from it by any means at all, because it does not understand the righteousness of faith."[1]

As New Testament scholar Darrell Bock has said:

> If the church is in a fog on the gospel, then the church very much risks losing its reason for being. A misdirected gospel message robs the church of valuable momentum in the world. Nothing leads to stagnation more quickly than for an institution to forget why it exists. A plethora of messages from the church might lead to no message from the church. In sum, in many locales the gospel has gone missing, and wherever that takes place, the church suffers, God's people lose their way, and the world lacks what it so desperately needs—an experience of God's presence.[2]

Luther discovered the key to joy and peace with God in Galatians. So precious a discovery was it to him that he said, "The Epistle to the Galatians is my epistle. To it I am as it were in wedlock. It is my Katherine."[3] Under God's hand, Luther was the central driving force to recover the gospel in the second millennium.

All of this simply alerts us to the critical message Galatians contains—a message which must be heard and heeded again in our era. It takes us into the heart of an experience—the enjoyment of God's presence and everlasting peace—which sets us free to love and be loved. It's a light we can't afford to hide under the proverbial basket.

Why this commentary, in this style? Because Paul wrote the message of Galatians to a group of churches needing to be reformed, and because Luther discovered in Galatians a message that illuminated his own mind and soul and thus helped fuel the Protestant Reformation, Dan embarked upon a six-month journey into Paul's passionate defense of the gospel shortly after being called as a revitalizing pastor to a church in northern Kentucky. The sermon series that resulted became the genesis of this book. Noel, in turn, prepared his own research and thoughts on the 24 messages; this book is the result of an international, intensely collaborative process spanning more than two years.

Although this book expounds the whole of Galatians, this is not an academic commentary. Instead, we aim to draw out the spiritual message contained within Paul's words, showing you how to apply it to your mind and soul. We hope that, through this book, you may experience the presence of God as saints before us have.

Robert Farrar Capon tells of our forebears' discovery:

> The Reformation was a time when men went blind, staggering drunk because they had discovered, in the dusty basement of late medievalism, a whole cellar full of fifteen-hundred-year-old, two-hundred proof Grace—bottle after bottle of pure distillate of Scripture, one sip of which would convince anyone that God saves us single-handedly. The word of the Gospel—after all those centuries of trying to lift yourself into heaven by worrying about the perfection of your bootstraps—suddenly turned out to be a flat announcement that the saved were home before they started ... Grace has to be drunk straight: no water, no ice, and certainly no ginger ale; neither goodness, nor badness, not the flowers

that bloom in the spring of super spirituality could be allowed to enter into the case.[4]

We pray this book would be the door that leads to stumbling upon the delights in the cellar once more, that it participates in the coming of a new reformation, that you would discover herein both your need for repentance and the sweetness of grace. That in discovering the gospel anew, you would live in the liberty of God's grace.

GALATIANS 1:1–5

Paul, an apostle—not from men nor through man, but through Jesus Christ and God the Father, who raised him from the dead—and all the brothers who are with me,

To the churches of Galatia:

Grace to you and peace from God our Father and the Lord Jesus Christ, who gave himself for our sins to deliver us from the present evil age, according to the will of our God and Father, to whom be the glory forever and ever. Amen.

CHAPTER 1

BACK TO THE GOSPEL

To journey into the book of Galatians is to venture into a hostile and confused mob, where outbursts of anger, jealousy, and bitterness are vented in a chaotic cacophony. One voice cuts through the bedlam—"Back to the gospel." All stop to listen, but will all hear?

That voice is Paul's, and his announcement is broadcast to us no less than to the churches in southern Galatia, churches in the region of modern-day Turkey, nearest the Mediterranean Sea, that he had planted on his first missionary journey. Galatians may well be Paul's earliest letter, written about 15 years after Jesus' ascension, and it's charged with an emotional intensity we can't afford to miss. While the letter is profoundly pastoral, Paul isn't trying to be particularly "pastorally sensitive." He's confronting something extremely dangerous.

Agitators, likely Jewish Christians from Jerusalem, had entered the churches he'd already gained for Christ—avoiding unreached fields and the hardships of such work—undermining his authority, persuading the believers that Paul hadn't known Christ or been commissioned by him. As a consequence, they argued, Paul's message wasn't to be believed; his gospel was at best deficient, at worst heretical. Their line of attack might be imagined: "Who is Paul anyway? Wasn't he one of the last converted, if indeed he's been converted at all? We, however, are pupils of the true apostles. We saw Jesus perform miracles, we heard him preach. We're ministers of Christ. We've got the Holy Spirit—it's impossible we should err. Moreover, we're from the mother church; Paul is a rogue itinerant whose message undermines God's law and erodes holiness."

Like attorneys trying to discredit a witness, the personal attack was aimed at discrediting Paul's testimony: justification by grace alone, through faith alone. These agitators insisted that in addition to faith in Jesus, God required circumcision, kosher eating, and Sabbath observance. In other words, salvation required Christ *plus* the law of Moses. This was no mere difference of opinion. Paul's aim, then, is to take the Galatians back to the true gospel, to liberate them from the agitators' lies. Their message might have sounded good, but it actually led to a devilish combination of thought and action that would have negated grace and established Pharisaic legalism at the heart of the church.

Therefore, as Philip Ryken has astutely noted, "Galatians is a letter for recovering Pharisees. ... The Pharisees were hypocrites because they thought that what God would do for them depended on what they did for God."[1] So they diligently pursued worship, orthodoxy, and morality, but failed to grasp that God's grace can't be earned. The way out of Pharisaism is the gospel—that is, rejecting our own righteousness and trusting the sufficiency of Jesus'. This alone can transform the Galatians, and us, into "ex-Pharisees."

OUR ABIDING TENDENCY IS TO PERFORMANCE-BASED RELIGION

Ex-Pharisees, however, struggle to leave legalism behind. "God loves us," we say, yet we secretly feel his love and our salvation are contingent on how we are doing in the Christian life. We constantly want to base justification on sanctification, to take what is free and slap a surcharge on it. Our abiding tendency is to performance-based religion, not knowing how to live by grace. Or we fear a message solely of grace will devalue God's standards.

Martin Luther knew our struggle. He was also an ex-Pharisee:

> I was a good monk and kept my order so strictly that I could claim that if ever a monk were able to reach heaven by monkish discipline I should have found my way there. All my fellows in the house, who knew me, would bear me out in this. For if it had continued much longer I would, what with vigils, prayers, readings and other such works, have done myself to death.[2]

Luther's conscience bothered him. He thought he wasn't good enough for God. The breakthrough came when he discovered Christianity wasn't about what he had to do for God, but about what God had done for him—Christ crucified.

The free grace of God in Christ, received by faith, was the theme of Luther's *Lectures on Galatians*, which he began by saying:

> I do not seek [my own] active righteousness. I ought to have and perform it; but I declare that even if I did have it and perform it, I cannot trust in it or stand up before the judgment of God on the basis of it. Thus I ... embrace only ... the righteousness of Christ ... which we do not perform but receive, which we do not have but accept, when God the Father grants it to us through Jesus Christ.[3]

The attack on Paul's authority, therefore, was an attack on the gospel. In reply, Paul lifts his voice with passion, not simply to defend his apostolic calling but to preach the gospel again to his beloved Galatian converts. Liberation from legalism lies in seeing God's grace not only as completely sufficient for salvation, but also as the wellspring for every facet of life.

LIBERATION FROM LEGALISM LIES IN SEEING GOD'S GRACE AS THE WELLSPRING FOR EVERY FACET OF LIFE

A MESSENGER SENT

The emotional intensity of Paul's greeting demands we pay full attention to the rest. His apostolic urgency can be gleaned from what is absent from the greeting, in addition to what is included.

Unlike his other letters, this one contains no commendation of the church, no notice of evidence of grace among them, and no expression of thanksgiving for them. Indeed, throughout the letter we meet a brusquely direct tone: "I am astonished," he writes in 1:6; "O foolish Galatians! Who has bewitched you?" in 3:1. And in rapid fire in chapter 4, Paul says, "I am afraid I may have labored over you in vain" (4:11); "Have I then become your enemy by telling you the truth?" (4:16); "My little children, for whom I am again in the anguish of childbirth until Christ is formed in you!" (4:19). This is no warm, fuzzy letter. Paul's not trying to be affable; he's concerned with the gospel's integrity. That integrity was wrapped up with his authority as an apostle, a position he was forced to defend.

The Greek word *apostolos*, from which we get "apostle," simply means "one who is sent," a title used to denote commissioned representatives. But the early Christians, both Jews and Gentiles, mainly understood it as applying to those who spoke with Christ's authority. The title was reserved for the Twelve and a couple of others who had been eyewitnesses of Christ's ministry and whom he appointed through the agency of the Spirit (e.g., Acts 1:16–26). In using the term in his letters, Paul shows "that while there were apostles *before* him, there were no apostles *after* him. According to Paul he is both 'the least' and 'the last' of the apostles."[4]

The point was that New Testament apostles weren't self-selected; hence Paul's status as an apostle was hotly contested by his opponents. Who really spoke with true apostolic authority? Paul's defense effectively proceeds thus: "No matter how much these vipers may brag, their provenance is lacking. They may boast that they have come either 'from men'—that is, on their own, without any call—or 'through men'—that is, being sent by someone else. But as for me, I have been called and sent neither *from* men nor *through* men but by Jesus Christ. In every way my call is like that of the apostles, and I am indeed an apostle." He didn't need the support of those who agreed, such as those in Antioch—Paul refers only to Jesus and the Father.

When Jesus revealed himself to Paul on the Damascus road, Paul became an eyewitness to his ministry. And it was there he was also commissioned, according to the book of Acts:

> Now as he went on his way, he approached Damascus, and suddenly a light from heaven shone around him. And falling to the ground he heard a voice saying to him, "Saul, Saul, why are you persecuting me?" And he said, "Who are you, Lord?" And he said, "I am Jesus, whom you are persecuting. But rise and enter the city, and you will be told what you are to do." ... Now there was a disciple at Damascus named Ananias. The Lord said to him in a vision, "Ananias." And he said, "Here I am, Lord." And the Lord said to him, "Rise and go to the street called Straight, and at the house of Judas look for a man of Tarsus named Saul, for behold, he is praying, and he has seen in a vision a man named Ananias come in and lay his hands on him so that he might regain his sight." But Ananias answered, "Lord, I have heard from many about this man, how much evil he has done to your saints at Jerusalem. And here he has authority from the chief priests to bind all who call on your name." But the Lord said to him, "Go, for he is a chosen instrument of mine to carry my name before the Gentiles and kings and the children of Israel. For I will show him how much he must suffer for the sake of my name" (Acts 9:3-6, 10-16; see also Acts 26:15-18).

If Paul's commission was so clear, why does he assert his apostleship so strongly? Was he a braggart, resentful of those who had stepped on his turf? No! He defended his apostolic calling because the gospel he carried to Galatia was in jeopardy. If he carried Christ's authority, his hearers would attend to his message. But if Paul wasn't an apostle—as his opponents implied—his message could be discarded. The defense of his calling was a defense of his message. He's not possessive; he's intensely passionate for the liberation and transformation of those to whom he preached the gospel.

A MESSAGE PROCLAIMED

C. J. Mahaney has suggested the liberating and transformative gospel can be traced along three lines.[5] These distinctions are helpful—so we want to linger on them below.

One: The Gospel Is God-Centered, Not Man-Centered

Paul wastes no time proclaiming where hope is really found. The hope of salvation is found only in grace. Grace forgives sin, and this alone leads to a peace that stills the conscience.

The law, and legalistic observance of it, accuses and terrifies; the more we sweat to extricate ourselves from sin, the worse off we are. Legal striving knows no end, provides no peace in the conscience, causes quietness to flee, robs our joy. Why? Doesn't striving *end* sin by making us better people? No, because salvation isn't man-centered; it's God-centered.

Notice *who* is emphasized in Galatians 1:1–5: not us, but God. The Father is mentioned thrice, the Son twice. When we are mentioned, it's in connection with our need for deliverance. Since we're incapable of altering our being, we're enslaved to the present evil age.

> SALVATION ISN'T MAN-CENTERED; IT'S GOD-CENTERED

The gospel's radical negation of ceaseless striving and hard work is unfathomable to us. Our thoughts can't produce it; our will doesn't originate it. It's otherworldly, "according to the will of our God and Father" (Gal 1:4). Christ suffered not because we are worthy, or because we moved him to act, but only because it was the will of God. "This Jesus, delivered up according to the definite plan and foreknowledge of God, you crucified and killed by the hands of lawless men," says Peter (Acts 2:23). It's hard to imagine a statement better calculated to oppose the intrusion of human will in salvation.

Divine grace, therefore, is God's unconditional goodwill toward humanity, irrespective of any human merit; it alone brings peace, a state of life enjoyed by those who have experienced this grace. Grace and peace are tied to Jesus' work, not ours.

Two: The Gospel Is Objective, Not Subjective

At the center of the gospel is the historical fact of Christ's substitutionary death upon the cross, his laying down his life freely. This was exactly how Jesus saw it; he said, "I lay down my life that I may take it up again. No one takes it from me, but I lay it down of my own accord" (John 10:17–18).

Jesus' death wasn't a simple display of love, nor was it an example of heroism. It was a sacrifice for sin. He laid down his life *for* ("on behalf of") his sheep (John 10:11). It's helpful to think of the cross as having two sides. The first side is that all of your sins were placed upon Jesus, and he endured the full wrath of God against them. The other side is that all of Christ's righteousness was put into your account. God sees you mercifully through the blood of Christ. One side is God's wrath against sin; the other, his mercy extended to us. You are justified; you stand in a right relationship with God, not on the basis of what you have done, but on the basis of what Jesus did.

THE GOSPEL ...
IS NOT A
FEELING

The gospel, therefore, is not a feeling, not a subjective experience, not repentance and faith. All of these wonderful things correspond to the gospel, and the gospel brings them about. But they are not the gospel.

When the gospel is viewed subjectively it becomes exposed to interpretation and alteration. Mahaney puts it well: "When we view [the gospel] objectively we are invited to trust in God for a salvation that is gracious and free. When we view it subjectively we are compelled to work for a salvation that must be earned."[6] Such work can never transform our hearts; it leaves them stuck, endlessly striving. Yet the gospel transforms!

Transformation occurs precisely because when the gospel is viewed objectively, we're assured of God's love located in the person and saving event of Christ, which is outside us—not dependent upon us. But if we view the gospel subjectively, God's love is held captive to our emotions and becomes dependent upon our performance, which is never complete. Instead, let Jesus' words from the cross echo in your heart: "It is finished!" (John 19:30).

Three: The Gospel Is Complete

It is important to realize how sufficient and complete the gospel is. The more we know the grace of God in Christ, the more we see the severity of our own personal sin, as well as the evil age from which we're delivered.

If sin is just a mistake, it could be sorted out with a moral fitness plan like a weight-loss regime; a resolution could be made, knowledge gained, training obtained. Christ's death, however, speaks to the severity of my sin: *It is severe enough to require death.* In fact, sin is death. Death and sin are two sides of one ugly coin. Sin is death dealing to our relationship with God, to the knowledge of our true nature, and even to our physical bodies. God's giving us over to this penalty also demonstrates his utter holiness. Even the minutest, most mundane sin can't stay in his presence. Sin's severity isn't defined by comparing ourselves to others, but to the holiness of God.

Jesus also gave himself up "to deliver us from the present evil age" (Gal 1:4). Paul contrasts this current age with the coming kingdom of God. When the New Testament sets off nature from grace, flesh from Spirit, or the old man from the new man, it is making the same contrast. The present age is dominated by an ethos opposed to the will of God. We can't transform this age into the age to come. It must pass away, or we must pass from it.

Because it is all-embracing (affecting our mind, emotions, and will, as well as the very social, political, and economic systems we live in), we can't remove ourselves from it.

But Jesus can do what we cannot. He frees each of us from "the present evil age" by orienting us away from ourselves and toward God, birthing in us a radical change in thinking, feeling, and acting. He builds within each of us a longing for God and a passion to obey. This deliverance isn't, however, out of the physical world—remember Jesus' prayer, "I do not ask that you take them out of the world, but that you keep them from the evil one" (John 17:15)—it is liberation from the God-opposed spirit of the world.

The gospel is sufficient to deliver us both from the penalty of sin and from the present evil age. It is wholly complete; nothing can be added to it.

This is why Paul effectively says, "Submit to my authority" (the assertion of his apostleship in Galatians 1:1). At first glance, this command seems to contradict Galatians 1:4, which could be paraphrased, "Christ has been crucified; you are delivered from the world, from this age that holds you enslaved. Be free; don't be subject to anyone." Is this a contradiction? Submit to me, but don't be subject to anyone? It is surely a paradox, but it's solvable.

The freest people on earth are those who submit most humbly and thoroughly to Jesus, who says, "It is finished! My grace is sufficient for you" (John 19:30; 2 Cor 12:9).

Because the gospel is complete, Paul is intensely passionate to preserve what he preaches as an apostle of Christ. Add anything to the gospel—religion, feelings, obedience to biblical imperatives—and you nullify its sufficiency. It is complete—nothing else is needed. It is objective—standing true regardless of your feelings in a given moment. And it is God-centered—it's about what he has done, not what you do.

> ADD ANYTHING TO THE GOSPEL ... AND YOU NULLIFY ITS SUFFICIENCY

A Mercy Shown

The gospel effects a dramatic subjective experience that continues to deepen as we go.

Paul knows this experience better than most. He was a very pious Jew, more legalistic and Pharisaical than Martin Luther. His zeal for the law led him on a manhunt for Christians and made him an accomplice to murder, all with the aim of eradicating the church. He truly believed he was doing God's bidding, yet all the time he was battling *against* God. Similarly, we become enemies of God when we pursue the law as a way to merit God's favor or to fix other people. Paul, however, was changed from the inside when the Light of the world shone upon him and the Word of God spoke to him, saying, "Saul, Saul, why are you persecuting me?" (Acts 9:4).

As Paul recalls this and reflects on the mercy of God at Calvary, he cannot but break into doxology: "to whom be the glory forever and ever. Amen" (Gal 1:5).

This doxology isn't a statement of superfluous wordiness. It places the gospel above both criticism and self-glorification. Look again at who is uttering these concluding words: It is Paul, the zealous Pharisee who no longer boasts about his efforts or work but trusts in the gospel of Jesus Christ alone.

Luther somewhere said, "It is the purpose of all Scripture to tear us away from our works and bring us to faith." Paul was torn away by Jesus, as we are torn away by the Holy Spirit, who impresses the message of Jesus upon us. Paul glories only in the mercy of God, for he knows the grace and peace of being ripped away from his works of righteousness and his self-reliance.

Have you been severed from your acts of goodness, your acts of religion, your acts of morality as the basis of your acceptance to God? If not, then hear the message of Galatians!

GALATIANS 1:6–10

I am astonished that you are so quickly deserting him who called you in the grace of Christ and are turning to a different gospel—not that there is another one, but there are some who trouble you and want to distort the gospel of Christ. But even if we or an angel from heaven should preach to you a gospel contrary to the one we preached to you, let him be accursed. As we have said before, so now I say again: If anyone is preaching to you a gospel contrary to the one you received, let him be accursed.

For am I now seeking the approval of man, or of God? Or am I trying to please man? If I were still trying to please man, I would not be a servant of Christ.

CHAPTER 2

NO GOSPEL AT ALL

Paul's sense of pastoral urgency is as strong as his sense of astonishment. How can the Galatians turn to a different voice so quickly?

A surface reading might suggest Paul is an insecure control freak, not wanting anyone to muscle in on his patch. But nothing could be farther from the truth. His motivation is love, and he writes with fire to combat the death-dealing influence of the false teachers now plaguing the Galatians. It's not a choice between two equally valid "gospels." "Gospel" means "good news"—and there's *no other gospel* than that of the grace of God in Jesus Christ, the very thing that Paul proclaimed. This gospel is the voice of God, albeit delivered through Paul's person. Little wonder he was horrified by what was occurring.

DESERTING THE GOSPEL: ABANDONING CHRIST

The Galatians weren't turning away from a survey canvassing their opinions, or merely from one point of doctrine or another, but from the *person* who'd called them: "I am astonished that you are so quickly deserting him who called you" (1:6).

The voice they heard in the gospel was Christ's. He alone can proclaim what he's done, and—though the Spirit of Christ does it through human lips—*he* speaks. His sheep hear *his* voice (John 10:3, 4, 16, 27). But false shepherds had infiltrated the Galatian churches with loud and persuasive preaching, drowning out the "good news" and replacing it with something else. Just what this replacement looked like will become clear as we go through the letter; suffice it to say, it turned people away from the finished work of Christ, shouldering them with the burden of their own salvation.

At one level, it was a clash of doctrine. Paul's opponents were armed with strong doctrinal statements, which, as we'll see, Paul rebuts with strong doctrine of his own. Good doctrine is just as important as a reliable GPS—but, as the line on the screen only points to the actual street, doctrine points to a person: Christ. If it doesn't point to him, it's not good doctrine.

In this respect, Paul wouldn't have any time for the simplistic notion that "all you need is love." While he would agree that love is greatest of all, even above faith and hope (1 Cor 13:13), he wouldn't agree to toss out doctrine in order to find it. In fact, the opposite is the case; love flows *from* the gospel. And this loss of love was being borne out in the Galatians' own experience. The fruit of the Spirit (love, joy, peace, patience, etc.) was withering on the vine while the deeds of the flesh (immorality, bitterness, strife, etc.) were growing like weeds. This is why Paul is so vehement.

Heart transformation comes from encountering Jesus. Hear him, meet him, be loved by him, and you'll have your heart changed—and only changed hearts truly engage in unity and love. Jesus' prayer to the Father "that they will all be one, just as you and I are one ... and may they be in us so that the world will believe you sent me" (John 17:21 NLT) rests on the full power of his death and resurrection.

> ONLY CHANGED HEARTS TRULY ENGAGE IN UNITY AND LOVE

In other words, both the fruitfulness and direction of our Christian life are directly related to the gospel. Why? Because in the gospel we see God as our Father. To understand and trust the gospel is to understand and trust its Author.

In this, the gospel isn't afraid to confront us; God isn't sympathetic to our preferences, allowing us to work out our spiritual lives as we will. To desert the gospel is to leave the *person* behind it, to transfer allegiance; hence Paul's astonishment.

Paul's statements, therefore, are not exaggerated. The Judaizers (agitators) had "distorted" the gospel and by doing so had deeply "troubled" the Galatians (1:7). But none—not the most spectacular angelic messenger, nor even Paul himself—should be believed if they preach another so-called gospel. Instead, they should be "accursed" (1:8–9), because that's where their message leads.

For the Galatians, such desertion was a work in progress: "I am astonished that you are so quickly deserting" (1:6). Spiritual desertion is a slide—an ongoing present problem—into which Paul was speaking as he wrote. The reasons for this slide will become even clearer as we go, but it essentially stems from losing focus on the fixed and final point of salvation—Christ.

It's easier to lose sight of that fixed point than we would like to think. Have you ever gone swimming in the ocean? When Dan was a preteen, his family took a trip to Cocoa Beach, Florida. While body surfing on the waves, he was caught in the longshore drift and ended up a quarter mile down the beach, out of sight of his family's umbrella. It's the same with spiritual desertion; all it takes is turning our eyes away from the fixed point of the cross, and we're lost—seeking a relationship with God on the ground of our merit. As pastor and theologian Sinclair Ferguson wrote, "The glory of the gospel is that God has declared Christians to be rightly related to him in spite of their sin. But our greatest temptation is to try to smuggle character into his work of grace."[1]

The true gospel, says Paul in Acts, is "the gospel of the grace of God" (Acts 20:24). This isn't an admixture of man's character and work or an alloy of a bit of human effort and a bit (or even a lot) of God's grace. Hunting for the "what do I dos" is pursuing law-keeping as my means of salvation; it's deserting the gospel of grace; it's abandoning Christ.

Distorting the Gospel: Opposing Christ

The Judaizers' message wasn't "good news." If you had been there, you would have heard a hard and challenging word based, chapter and verse, on the Old Testament. You could respond to alleviate your sense of shame—by deeper commitment, more rigorous discipline, and promises of greater obedience—and thus be launched into a world of competitive self-righteousness. With a conscience clouded by guilt, you'd become judgmental, legalistic, and hard. You'd start to despise the man who first told you that believing in Jesus was freedom. Anything you heard would add more weight to your backpack as you were force-marched through God's boot camp. Then, desperate for air, you would kick over the traces and become completely licentious.

Legalism and licentiousness aren't opposites; they're just different expressions of the same hostility to grace. Going the Judaizers' way, you'd have to perform well enough for God to save you—and then ensure you worked hard enough at being godly to keep his love for you alive.

Go ahead and try it. You'll fail, no matter how hard you strive. Just try controlling your tongue, or your thoughts behind it, for a day. Anger, self-pity, frustration, sarcasm, complaint, criticism and so on find their way from the heart to the tongue. A man might control his tongue for a week by taking a vow of silence, but what would this prove? The law doesn't merely apply to our actions; it also applies to our thoughts and our motives. In the Sermon on the Mount, Jesus basically said, "You're all stuck, you're all in a pickle. Your thoughts, motives, and your actions make you all guilty. None of you is clean, none of you is pure." Or, in the words of James, "Whoever keeps the whole law and yet stumbles in one point has become accountable for all of it" (Jas 2:10).

Redoubling effort doubles failure—not only because striving is depressingly ineffective, but also because our efforts move us decidedly away from reliance on Christ's righteousness.

So: Live by the law, and you'll know insecurity, not security; panic, not peace. Like Luther, you'll discover that even repentance isn't good enough, for it's tainted with the motive of recommending yourself to God. How do you know if even your repentance is sincere or complete? Luther discovered the truth: It's neither! That's why grace is the only hope. That's why Paul burst into doxology: "To *God* be the glory, forever and ever, Amen!" (Gal 1:5).

Those troubling the Galatians were saying, "You need Christ; you need to be on that team. But what really makes the whole thing work is how hard you yank on your bootstraps. It's what you do for God that counts." And if we're honest, we probably speak this way (to ourselves and others) far more than we'd like to admit. Do you see how distorted this picture of the gospel is? Because from this view, there's no true end to the boot tightening. Where do you find hope that your laces won't become untied as you walk? When do you know that you've done enough work? How do you know you've prayed enough, said the right prayers, used the right words, had the right motive, prayed out of a pure enough heart? And, worse still, because it is a gospel of self-effort—with you and your commitment at the center, rather than Christ—it can never lead to true adoration, only to self-righteousness. It spawns pride, not doxology.

Grace undercuts all human pride, so we don't really want it. We want reward and glory—and grace doesn't give us these. So we functionally oppose Christ because our hearts will not allow us to be totally, radically, and completely wrong. We still want an island—even a little one—on which we can plant our flag and recommend ourselves to God and each other. Who gets the glory if we follow a legalistic,

> GRACE
> UNDERCUTS ALL
> HUMAN PRIDE

self-justifying path? We do. Yet Paul is adamant: The glory belongs to "God the Father ... forever and ever" (Gal 1:4–5).

For those who turn the gospel upside down, Paul has strong words: "Let them be accursed." This statement really is "*anathema*"—i.e., "Let God's judgment fall on them."

Isn't Paul a bit harsh? It might seem so in an age of tolerance. But he's in line with a comment of Jesus': "Whoever causes one of these little ones who believe in me to sin, it would be better for him if a great millstone were hung around his neck and he were thrown into the sea" (Mark 9:42). Paul's in line with Christ because *we* are the little ones, children of God. Turning the gospel upside down causes me to sin because it causes me to trust in myself instead of Christ. Therefore, the harshness is fitting—so Paul repeats himself.

> But even if we or an angel from heaven should preach to you a gospel contrary to the one we preached to you, let him be accursed. As we have said before, so now I say again: If anyone is preaching to you a gospel contrary to the one you received, let him be accursed (Gal 1:8–9).

Don't we need to obey the law, do some righteous things? Ah, that's the stealth of it. Legalism gains its power by appealing to the Christian's passion to obey God, to fulfill the law. But it also appeals to the sinful passion within us that wants to earn our acceptance before God. There is a place for active righteousness, but it's got nothing to do with your standing before God. If you drive down Interstate 75 at 88 miles an hour, you won't end up *Back to the Future* in 2025—but you will have a red light in your rearview mirror. Though you cry out, "I'm righteous in Christ," the state trooper will still give you a ticket. But your obedience to the law in any of its forms isn't what saves you, nor does it keep God loving you. He loved you even before you knew the obedience of faith. Obedience is only ever a thankful response to being saved, and if anything—even obedience—is added to the equation of grace, it's no longer grace. We can't get the gospel a little bit wrong; to distort its freedom results in losing it entirely.

Only Christianity places grace at the center of salvation; every other worldview places obedience to the law at the center. Jesus nipped a "law versus grace" question in the bud when he was asked: "What must we *do*, to be doing the works of God?" He responded, "This is the work of God, that you *believe* in him whom he has sent" (John 6:28–29). Justification is based on faith in Christ's work, not faith in yours.

> "THIS IS THE WORK OF GOD, THAT YOU BELIEVE IN HIM" (JOHN 6:28–29)

We have likely heard others—or ourselves—tell pastors or friends, "You keep telling me about the gospel. I know the gospel. I believe the gospel. But I don't see how it applies to my situation. Give me something that's going to really help, tell me what to do!" But what that's really saying is that God isn't enough for our problems. It's opposing Christ, rejecting his sufficiency for all our needs, blinded from the the gospel by the cloud of our own self-righteousness.

Defending the Gospel: Serving Christ

The harshness of Paul's words show he's not concerned about pleasing men and women. Nevertheless, some felt he was preaching a law-free gospel to please people and reel them in—a fantastic deal, too good to be true.

Maybe you were like us growing up: your mother made you eat breakfast cereal every morning, and you, in turn, nagged her to send away for the free gifts advertised on the box. You know the sorts of things: plastic toys, magic tricks, Captain Crunch iron-ons. But there was fine print; to get the prize, you had to send in 10 UPC symbols and 5 dollars for shipping and handling. It wasn't really free.

The Judaizers saw themselves as cleaning up Paul's mess by reading the fine print for the Galatians. But grace isn't easier to believe in than the law. Our hearts are constantly warring against it, yelling, "That's mine; I did that!" We want something we can point to.

We are daily engaged in "stealth warfare." The stealthy tendency of the flesh is constantly present—attempting to smuggle character into the mix; to recommend ourselves to God; to compare ourselves with others. This leads to defeat. When we're full of self-pity because we're not yet perfect, or beat ourselves up to atone for our failure, or work hard to justify ourselves in the eyes of others, we've taken our eyes off Christ. We've given an ear to another voice. Spiritual depression enters through this route. So we need to defend the gospel in our own hearts, and even more in the hearts of one another. Hearing the absolving word from the lips of another human being is more powerful than hearing it from our own inner voice. Faith comes by *hearing* (Rom 10:17)—not just at our first encounter with the gospel, but as the staple of the Christian life.

Preaching the gospel to ourselves—and to each other—is serving Christ. To be as unbending as Paul over the nature and substance of the gospel is not intolerance, it's service to Christ. To defend the gospel isn't to push the law on each other but to lead each other to Jesus. To defend the gospel is to fight against the subtle tendency to confuse law with grace. Luther said, "The law says, 'do this,' and it is never done. Grace says, 'believe in this,' and everything is already done."[2]

What's your emotional state tied to? Is it tied to what you did or didn't do yesterday, or even what someone else did or didn't do this morning? Are you enjoying the gospel, or is it a stale side dish? Are you satisfied with the gospel, or are you starving for a different meal? Do you fully taste the sweetness of the gospel?

To hand each other the freeing message of the gospel is to serve Christ by pointing one another to him. For there is no gospel at all outside or beyond his grace—Christ is enough!

For I would have you know, brothers, that the gospel that was preached by me is not man's gospel. For I did not receive it from any man, nor was I taught it, but I received it through a revelation of Jesus Christ. For you have heard of my former life in Judaism, how I persecuted the church of God violently and tried to destroy it. And I was advancing in Judaism beyond many of my own age among my people, so extremely zealous was I for the traditions of my fathers. But when he who had set me apart before I was born, and who called me by his grace, was pleased to reveal his Son to me, in order that I might preach him among the Gentiles, I did not immediately consult with anyone; nor did I go up to Jerusalem to those who were apostles before me, but I went away into Arabia, and returned again to Damascus.

Then after three years I went up to Jerusalem to visit Cephas and remained with him fifteen days. But I saw none of the other apostles except James the Lord's brother. (In what I am writing to you, before God, I do not lie!) Then I went into the regions of Syria and Cilicia. And I was still unknown in person to the churches of Judea that are in Christ. They only were hearing it said, "He who used to persecute us is now preaching the faith he once tried to destroy." And they glorified God because of me.

CHAPTER 3

NOT MAN'S GOSPEL

R eading Paul is like hearing one side of a telephone call—you don't directly catch the other voice, but you can still follow the conversation. The final part of this chapter, together with what we know from his other letters, gives a pretty clear picture, but to understand much of what happens next, we need some context.

BACKGROUND FROM PAUL'S TIME

The Pharisees were one of the three main religious parties in Judaism (the others being the Sadducees and Essenes). The Sadducees were theologically liberal, belonged to the aristocracy, and were in bed with the Romans; the Essenes had declared a plague on both their houses, having retreated to the desert to wait for God and perfect holiness. The Pharisees were the conservative students of the law and Israel's history. They were highly visible, vocal, and sometimes violent. Zeal was their watchword. If you were to be stoned to death, a Pharisee would be the one to pick up the first rock. In many ways, they were Judaism's Puritans—theologically literate, concerned that the law be honored, and methodical in its observance. And the flesh is never uglier than when it's dressed for worship, wearing its religious face.

Paul had been a strict Pharisee and the son of a Pharisee. His zeal was white hot.

Though born a free Roman citizen, Paul—then known as Saul—was Jewish through and through, a Hebrew's Hebrew (Phil 3:5). He'd been educated in the university city of Tarsus, was multilingual, had a towering intellect, knew the Hebrew Scriptures inside out, and had studied under one of Judaism's most revered teachers, Gamaliel. He was an Ivy League religious lawyer and saw himself as *the* defender of the faith.

But during one of Saul's crusades against the church, the Light of the World blinded him and spoke to him (Acts 9:1–22; see also Acts 22:1–21; 26:12–23). Jesus not only called Saul to account, he called him to be his servant. He who thought he saw so clearly was led meekly into the city, where he waited in darkness for three days. On the third day he rose a new man, with a new name and a new mission. Everything he believed was turned inside out. The rest of his life would be spent defending the very gospel he once sought to destroy.

All of this brings us to the passage at hand. Paul was very clear about his apostolic authority: "For I did not receive [the gospel] from any man, nor was I taught it, but I received it through a revelation of Jesus Christ" (1:12). While this essentially repeats Galatians 1:1 ("Paul, an apostle—not from men nor through man, but through Jesus Christ"), the very repetition stresses the high stakes. The agitators were trying to torpedo his apostolic authenticity.

You can hear the echo of their words. "Paul's not a true apostle, but a trainee, and he's botched the teaching," they might have said. "He's not from the mother church at Jerusalem as we are. He's spent his so-called-ministry in the boondocks, and no one of consequence wants to know him. If he were genuine, he'd be at the center of things, like us!" To this, Paul responds, "The gospel that was preached by me is not man's gospel—I didn't botch it up! And my story proves it."

God unveiled his power through Paul's transformation. In the gospel God breaks in from the outside, captures us, radically reorienting our worldview. It's a Copernican revolution of the soul, where the Son is suddenly at the center. If the gospel came merely from man—from inside our humanity—it would only extend and display the current heart of man; it couldn't forge a new one.

By contrast, the false teachers' message is "man's gospel"; it caters to self-assertion. The flesh, the old nature, always prefers self-reliance and self-protection. It wants to avert wagging fingers and establish its own righteousness. It's intriguing that one possible

> IN THE GOSPEL
> GOD CAPTURES
> US, RADICALLY
> REORIENTING
> OUR
> WORLDVIEW

derivation of the word "Pharisee" is "one who specifies"—that is, who points the finger, nominating who's in and who's out, who's righteous and who's not. The false teachers were using the Old Testament law (especially circumcision, dietary requirements, and Sabbath observance) as the basis for their specifying. They wanted Paul's Gentile converts to become observant Jews—and declared it to be the only way for them to become completely legitimate members of God's family.

The gospel Paul preached has been under fire since the very beginning. Even Thomas Jefferson said, "Paul was the great Coryphaeus, and first corrupter of the doctrines of Jesus."[1] Wherever the gospel is truly preached it will come under fire, because its message crucifies the flesh: Your self-assertion and self-reliance get you nowhere with God. False gospels, however, appeal to the flesh: You get somewhere with God when you get all of the steps right.

Let's be honest. You probably haven't had someone enter your church demanding that the men be circumcised and that you only eat kosher food. Although we don't dance to that tune, there's no shortage of people "specifying" which dance steps *are* acceptable. Or whether it's acceptable to dance at all!

Our flesh wants a hill—any hill—on which to raise our flag. Self-help books sell so well for a reason; we desperately want to get the steps right, and prove to ourselves and others that we are a success. But the true gospel opposes this, calling out this false salvation. It's bondage—not liberty.

It's a hard truth to hear. The sinful human heart wants to be at the center. It desperately believes it's not *that* sinful and, therefore, can make itself righteous any time it chooses.

But the gospel is God's grand "no" to all human pride, religion, self-trust, and self-assertion. It's his "no" to your conviction that you can fix things. In other words, to hear the gospel—even to hear it deeper and louder—you have to give up reliance on yourself, confess your true poverty and powerlessness.

This is what Paul's biography shows: He confesses the power of the gospel by confessing his own powerlessness. Paul's story proclaims that the gospel doesn't come from men. They preach power, not poverty. The gospel is from Jesus Christ. God's blessing is "yes" in Jesus alone—and that "yes" is simultaneously his "no" to all human religion, law-keeping, and attempts at holiness. The gospel refutes human ambition; it alone brings glory to God.

THE GOSPEL REFUTES HUMAN AMBITION

There is a solid reason to believe Paul's gospel over that of the Judaizers. Had tradition and law-keeping brought true salvation, Paul wouldn't have turned from them; he more than anyone had grounds to boast. In Philippians, he says:

> If anyone else thinks he has reason for confidence in the flesh, I have more: circumcised on the eighth day, of the people of Israel, of the tribe of Benjamin, a Hebrew of Hebrews; as to the law, a Pharisee; as to zeal, a persecutor of the church; as to righteousness under the law, blameless (Phil 3:4-6).

No emotional state or psychological device was going to unseat Paul's mind. Moreover, he says in Galatians, "I was advancing in Judaism beyond many of my own age among my people, so extremely zealous was I for the traditions of my fathers" (Gal 1:14). The book of Acts records this zeal: "I not only locked up many of the saints in prison after receiving authority from the chief priests, but when they were put to death I cast my vote against them" (Acts 26:10). The only court that had such power was the Jewish Sanhedrin, the supreme court of 71 members. So there is reason to believe Paul was quite possibly the youngest member of the Sanhedrin, casting his vote in the court. It also explains how he managed to obtain a letter from the high priest to arrest Christians in Damascus. If traditions and law-keeping were the ticket to success, Paul had several. He'd been far more vigorous than the false teachers who were bothering the Galatian churches, so on that score they could teach him nothing.

It's common in the church to say that "this is the way we've always believed; this is the way we've always acted." It's common to see tradition and law-keeping as the infallible rule and to judge ourselves against them as a barometer of our standing with God. Moreover, we like the approval of men because it doesn't go to the depth of our hearts. But when God comes, his gospel confronts us with who he *really* is, and in that light, we're confronted with who we really are.

> HIS GOSPEL CONFRONTS US WITH WHO HE REALLY IS, AND WHO WE REALLY ARE

Tradition and law-keeping are preferred because they're safe. They tell us how to avoid shame, and we've got *so* much invested in them. Paul realized that if Christianity was right, it would blow his Pharisaism to smithereens. It would call his world and life view into question. This was the gas line fueling his fiery, murderous contempt of Christians. And aren't we often ignited by the same fuel? We're so inflamed by others' failure because it calls our lives and traditions into question. It puts us on the spot, demanding that we answer: What's behind your ambitious striving, anyway? We don't like that question.

Paul answers, "Don't look at yourself, look to Christ; don't trust yourself and your tradition, trust Christ alone; don't try to impress God—you can't. I tried that way; it's a dead end. I was a fanatic, I was a bigot, and I was dead wrong while I thought I was dead right!" This is the theme behind his words in Philippians:

> Whatever gain I had, I counted as loss for the sake of Christ. Indeed, I count everything as loss because of the surpassing worth of knowing Christ Jesus my Lord. For his sake I have suffered the loss of all things and count them as rubbish, in order that I may gain Christ and be found in him, not having a righteousness of my own that comes from the law, but that which comes through faith in Christ, the righteousness from God that depends on faith (Phil 3:7–9).

There it is—"Righteousness *from God* [not from us] that *depends on faith* [not on our obedience to the law]." What a relief! Not us, not our ambition, not our holiness—but instead, God's grace!

This alone is the cure for our condemnation under the law's accusing finger. As Carl Walther wrote in the 19th century:

> When reading the Law, pondering it, and measuring our conduct against its teaching, we are terrified by the multitude of demands which it makes upon us. If nothing else were told us, we should be hurled into despair—we should be lost. God be praised! there is still another doctrine, the Gospel. To that we cling.[2]

THE GOSPEL IS REVEALED BY GOD

In Galatians 1:15 Paul says, "He who had set me apart before I was born, and who called me by his grace, was pleased to reveal his Son to me, in order that I might preach him among the Gentiles." The point is, God changed his course—God arrested him. Paul's raging fanaticism, which had caused him to torture, imprison, and kill others, was no match for God's love. God chased him down, apprehended him, and cuffed his hands—by changing his heart.

Before Paul was even conceived, God had set him apart for his service. Certainly this wasn't deserved or requested; rather, it was in order to reveal God's glory. God opened Paul's eyes and heart to see Jesus not as an impostor, but as the promised Messiah.

It's God's initiative at each step; changing a violent fanatic into a preacher of the message he once oppressed doesn't result from initiative on our side. It's not a transformation Paul desired, nor is it "a result of works, so that no one may boast" (Eph 2:9). It was God's doing—and it still is! The grace which stops us in our tracks is the same grace which goes on transforming us. Paul never suggests that he was saved because he made a decision for God. He was saved because God "was pleased to reveal his Son to [him]" (Gal 1:16).

Only irresistible grace overcomes self-assertion, self-reliance, and self-protection. As Isaiah says, "All of us, like sheep, have strayed away. We have left God's paths to follow our own" (Isa 53:6a NLT). We aren't interested in God or grace. Our interest is in hills and flags. "Yet the LORD laid on [Christ] the sins of us all" (Isa 53:6b NLT).

> IRRESISTIBLE GRACE OVERCOMES SELF-ASSERTION, SELF-RELIANCE, AND SELF-PROTECTION

Since the true gospel isn't man-made, it doesn't glorify us. It doesn't say, "You can reach heaven, you can fix the woes of your life, you can overcome the wounds by getting the dance steps right." Rather, it says, "You've got the steps all wrong, but don't fear—there's a partner whose feet you can ride on—heaven is reaching down for you." In Jesus, God entered human history and human hearts; in Jesus, God invites you to come and join the dance.

Luther knew how hard it was to cling to the truth of the gospel and trust it implicitly. He wrote, "It is easy to say what the Gospel is nothing but the revelation of the Son of God or the knowledge of

Jesus Christ and not the revelation or knowledge of the Law. But in the conflict of conscience and in practice it is difficult even for those who have had a lot of experience to hold to this for certain."[3]

Like us, you might have shared the gospel with a friend who pushed it away with the words, "It's too easy—you have to *do* something." He couldn't fathom grace. And we're prone to encountering the same hazard. We trip over grace and slide into the ditches of pity or assertion. We ask, "Why hasn't God answered me? Maybe if I clean up my act he will? What does he want me to do? Perhaps the atheists are right!" This isn't remembering the gospel, preaching it to yourself. It's self-pity chasing self-assertion. It's a passion for self. It's not worshiping God. It's trying to use him, then angrily dismissing him when he proves unhelpful.

The gospel proclaims nothing but free and divine grace, and because this is anything but self-evident, it's so hard to hold on to. Our hearts need to be taught over and over what our heads learned a long time ago.

The gospel proclaims the divine work of sheer grace; neither human reason, nor wisdom, nor the law of God teach this. We dance with the Trinity when, empowered by the Holy Spirit, we take the message of Christ into our hearts and trust it more than all other messages.

The Gospel Brings Glory to God

Paul credits God with the radical transformation he experienced. Galatians 1:16 actually says in Greek that God "was pleased to reveal his Son 'in' [not 'to'] me." The point is that Jesus entered Paul's heart; note his words in Galatians 2:20: "It is no longer I who live, but Christ who lives in me." His change was from the inside out.

His knowledge of God went far beyond the historical and factual—a grasp of morality, tradition, and ritual. It became spiritual and personal. It's why he gives us his timeline: three years in Arabia, only 15 days with Peter and James in Jerusalem, then a decade or more in Syria and Cilicia. No other explanation accounts for Paul's life and ministry—he had come to know the risen Lord himself.

Only the gospel, nothing else. No psychology, no philosophy, no political ideology, no traditions, no law-keeping can take us from where we are to where we ought to be. If they could, we'd get the glory, not God, and Christ would have died in vain.

When you begin to hear the music of the gospel in your heart, listen to it—don't quench the Spirit. Savor it. Come back to it again and again. You'll find yourself glorifying God for the work of his gospel in you, not man's gospel—just like the churches of Judaea glorified God for the report of Paul's transformation.

Then after fourteen years I went up again to Jerusalem with Barnabas, taking Titus along with me. I went up because of a revelation and set before them (though privately before those who seemed influential) the gospel that I proclaim among the Gentiles, in order to make sure I was not running or had not run in vain. But even Titus, who was with me, was not forced to be circumcised, though he was a Greek. Yet because of false brothers secretly brought in—who slipped in to spy out our freedom that we have in Christ Jesus, so that they might bring us into slavery—to them we did not yield in submission even for a moment, so that the truth of the gospel might be preserved for you. And from those who seemed to be influential (what they were makes no difference to me; God shows no partiality)—those, I say, who seemed influential added nothing to me. On the contrary, when they saw that I had been entrusted with the gospel to the uncircumcised, just as Peter had been entrusted with the gospel to the circumcised (for he who worked through Peter for his apostolic ministry to the circumcised worked also through me for mine to the Gentiles), and when James and Cephas and John, who seemed to be pillars, perceived the grace that was given to me, they gave the right hand of fellowship to Barnabas and me, that we should go to the Gentiles and they to the circumcised. Only, they asked us to remember the poor, the very thing I was eager to do.

CHAPTER 4

GOSPEL-SHAPED UNITY

O nce Paul had been at the very heart of things, probably a
member of the Sanhedrin itself. Now he was "missing in action," absent from Jerusalem for more than a decade, consorting
with Gentiles somewhere beyond the horizon.

Being born on the right side of the tracks is one thing. Leaving
it all behind to live on the other side is another—it's altogether
more culturally threatening. Those back home gossip about your
degeneration and theorize in hushed tones about how it started
and where it'll end. The feedback is seldom positive. Paul would
have been pilloried for his remote ministry among the Gentiles,
likely painted as too insecure to show his face to the high hege-
mons in Jerusalem, while the false teachers painted themselves
as belonging to the favored inner circle.

But there's more. The men who had come down from
Jerusalem were Jewish—probably ex-Pharisees (see Acts 15:1,
5, 24)—whose rusted-on zeal was still corroding their message.
The greatest visible division in the New Testament world was
between Jew and Gentile; it was historic, deeply ingrained, and
filled with prejudice.

So Paul failed this test too. Not only was he an outcast from
the citadel of Jerusalem, but he was fraternizing with the Gentiles

in the worst possible way. The old boundary markers of circumcision, Sabbath keeping, and dietary laws no longer applied to him or his converts. He'd not only jumped the fence to eat with them, he'd torn down the enclosure entirely. What would become of the rest of the law if such erosion should continue? Surely God couldn't condone such fraternizing, especially when his clear commandments were being ignored! If Paul's way were to continue, Judaism would be culturally overthrown; his gospel was a Trojan horse that had to be exposed.

THE TWO TYPES OF UNITY

We're faced with two types of unity here. The one, from Paul's side, is the unity of the gospel. Its genesis is grace; its currency, love; and its power, the Spirit of Jesus. The other is the unity of conformity. Its genesis is the flesh; its currency, the law; and its power, coercion leveraged on fear.

In this highly charged setting, we read of a meeting in which the stakes couldn't have been higher. Which would prevail? The relational unity of the Spirit, or the legal unity of the flesh?

Paul has already claimed that his gospel was not from man, but from God. He stressed the validity of his gospel message by telling how he didn't go to Jerusalem to learn from the leaders there, but was taught directly from Jesus. He was no less an eyewitness of Jesus' resurrection than the original apostles (Acts 1:3).

Now, with the gospel itself at stake, he tells of his visit to Jerusalem: "after fourteen years [since the Damascus road experience] I went up because of a revelation and set before them … the gospel that I proclaim among the Gentiles, in order to make sure I was not running or had not run in vain" (Gal 2:1–2). Paul had been to the Jerusalem congregation once before, for 15 days (Gal 1:18), but that visit didn't have the critical importance of this one.

This isn't a traveler's itinerary or biographical sketch. Rather, Paul is showing how the gospel shapes the church. He went up to Jerusalem not because of a summons, but in response to divine revelation. He goes not to have the gospel he'd been preaching for

14 years corrected, but for support and unity—because *gospel* unity would disarm the agitators. Love alone must win out. Without

this outcome, Paul would have run in vain. The Judaizers would have stolen the keys of the kingdom and imprisoned the church under the law.

Gospel-Shaped Relational Unity

Paul traveled to Jerusalem with two companions: Barnabas and Titus. This was typical for Paul—he always lived in close relational connection with a community of faith, not as a strategy, but as the overspill of the gospel. His closest ministry associates were the fruits of the gospel, often his direct converts. The love they shared was the harvest of the Spirit's life among them, the motive and power for their mission.

Barnabas was a Jew from Cyprus, a Levite who may also have studied under Gamaliel; he was certainly a capable and gifted man since he was sent to lead the church in Antioch. But since the work was so extensive, he sought out Paul and brought him back as a ministry partner (Acts 11:25). Later, he and Paul undertook the first missionary journey together (13:1–3).

Titus, a convert of Paul's preaching, was an uncircumcised Greek. Because of this, Titus became the test case on which the visit would succeed or fail. If you were a Jew, to eat with a Gentile or to step into a Gentile home rendered you ritually unclean. Paul took Titus not just to dinner, but into the headquarters of the Christian church and into a private meeting with key leadership under the watchful eyes of zealous ex-Pharisees (whose zeal was not too "ex"). At the very least, this was a likely way to provoke an argument! But that wasn't Paul's purpose. Rather, he aimed to establish the truth of the gospel, with Titus as a bold object lesson.

Certainly Paul must have known this would enrage the Judaizers. Galatians 2:4 reads, "False brothers secretly brought in—who slipped in to spy out our freedom that we have in Christ Jesus." So there were some who were trying to force Titus to be circumcised, yet Paul's party "did not yield in submission even for a moment" (2:5). It seems as though those of the circumcision lobby had infiltrated the meeting with big guns of their own to argue the case against Paul. Had they won, Titus would have been circumcised on the spot, and the church would have become but another sect of Judaism.

We can barely fathom the heat and pressure they applied. Legalistic religion schools consciences, shapes cultures, and thereby defines who's "in" and who's "out." The social control exercised by this combination is potent; upon this anvil, many a twisted church policy has been hammered. This was a crucial battle, *not* merely a question of circumcision versus uncircumcision.

Paul was remarkably free in these things. He insisted that Timothy be circumcised (Acts 16:3), but strictly forbade anyone laying a finger on Titus (for which Titus was likely exceedingly glad!). Why the difference? Because in Timothy's case it wasn't about his standing before God or his relationship to the law. Timothy needed to be circumcised *for the sake of* the gospel. He was to share with Paul in ministry among Jewish people, and because of his own family background (having a Jewish mother) he couldn't enter synagogues and debate alongside Paul if he wasn't circumcised. Titus was Gentile through and through. He was *not* to be circumcised *for the sake of* the gospel. His ministry was to be among other Gentiles. His circumcision would have sent the message to everyone else: To become a Christian is to become a Jew in culture and custom.

Legalistic religion can't cope with this. It wants black and white rules all the time, about every detail. The hospitality of grace—in which one is as at home among the Jews as the Gentiles (e.g., 1 Cor 9:19–23)—confounds it. Where the currency of fellowship is love, the liberty of the Spirit sets a broad and welcoming table. Where the currency is coercion, fear patrols the gates, making sure that only law-abiding citizens come in.

So would the apostles be unified in a law-free gospel? We can imagine Paul arguing to exhaustion, or the wisdom of the Spirit confounding the clanging gongs who were his opponents. But, however it came to be, Titus was accepted as an equal brother with equal standing *without circumcision*.

A law-free gospel doesn't mean that good works aren't to be done. This is the very thing Paul was keen to promote, not least to do good to the poor (2:10), just as his Gentile converts had done in their love gift to the Jerusalem church. The gospel doesn't negate the Ten Commandments as moral law. Rather, a law-free gospel means no one is *right* before God on the strength of upholding these commandments—performing good works and keeping good morals. Salvation is by grace through faith. And only that gospel yields deep relational unity. Paul's acceptance of Titus, as well as the other apostles' acceptance of him, reveals not only their doctrinal coalition, but the transformation of their hearts; "when the gospel shapes our relationships, the fruit is miraculous."[1]

Let's put more flesh on these bones. We have a tendency to rank sin. Since pride and lust are common, we say, "Yeah, I struggle with that too—welcome to the club." But if you're battling depression, suffering marriage problems, have been abused, tempted toward homosexuality, or succumbed to substance abuse, you'd better remain silent. Otherwise someone will discover you don't belong in the church.

Maybe you played on a high school football team. If so, you were likely drilled in sidestepping and spinning free from tackles. For many of us, these type of maneuvers also describe the experience of our Christian lives, spinning free from tackles—real or perceived—by other Christians, hoping to move the ball another 10 yards down the field. But some of us feel we've been tackled so much that we've quit the game and are sitting in the bleachers. We're unsure about God and uninterested in church. It's a hard place to be—made so precisely because it's not gospel living; it's not living by faith. It's living by the law—legalism, life on the treadmill.

When we realize grace isn't contingent on our performance, our hearts will be quieted and open. And when we can rest in the knowledge that we're saved by grace, we're able to see that our neighbors are also saved by that grace! You're also a sinner whose name is Beloved; you're on the same road of transformation, held in union with the same Christ. And having our identities shaped by the same gospel renders your "sin" color, your skin color, your political color, your hair color, your favorite color inconsequential. For in Christ we're the same: sinners saved by grace.

Do you want to know if your head and heart, your belief and life, have been shaped by the gospel? Do you want to know if the gospel governs your relationships? Then ask yourself, "Is there anyone I'm at odds with?" A spouse, child, relative, coworker, friend, acquaintance? If so, let the gospel have its way in you. Jesus is grace and life. Humbly go to each other with a passion to forgive as God has forgiven you. That's life in the gospel.

Tracing the details of "the wrong" isn't what's important. Assigning blame, marking out potholes so they can be avoided, and noting your neighbor's lack of change aren't important either. Why? Because that's treadmill living; it's demanding a righteousness from others that God alone gives.

What *is* important is a heart that experiences grace and longs to pour it out to others. This is the relational unity the gospel creates.

Gospel-Shaped Missional Unity

The gospel is not simply a message to be preached, it's the powerhouse of the church's mission. We don't evangelize *with* the gospel, but *because* of it. In many instances, the church itself needs to be "regospelized," so dead is it to the reality of the grace and love of God. If the liberty of the Spirit through the gospel isn't the beating heart of a congregation, it will turn to one program after

> THE CHURCH ITSELF NEEDS TO BE "REGOSPELIZED"

another to do its "outreach." But the church is never revived by the law, even if it's dressed up as an evangelistic program.

Paul set the gospel that gripped his life and changed it so radically before Peter, James, and John.

> When they saw that I had been entrusted with the gospel to the uncircumcised, just as Peter has been entrusted with the gospel to the circumcised ... and when James and Cephas and John, who seemed to be pillars, perceived the grace that was given to me, they gave the right hand of fellowship to Barnabas and me, that we should go to the Gentiles and they to the circumcised (Gal 2:7–9).

Peter, James, and John perceived Paul was in possession of the true gospel; or, better, that the true gospel was in possession of Paul. So they didn't edit it, trim it, change it, or supplement it. The false brothers wanted to take an Olympic gold medal and have it bronzed. But Peter, James, and John accepted Paul's gospel as perfect, and gave him the right hand of fellowship.

The right hand of fellowship symbolizes partnership in the gospel. It's saying, "Paul, we preach the same gospel as you do; we're in fellowship with you for that reason. Our teaching is neither better nor more sublime than yours. Our labor might be divided into different fields, but the true gospel unites our mission."

The apostles saw the gospel wasn't just for their own benefit. It had been entrusted to them for the purpose of passing it on. Jesus hits this home in the parable of the Talents, saying:

> A man going on a journey ... called his servants and entrusted to them his property. To one he gave five talents, to another two, to another one, to each according to his ability. Then he went away. He who had received the five talents went at once and traded with them, and he made five talents more. So also he who had the two talents made two talents more. But he who had received

the one talent went and dug in the ground and hid his master's money. Now after a long time the master of those servants came and settled accounts with them (Matt 25:14–19).

To the ones who had received five and two talents he said:

"Well done, good and faithful servant. You have been faithful over a little; I will set you over much. Enter into the joy of your master" (25:21, 23).

But to the one who received one talent he said:

"You wicked and slothful servant! ... Take the talent from him and give it to him who has the ten talents. ... And cast the worthless servant into the outer darkness" (25:26–30).

Being entrusted with the gospel has two purposes. The first: to treasure it and be transformed by it. The second: to pass it on, to multiply it—not to hoard it. This is what the good servant does.

When you have something of great value, something you treasure and delight in, don't you want to show it off, share it, bring others into the joy of your delight? Have you ever tasted a bit of food and said, "This is marvelous, try this!" Tasting the delightfulness of the gospel, knowing its sweetness, is what binds us together in unity. And it's what propels us into the world with something too delightful and too life-changing to hoard.

Since the apostles had the common experience of delighting in the gospel, they freely celebrated each other's calling. They weren't possessive or jealous. They were free to be of one heart and purpose, albeit in different fields. Paul and Titus (fully intact) left the gathering, having been affirmed in the nature of the gospel itself, through the unity the gospel created.

But the battle wasn't over yet. Not by a long shot.

GALATIANS 2:11–14

But when Cephas came to Antioch, I opposed him to his face, because he stood condemned. For before certain men came from James, he was eating with the Gentiles; but when they came he drew back and separated himself, fearing the circumcision party. And the rest of the Jews acted hypocritically along with him, so that even Barnabas was led astray by their hypocrisy. But when I saw that their conduct was not in step with the truth of the gospel, I said to Cephas before them all, "If you, though a Jew, live like a Gentile and not like a Jew, how can you force the Gentiles to live like Jews?"

CHAPTER 5

STAYING IN STEP

Winning a battle doesn't win a war. After the Allied victory over Rommel's forces in North Africa—their first victory of World War II—Winston Churchill said, "This is not the end. It is not even the beginning of the end. But it is, perhaps, the end of the beginning." Had Paul heard Churchill, he would have said, "Winston, I've said that a thousand times myself!" Most of our New Testament letters arise because of new battle fronts opening—different terrain, different issues, but always the same weapons (see 2 Cor 10:3–5).

No battle, however, was as intense as this, or as critical; in this mêlée, some of the key generals had changed sides after being carried away by the false teachers' rhetoric. It must have been pretty persuasive, and before long we'll see why it was so. But imagine Paul's mind and state of heart as he spoke publicly about these esteemed leaders—his brothers in the Lord. We do him a great injustice if we reckon it was easy. The old Paul—whose angry zeal drove him—had gone. He was confirmed in his weakness (see 2 Cor 13:4) and habitually knew fear, inadequacy, isolation, and grief. Any fracture in the newfound love that bound the Father's children together struck him to the core.

Perhaps if it had been any other issue, and any other person, he may have had a choice to act differently. But given what was at stake, he couldn't.

Since Paul verbally confronts Peter, we might charge him for unsportsmanlike conduct—not just giving him a yellow card, but pulling out the red card and ejecting him from the game! After all, isn't Paul responsible for the quarrel?

No. The quarrel doesn't mark Paul's failure with the gospel, but Peter's. Paul's the referee: blowing the whistle, stopping play, calling a penalty that threatens the game for everyone. Where everyone should be enjoying good fellowship and food at an ancient potluck, Peter has given in to pressure, crossed the hall floor, and separated from the Gentiles. He had started eating only with Jews, and only kosher food. In so doing, he was saying, "If I eat like a Jew I am righteous; if I eat like (or even with) a Gentile I am condemned. Therefore, righteousness is a matter of keeping to the rules!"

Because of his stature, Peter's actions encouraged others to follow suit. In other words, he'd turned aside from the boundless freedom of the gospel, retreating behind boundaries that reestablished ancient enmities and had cemented division for generations.

How could this have happened? And to Peter, no less—the man who received the visions of Acts 10 and had seen the Spirit fall on the Gentiles in Cornelius' house?

The false teachers' argument must have had both logical force and theological weight. Perhaps it went like this: "The signs of circumcision, food laws and Sabbath observance were given to Abraham and Moses by God! They were part of the great covenants with Abraham and Moses, to which all the people of Israel were pledged! They are so important that they're eternal (e.g., Gen 17:13: "both he who is born in your house and he who is bought with your money, shall surely be circumcised. So shall my covenant be in your flesh an everlasting covenant"). Did not

Israel go into exile for treading underfoot the laws relating to the Sabbath, for eating unclean things, for neglecting to circumcise their children? Did not the returning exiles vow to keep the laws again (e.g., Neh 13)? And what about these hundreds of years, striving with all our might to maintain our identity against Greece and Rome? And what about all the sacrifices of our forefathers? If you continue like this, you'll bring God's wrath on us all. Yes, the Gentiles can come in, but the promises were that they'd be children of Abraham—that they would join themselves to the Jews, as they should. We must be pleasing God in all respects! The Gentiles cannot be allowed to join us in a way that compromises the high standards of righteousness that God expects! As for Paul, we've already told you what sort of fellow he is. His credentials are worthless. He's disqualified himself, because he's encouraging you to do the very things that brought God's wrath upon our ancestors."

Then, add this thought to the mix: They had no New Testament. While we tend to settle our debates by referring to the New Testament, Paul only had a novel interpretation of the ancient writings against the false teachers' citation of the Old Testament, chapter and verse. No self-respecting rabbi would sanction such a reading of the Scriptures.

So it's not hard to see why Peter and Barnabas buckled. Their opponents' logic was coercive, leveraged on fear, and, because of this, irrefutable—except by the gospel itself.

Paul recounts this story to the Galatians to emphasize the nature of Christian freedom, by stressing the gospel's sufficiency to make us right with God and each other. Paul didn't exceed the bounds of Christian modesty and humility, nor was he afraid that people would see him as stubborn or proud. As Paul called Peter to stay in step with the gospel, he calls the Galatians—and us—to do so as well. And we can understand what this means through three developments in Paul's brief story.

ATTENDING TO REPUTATION

New Testament scholar Joachim Jeremias notes:

> In Judaism, table-fellowship means fellowship before God, for eating of a piece of broken bread by everyone who shares in the meal brings out the fact that they all have a share in the blessing which the master of the house has spoken over the unbroken bread.[1]

Peter's eating freely with the Gentiles in Antioch expressed that they were all under the same blessing. This was in accord with Jesus' teaching that all foods were now clean (Mark 7:6-23) and was certainly the view of Paul, the converted Pharisee, who saw that nothing *of itself* was unclean. Rather, all was given to be enjoyed (see Rom 14:14, 20; Titus 1:15).

The vision Peter had in Acts 10 radically altered his lifestyle, showing that the Gentiles were saved by grace through faith just as he was. And so Peter was free, so to speak, to be a Gentile.

> Peter went up on the housetop about the sixth hour to pray ... he fell into a trance and saw the heavens opened and something like a great sheet descending, being let down by its four corners upon the earth. In it were all kinds of animals and reptiles and birds of the air. And there came a voice to him: "Rise, Peter; kill and eat." But Peter said, "By no means, Lord; for I have never eaten anything that is common or unclean." And the voice came to him again a second time, "What God has made clean, do not call common" (Acts 10:9-15).

It was as though God told him, "A new stage of redemptive history has dawned. The Old Testament sacrificial and ceremonial laws have done their part; let them fall."

After this vision, the Lord brought Peter to the house of Cornelius, a Roman centurion, where they were already waiting for him to preach the gospel! God had orchestrated a wonderful divine appointment, using dreams, visions, and angelic messengers. The hand of God on this event could not be denied.

But on returning to Jerusalem, Peter was confronted by the legal zealots: "You went to uncircumcised men and ate with them" (Acts 11:3). His defense is telling: "As I began to speak, the Holy Spirit fell on them just as on us at the beginning. ... If then God gave the same gift to them as he gave to us when we believed in the Lord Jesus Christ, who was I that I could stand in God's way?" (11:15, 17).

Israel had been called by God to be a priest to all nations (Exod 19:6). The law, which included food laws, set them apart from the nations. Therefore, food laws concerned more than an ethnic division: They announced that the Jews belonged to God. But now it wasn't food laws that announced who belonged to God, but the Holy Spirit himself. Circumcision and food laws weren't needed for salvation. Yet the Jewish Christians could still keep their cultural heritage.

In Jerusalem the church was largely monoethnic, but in Antioch it was mixed. So it is in Antioch that the questions arose: How are Jews and Gentiles to relate within the same congregation? Do they dine together?

God's answer was clear to Peter—and he ate with Gentiles. But when James' groupies showed up—groupies who lacked James' own balance and character—the scuttlebutt began buzzing. Peter grew afraid. Why? Because he was concerned about what others were saying; his reputation was in question. He was face-to-face with complaints and criticism; he likely was feeling discouraged, his spirit being pulled down. Why was he losing his joy and freedom? All the static over his actions was undermining his confidence in the gospel. He returned to a practical legalism, then, to lessen the impact of the cultural police force around him. But in so doing, his law-keeping was entirely unlawful.

STATIC OVER PETER'S ACTIONS WAS UNDERMINING HIS CONFIDENCE IN THE GOSPEL

How often do we fall into this same hole of unlawful law-keeping? Like Peter, how often do we yearn for reputation before others? How often do we look to our actions to prove our goodness? How often do we want nods of approval and acceptance?

The revivalist author Stanley Voke writes:

> We are all reputation-conscious. Some of us have a reputation—it may be for piety, efficiency, leadership, preaching, housekeeping, anything! Others of us wish we had a reputation. Once acquired, or assured, it can haunt us, dog us, browbeat us, wear us to shreds. Bondage to reputation can be sheer slavery, and yet did we but know, it is only a form of struggle for our own righteousness. We are unwilling to be known as failures along any line.
>
> The struggle for righteousness consequently becomes a struggle for appearance which simply means that somewhere we end up being dishonest about ourselves. ... What a relief when we see Christ as the end of all this. He is the end of the struggle for righteousness since He not only fulfilled the law for us, but was cursed for us as well. He has not only attained our perfection but atoned for our imperfection. There is nothing more to struggle about, for He has done all for us and God asks nothing now but our repentance and faith.[2]

Attending to reputation is what led Peter not only to separate from the Gentiles, but to shrink back from the gospel.

SHRINKING FROM THE GOSPEL

Paul writes in verse 13 that Peter's actions were hypocritical. How so?

They weren't hypocritical because he got his doctrine wrong, or because he was ignorant. Hypocrisy is present because Peter wholly believed one thing and did another. He was two-faced.

He caved to the sociocultural board of governors, the gatekeepers of reputation.

Peter was a great man, a great church leader, yet even great followers of Jesus are not immune to failures and foul balls. This was no less than Peter's fourth failure over the same issue; recall his three denials of Jesus (Matt 26:69–75). His fear of other people's opinions repeatedly overthrew his trust in God. When this happens, to Peter or to us, a practical denial of the gospel in our own hearts is followed by one in our words or actions.

> DENIAL OF THE GOSPEL IN OUR OWN HEARTS IS FOLLOWED BY ONE IN OUR WORDS OR ACTIONS

In 1520, Pope Leo X condemned Luther's Protestant views as heretical and summoned him to either renounce or reaffirm them at the Diet of Worms in April 1521. When Luther appeared before the assembly he was presented with a table filled with copies of his writings. When asked if he still believed what the writings taught, he asked for time to think about his answer. He was granted an extension. Luther prayed and consulted friends and mentors. The next day the same question was put to him. He apologized for the harsh tone of many of his writings, but said he could not reject the majority of them or the teachings in them. Luther respectfully but boldly stated, "Since then Your Majesty and your lordships desire a simple reply, I will answer without horns and without teeth. Unless I am convicted by Scriptures and plain reason—I do not accept the authority of popes and councils, for they have contradicted each other—my conscience is captive to the Word of God. I cannot and I will not recant anything, for to go against conscience is neither right nor safe. Here I stand, I cannot do otherwise. God help me. Amen."[3]

The struggle of the Christian life is the struggle to believe the gospel. It is the struggle to really live out of the belief that the cross provides all the stability and security we need. When we're centered in the divine love and faithfulness of Jesus, as Luther was at that point, hypocrisy is denied a foothold. But you can't overcome hypocrisy by merely trying harder not to give in—will power isn't the answer. The gospel is. Peter's will wilted, because the gospel was occluded by the board of governors on his shoulder.

OPPOSING FOR THE GOSPEL

Peter's lifestyle wasn't in step with the gospel—and he was causing others to get out of step also.

Picture a high school marching band. Getting out of step is common when marching. The remedy is to look at the feet of the person in front of you. Those in the back look forward, those in the middle look forward, and those in the front look at the drum major. If the drum major is out of step, soon the entire band is confused.

Peter, the Rock, was the drum major—and he was out of step. When he drew back from table fellowship with the Gentiles, the Jews—and even Barnabas—followed. This is why Paul publicly opposes Peter to his face: "But when I saw that their conduct was not in step with the truth of the gospel, I said to Cephas before them all, 'If you, though a Jew, live like a Gentile and not like a Jew, how can you force the Gentiles to live like Jews?'" (Gal 2:14).

Peter could have said, "Come on, Paul. I'm not preaching that the Gentiles need to observe food laws to be saved"—to which Paul might have responded, "When, as an apostle, you cut off table fellowship with Gentile brothers and sisters, the Gentiles can't escape the impression that they aren't fully Christians because they aren't fully Jews. That's compulsion, Peter." It's like being in Greensboro, North Carolina in 1960 and letting African Americans come into Woolworths but barring them from the lunch counter. You're telling them they've got to change their ethnicity to be acceptable; it's not enough to be a legal citizen. Just as Paul would not yield in Jerusalem, neither would he in Antioch, not even for a moment.

If we're honest, we all struggle with wanting to be accepted and approved of. But the only way to enjoy the truth of my acceptability, to experience its full weight and significance, is to "live by faith in the Son of God, who loved me and gave himself for me" (2:20). Staying in step with the gospel, then, means continually facing up to your own sinfulness—be it succumbing to fear, reputation-seeking, hypocrisy, or practical legalism—and fleeing to Jesus, resting by faith in his righteousness. It means living in the truth that God has removed your transgressions from you as far as the east is from the west (Psa 103:12). It's seeing that Christ is the end of the struggle for acceptance and approval (righteousness) by God and others.

> STAYING IN STEP IS ALL ABOUT HEARING THE GOSPEL

Staying in step with the gospel is the only true way to peace and joy because it's the only way to experience Christian freedom. And, as we'll come to see, staying in step is all about hearing the gospel, God's greatest gift to the world.

GALATIANS 2:15–21

We ourselves are Jews by birth and not Gentile sinners; yet we know that a person is not justified by works of the law but through faith in Jesus Christ, so we also have believed in Christ Jesus, in order to be justified by faith in Christ and not by works of the law, because by works of the law no one will be justified.

But if, in our endeavor to be justified in Christ, we too were found to be sinners, is Christ then a servant of sin? Certainly not! For if I rebuild what I tore down, I prove myself to be a transgressor. For through the law I died to the law, so that I might live to God. I have been crucified with Christ. It is no longer I who live, but Christ who lives in me. And the life I now live in the flesh I live by faith in the Son of God, who loved me and gave himself for me. I do not nullify the grace of God, for if righteousness were through the law, then Christ died for no purpose.

CHAPTER 6

JUSTIFIED BY FAITH

I f you were a town crier how would you announce the gospel? What would your central message be?

How about something like this? "Hear ye! Hear ye! All rebels and opponents of the King! A great day of reckoning is coming. But hear this, inhabitants of the realm! Amnesty is published by the mercy of your Sovereign. A price has been paid, all debts abolished, all rebellion absolved. Cease your insurrection, kneel in submission, and receive the blessing of imperial favor. Then arise—not just a happy subject of your King—but coheirs with his only son, adopted into his family. Receive his kingdom as your everlasting possession!" That would be good news! But did you notice what's at the center? Amnesty.

Justification and the remission of sins are two sides of the one coin—and both are closely related to adoption. But there can be no verdict of *justified* if the penalty for sin has not been paid. If justification isn't at the center of our gospel, we don't have good news at all. Without justification, we're left trying to work out how to deal with the guilt of our sins. At best, we would have a half-finished work to proclaim: God's done all he can, now it's up to you, and don't blame him if you screw it up!

But if justification is real, then we have truly good news! For your justification can't be undone; it's not something you did in the first place.

Luther put it this way: "If the doctrine of justification is lost, the whole of Christian doctrine is lost."[1] As J. I. Packer has said, "When … the thought of justification drop[s] out of [our] minds: the true knowledge of salvation drops with it, and cannot be restored till the truth of justification is back in its proper place. When Atlas falls, everything that rested on his shoulders comes crashing down too."[2]

This truth is so important that Paul repeats the word "justified" three times in Galatians 2:16, making it the hinge on which the letter turns: "We know a person is not justified by works of the law but through faith in Jesus Christ, so we also have believed in Christ Jesus, in order to be justified by faith in Christ and not by works of the law, because by works of the law no one will be justified."[3] This principle is repeated in other places (e.g., Gal 3:10; 5:4; see also Rom 3:20), and it can also be stated thus: "If righteousness could come through the law, then Christ died in vain" (Gal 2:21).

The point is plain: Our righteousness is not based on something true of us, but on what is true of Christ. He's kept the law where we haven't; he's atoned for our sins when we couldn't. The gospel isn't self-referential in any way. In fact it's exactly the opposite. It teaches us to look away from ourselves and our performance, to Christ and his.

A Dead End Highway

It's similar to the story of a man who, on a wintery day years ago, decided to leave work early because a blizzard was coming. While in his truck, the radio reported that the highway he usually traveled had been closed. The reporter jokingly noted that an old narrow logging road up in the hills was still open. Young, half-fearless and half-foolish, he decided to take it. It was longer, slower, unpaved, and more perilous. He'd be at the mercy of the road; it was risky. But he took the old rough pass and eventually made it home.

The highway we gravitate to when trying to sort out our lives—the one that we think leads to the way to get right with God, or at least to ease our consciences—is eight lanes wide. It's straight, it's paved, it's easy traveling, no bumps, no risk. But it's completely blocked. All who hope to get right with God on the basis of what they've done, are doing, or will do, are traveling a blocked road and will never reach their destination.

What would you see if you went beyond my actions and looked into my heart, read my mind, examined my motives? Or I, yours? We'd find multiplied transgressions of God's law, a hatred of God, a spirit of evil totally offensive to God's holiness, and a stubbornness so ingrained we'd never humbly come to him on our own.

The innate goodness of the human heart and its ability to redeem itself are the world's grandest delusions, which every moral and religious system falls into. Religion crucified God when he visited us. His true goodness was so offensive to our tawdry religious endeavors, we drove nails through his flesh. Yet that event remains the very means of our rescue. This is the narrow mountain pass, which natural human reason finds totally unappealing because it requires relinquishing trust in one's self and placing that trust in the way we would rather not go.

That Way has a face and a name. Jesus said, "I am the way, the truth and the life, no one comes to the Father but through me" (John 14:6). Paul says this man is none other than "the Son of God who loved me and gave himself up for me" (Gal 2:20). There's no other way to be justified.

THE MEANING OF JUSTIFICATION

Paul unequivocally announces that we're justified by faith, not works of the law. But what does "justification" mean? And what "works of the law" is he referring to?

"Justification" is legal language. Its context is clear in Deuteronomy 25:1: "If there is a dispute between men and they go to court, and the judges decide their case, and they justify the righteous and condemn the wicked" (NASB). Another translation puts it this way: "If there is a dispute between men and they come into court and the judges decide between them, acquitting the innocent and condemning the guilty" (ESV). To be justified is to be legally acquitted. It's the opposite of being found guilty, or being condemned. It's to be in a right standing with the court—in this case, with God himself.

But how can we possibly be declared righteous? We've sinned and fallen well short of the glory of God (Rom 3:23). We're not righteous; we're guilty.

The Judaizers say: "God has provided a highway for you to drive on with clear signage. The way to be justified is by obedience to the law in every detail. Refrain from anything the law forbids. Revere God's name, honor your parents, avoid adultery, murder, theft, lying, coveting. Take your religion seriously by observing the ceremonial laws. Keep your nose in the Scriptures, pray, be charitable. Do all of this—don't fail—and you'll make the grade. The law will justify you, and God will accept you."

To many of us this sounds about right; we nod in agreement. We naturally think that the law is the highway back to God. Keep it, keep on it, and keep going. But in this perspective, we totally misunderstand the purpose of the law.

The law wasn't given to make us good. It was given to show us how bad we are. The Jerusalem Bible translates Romans 3:20 in a helpful way: "So then, no human being can be found upright at the tribunal of God by keeping the Law; all that the Law does is to tell us what is sinful" (JB). The law actually blocks the highway, turning us to the mountain pass where our confidence must rest in God, not in our ability to make ourselves like him.

This is counterintuitive. People the world over believe that the way to improve morals, establish righteousness, and make progress in holiness is to increase both obedience to the law and the number of laws to which we have to be obedient. And, for good measure, ensure that punishment is swift and strong.

The gospel speaks a different language—there's never any justification in the law, never any forgiveness, never release from guilt. The law never says a good thing about you. It's your worst nightmare, steadfastly pointing out failure, transgression, and sin. The law slays.

THE GOSPEL SPEAKS A DIFFERENT LANGUAGE. THE LAW SLAYS

But it also does something even more deadly. It establishes in you the foolish and futile pursuit of "righteousness according the law" (Phil 3:6). It sets you up as the self-righteous judge, jury, and executioner of others who have failed even more than you have. It allows you to stand with the Pharisee, thanking God that you're not like other sinners (Luke 18:11), treating your fellow human beings with contempt. Like a psychiatric patient undergoing an acute psychotic episode, we have no insight into our real situation—except that in our case, our ignorance is willful.

We need to interrupt ourselves for a minute.

Paul wrote in Koine Greek, and in that language he didn't have the luxurious range of legal sounding adverbs and adjectives that English has. We're used to fine differentiation—legal, legalist, legalistically, lawful, lawfully, and so on. Each is used in a particular way. Paul had one word (*nomos*) to stand for all these nuances. For example, he could speak of "the Law and the Prophets" (Rom 3:21), but in that same verse also uses the word "law" differently when he says that "righteousness has been revealed apart from the law" (Rom 3:21)—that is, apart from obedience to the law. He could speak of law as a principle (e.g., "the law of sin and death" [Rom 8:2]), as the good gift of God (Rom 7:12), or as a shorthand way of speaking about the Old Testament (1 Cor 14:21).

This helps us, then, understand his phrase "works of the law," which he uses at certain key junctures (Gal 2:16; see also 3:2, 10; Rom 3:20, 27-28). He's saying, "Any use of the law (any law!) by which we aim to present ourselves clean and right before God is a work of the law."

The law to which you're aligned will vary. It may be obedience to the cultural laws of circumcision, Sabbath-keeping, or dietary requirements; compliance to the Ten Commandments; seriousness in piety, strictness of self-discipline, regularity in any religious practice; devotion to works of charity, honesty in business, pride in your upstanding reputation; anything, in fact, that says we're accepted before God on the basis of something we've done, something true of us.

This highway is wholly blocked! That's the good news!

Consider Galatians 2:15: "We ourselves are Jews by birth and not Gentile sinners; yet we know that a person is not justified by works of the law." With more than a tinge of irony, Paul is saying, "Look, we haven't been outside the covenant like Gentiles have. We have a privileged birth and revealed religion. Yet with such a wonderful heritage, even we Jews are saved by faith alone." Remember Abraham? "He believed the Lord, and [the Lord] counted it to him as righteousness" (Gen 15:6). Abraham lived before the law was given, and he was justified by faith alone!

If I Muster Up Faith ... That's the Answer?

The text is clear: It's not works of the law, but *faith* that matters.

As soon as you read this, your flesh says, "Ah, so there is something I can do after all! I can get a righteous standing in exchange for faith!"

No, not one bit. This road is blocked too. Faith is the means, not the source, of justification. Grace is the source. You're justified *through* faith, not *because of* it.

FAITH TRUSTS
WHAT GOD IS
DOING

God giving his Son to pay for my sin is grace; God calling my name is grace; God removing the scales from the eyes of my heart is grace; God applying his promises to me is grace. God is the wholly active one, giving, calling, removing, applying. Faith, then, trusts what God is doing. And it, too, is a gift (Eph 2:8), for we don't naturally trust God.

Trust, however, is more than nodding at facts. Even the demons assent to facts about Jesus (Matt 8:28-29; Jas 2:19). Trusting Jesus is seeking refuge in him: "God is our refuge and strength, a very present help in trouble" (Psa 46:1). Trusting Jesus is seeking his mercy: "Have mercy on me, O God, according to your steadfast love; according to your abundant mercy blot out my transgressions" (Psa 51:1).

When King David was hounded by enemies and tormented by guilt, he didn't look to the law and ask for justice—that wouldn't have boded well for him. Rather, he called for God to save him on the basis of God's righteousness, not his own. In Psalm 143, he says:

> Hear my prayer, O Lord;
>> give ear to my pleas for mercy!
>> In your faithfulness answer me, in
> your righteousness!
> Enter not into judgment with your servant,
>> for no one living is righteous before you.
> For your name's sake, O Lord, preserve my life!
>> In your righteousness bring my soul out of trouble!
> (Psa 143:1-2, 11).

Even for David, "a man after [God's] own heart" (Acts 13:22), works of the law couldn't justify—only God could. See Psalm 65:3, "When we were overwhelmed by sins, you forgave our transgressions" (NIV); "When iniquities prevail against me, you atone for our transgressions" (ESV); "Our faults overwhelm us, but you blot them out" (JB).

The new covenant in Christ's blood is the ground on which God hears your cries for mercy and accepts you. It has nothing to do with your merit or worthiness. "'Because you believe in me,' God says, 'and your faith takes hold of Christ, whom I have freely given to you as your Justifier and Savior, therefore be righteous.'"[4]

Faith moves beyond merely acknowledging facts; it forsakes all hope of self-righteousness and trusts only in Jesus' righteousness. You're either contributing to your righteousness, or you're receiving it. You can't drive on two roads at once.

AN ALLEGATION AGAINST JUSTIFICATION BY FAITH

Feel the angry static from the other side of the conversation? The Judaizers—together with all forms of natural human reason—argue thus: "If God declared believers righteous by faith, why bother trying to become a better person? You're just handing out spiritual lottery tokens, giving away something for nothing. Your doctrine is highly dangerous, Paul. It's encouraging everyone to break the law. It certainly encourages the Gentiles to transgress the most important of the covenant signs: circumcision. If that goes, where's the limit? Doesn't your gospel make Christ a servant of sin?"

"Certainly not!" says Paul, "Christ is not a servant of sin" (see Gal 2:17). God isn't aiding and abetting sin by justifying people. Our sins are our fault; Christ can't be blamed. The antidote for sin is not more law, but more grace. "In fact," says Paul, "this gospel truly establishes the law" (Rom 3:31), not because it helps us become better people but because it throttles us, smarmy self-righteousness and all. Grace isn't resuscitation, but resurrection. It brings true, absolute, and total forgiveness by putting us to death in Christ.

> JUSTIFICATION IS NOT FICTITIOUS

Justification is law court language, but it's not fictitious, declaring people righteous when they're honestly anything but. Justification occurs as we are united to Christ by faith, and a real transformation is implied by this union: "If anyone is in Christ, he is a new creation. The old has passed away; behold, the new has come" (2 Cor 5:17). Yes, there is a new standing, a new status, but union with Christ means a new life has begun, and we can never go back to the old life.

This doesn't mean I'm sinless or that the struggle against sin is over. Paul certainly fought an ongoing battle; recall his statement, "For I do not understand my own actions. For I do not do what I want, but I do the very thing I hate" (Rom 7:15).

The point of transformation isn't so much freedom from sin—although new life leads to new purity—but the feeling of repugnance toward sin. In other words, the point of transformation is when a battle begins in our souls between who we were designed and long to be as Christians and the people we presently are. Before we knew Christ, there was no battle, no taking of ground.

We can't seriously contemplate returning to the old life, in which we knew neither God nor this battle in our souls. Once our eyes have been opened and the scales have fallen, they can't be reattached. It's like coming to know your husband or wife; regardless of whether your relationship is smooth or strained, you still know them. You can't return to the day before their existence was known to you. This is why Paul says, "The life I now live in the flesh I live by faith in the Son of God, who loved me and gave himself for me" (Gal 2:20). The groom is known, and this relationship has changed everything. Christ transformed Paul's heart, touched his character and reoriented his direction, and made him inseparably one with himself. The wedding ring of faith makes all the difference.[5]

AN ANSWER FOR JUSTIFICATION BY FAITH

Justification by faith isn't a pass for brazen licentiousness. It's heart transformation, not the law that fences me. Note Paul's words about the law: "For through the law I died to the law, so that I might live to God" (2:19). What does this mean?

The holy job of the law is to slay us, to make us sinners. As such it's like a schoolmaster, pointing us to Christ (Gal 3:24).

The law doesn't die; we die. It destroys all hope of justification by works. Once it has slain our pride and self-sufficiency, there's nothing more for it to do. Putting it differently, Paul says, "I have been crucified with Christ"—that is, in faith's coming we die to our own efforts to contribute to our righteousness, so that by faith's cleaving we might be raised up, receiving Christ's righteousness. New Testament theologian F. F. Bruce explains it well:

> All believers in Christ have "died in relation to sin" (Romans 6:2, 11), but the point stressed here is that, at the same time, they have "died in relation to law." ... Paul ... no longer lives under the power of the law; he has been released from its dominion and has entered into new life.[6]

The person who trusts God's work rather than his or her own shouts from the roof tops with Paul, "It is no longer I who live, but Christ who lives in me. And the life I now live in the flesh I live by faith in [or by the faithfulness of] the Son of God, who loved me and gave himself for me" (Gal 2:20). It's a joyous gospel exclamation in every part. Paul is still Paul, but every part of him is renewed through Christ. Christ has given him a new purity. By the blood of Jesus he is accepted and justified; he doesn't have to perform to be approved. Christ has given him a new identity: He is a treasured possession of God, no longer a murderer. It has given him a new inclination: He has new appetites, his heart actually wants to obey God—and yet his obedience isn't the basis of his justification. And it has given him a new power: The Spirit of God causes his hunger to increase for what God created him to be.

To rebuild the law would be to say that "Christ died for no purpose" (Gal 2:21); it would be to negate the center of the gospel.

GALATIANS 3:1–5

O foolish Galatians! Who has bewitched you? It was before your eyes that Jesus Christ was publicly portrayed as crucified. Let me ask you only this: Did you receive the Spirit by works of the law or by hearing with faith? Are you so foolish? Having begun by the Spirit, are you now being perfected by the flesh? Did you suffer so many things in vain—if indeed it was in vain? Does he who supplies the Spirit to you and works miracles among you do so by works of the law, or by hearing with faith?

CHAPTER 7

DEFEATING THE
LEGALIST WITHIN

How do you feel when you are reproved? Do the sinews of embarrassment, anger, and defensiveness stiffen in your neck? Do you commiserate with friends on the phone or Facebook, engage in gossip, and thereby justify yourself? This is, at least, how our flesh responds, but it doesn't have to be so.

As we step into the waters of Galatians 3 we meet a tidal wave of reproof. If Paul had been my pastor and doused me with the words, "O foolish man! Who has bewitched you?," I'd be looking for a new church. But I'd be desperately wrong. For such a response doesn't flow from a heart secure in the gospel; it flows from my insecure pining for praise and turns to the law for comfort.

A heart seeking to be justified by works of the law is always a man-pleasing, ego-stroking, legalistically aligned blowtorch. It not only identifies its righteousness before God with the respect garnered from its human audience, it also redirects its insecurity as emotional oxyacetylene, cutting down any detractors.

Paul knew this deadly concoction personally, and he wanted to liberate the Galatians from it. As they turned from grace to law, their joy had evaporated, their insecurity had increased, and their love for Paul had turned to hatred. They had lost all spiritual discernment. Paul's bold reprimand was a thump to the heart aimed at defibrillating their fluttering spirits, at restoring their consciousness.

A DISRUPTING INTERROGATION

Flattery is not friendship. Proverbs 27:6 says, "Wounds from a sincere friend are better than many kisses from an enemy" (NLT). Paul was being a true spiritual friend to the Galatians when he essentially said, "O you dear idiots of Galatia ... surely you can't be so idiotic" (Phillips). They needed to be brought up short.

As Luther said:

> It is legitimate for an apostle, a pastor, or a preacher to reprove those under him sharply in Christian zeal, and such a scolding is fatherly and holy ... therefore, unless [he] scolds when the situation demands he is lazy and useless and will never administer his office properly. ... Nevertheless, this anger must be moderated and must not proceed from envy; it must proceed only from fatherly concern and Christian zeal. That is, it must not be a childish ... show of temper that is out for revenge; its only desire should be to correct the fault. ... Paul is denouncing the Galatians here out of sheer zeal, not in order to destroy them.[1]

But how do we know if Christian zeal is proper? How do we discern that opinion, tradition, culture, or our own preferences aren't ruling the roost?

Only centering on the gospel is what prevents us from drifting into opinions, tradition, culture, trends, or our insecurities. Paul doesn't shrink from reproving the Galatians with bold intensity—seeking to disrupt them, to disturb their patterns of misplaced faith, and unsettle their comfort—because they were shrinking back from grace. They were supplanting gospel-centered living with legalism. Reproof is right only when its primary concern is with him who is himself the Way—when what we're seeking to address has to do with the articulation, understanding, and practical application of the gospel.

C. J. Mahaney has said, "Legalism is seeking to achieve forgiveness from God, justification before God, and acceptance by God through obedience to God."[2] Paul once held the patent on this life approach and the "reproof" which went with it—including incarceration, torture, and death. Rooting out disobedience had been his *raison d'être*, yet he was to find that it was he who had been disobedient (Titus 3:3). Therefore, he was focused only on "Christ crucified" (see 1 Cor 2:2); he wanted to prevent the Galatians from returning to the same place he had been.

"Bewitching" carries multiple connotations. The Galatians had encountered something beguilingly attractive, enchanting, and other-worldly. The so-called gospel of their new gurus was deeply appealing—it was couched in fascinating logic, and the flesh finds it innately attractive. What's more, the principalities and powers of the unseen realm turbocharge it with high octane spirituality. It's heady stuff, and if ever we meet the same mix, we're likely to respond in the same way. That is, unless a Paul is prepared to give us a thump on the chest.

APPEAL TO THE GALATIANS' EXPERIENCE

True doctrine never stands alone, as a cudgel in our hands with which to batter our opponents. The truth liberates, bringing us into a realm of love, joy, peace, goodness, and hope, heretofore entirely unknown. In short, the Truth, Jesus, speaks the truth of his gospel into our hearts, and the Spirit produces his fruit, launching us into true freedom.

When Paul preached the cross, the Galatians saw Jesus! It's not that he emphasized the mental and physical sufferings of Jesus until their hearts were moved to tears—you couldn't live in the Roman world without daily encountering staggering brutality; crucified men were a dime a dozen. What they understood and felt was the meaning of Christ's cross. In Acts, visions and other signs of the Spirit's presence often accompany the spoken word, especially in totally new situations. It was likely so with the Galatians. But, most important, they heard the preaching and understood the cross with crystal clarity, clarity that only the Spirit could bring.

The pundits from Jerusalm might have befuddled the Galatians' minds with their clever arguments, but they couldn't do any-

SIGNS OF
THE SPIRIT'S
PRESENCE
ACCOMPANY THE
SPOKEN WORD

thing to change their experience. Paul has simply to ask them, "Did you receive the Spirit by works of the law or by hearing with faith?" (Gal 3:2). Works of the law, neither pagan or Jewish, hadn't flooded their hearts with the Spirit. Indeed, they were under "the elemental principles of the universe" until faith came through Paul's message (Gal 4:3, 8–9). But when they heard the gospel, the gates of heaven were opened. Joy so great it carried them through the sufferings that accompanied their new life replaced their fear; surely, surely says Paul, this hasn't all been in vain.

The hallmarks of the Spirit's presence—love, joy, peace, patience, goodness, and on—don't begin when you first try to obey. They begin when you first believe! Likewise, the secret to ongoing fullness in the Spirit is to keep on hearing and believing the gospel.

By contrast, the false teachers were great at selling train tickets to the state of Guilt, where the Forest of Shame was always open. The devil loves to ally with those voices; he's the chief engineer and wants nothing more than to pull down the carriage blinds so you can't see the grace of the cross out of the window of your soul. The great jailer masks himself as the tour guide to freedom, but his doctrine can never produce the Spirit's fruit.

This is why Paul asked the Galatians to look back. What state were they in when they heard the gospel? What difference did it make when they heard it? How were they set free? And now look around. Is the same fruit being produced? Is the same liberty of the Spirit present? If not, what's changed? The difference lies in what you're hearing. But their problem is so often ours. If we began with God in one way, why do we assume we'll continue with him in another? Why, having begun by the Spirit, do we so often attempt to perfect ourselves by the flesh?

WE CONFUSE OUR
POSITION BEFORE
GOD WITH
OUR PRACTICE
BEFORE GOD

One of the chief reasons is because we confuse our justification with our sanctification; that is, our position before God with our practice before God. The law can neither justify nor sanctify you; it can no more declare you holy than it can bring lasting change to your heart.

But the flesh loves to hear that it has a role to play. If, for a moment, it gives up believing it can justify itself, it immediately turns to the path of holiness to sanctify itself. Either way, it thinks the law is the answer. It can't be educated or reasoned with on this point. It's inimical to the Spirit in every way, believing it can still reform itself.

Certainly there is struggle and effort to the Christian life, but it is not where we think. It is not a struggle to be holy and practice holiness; this is trying to be perfected in the flesh. It is a struggle to continue in the way we began—namely, to believe our justification is true. Gerhard Forde put it well when he said that "sanctification is the art of getting used to justification."[3]

Sanctification is forgetting about ourselves and looking at Jesus in the way John the Baptist did: "He must increase, but I must decrease" (John 3:30). The Christian life is always the life of faith. Active righteousness (or performance) is never the ground of our justification; it is the evidence of it. We bring nothing to the party except our sin. As John Bunyan experienced this very truth:

> One day, as I was passing in the field, and that too with some dashes on my conscience, fearing lest yet all was not right, suddenly this sentence fell upon my soul, Thy righteousness is in heaven; and methought withal, I saw, with the eyes of my soul, Jesus Christ at God's right

hand; there, I say, is my righteousness; so that wherever I was, or whatever I was a-doing, God could not say
of me, He wants my righteousness, for that was just before Him. I also saw, moreover, that it was not my good
frame of heart that made my righteousness better, nor
yet my bad frame that made my righteousness worse;
for my righteousness was Jesus Christ Himself, the
same yesterday, and to-day, and forever (Hebrews 13:8).
Now did my chains fall off my legs indeed, I was loosed
from my affliction and irons, my temptations had fled
away; so that, from that time, those dreadful scriptures
of God left off to trouble me now; now went I also home
rejoicing, for the grace and love of God.[4]

Appeal to God's Activity

What sent Bunyan home rejoicing was that his salvation was
secured by grace *alone*. The flesh may reluctantly admit that it
needs a modicum of grace, but baulks at the "alone" bit. Yet that
is where our security lies; there, it is all God's work, not ours.
And, as he has begun, so he will continue: "Does he who supplies
the Spirit to you and work miracles among you do so by works of
the law, or by hearing with faith?" (Gal 3:5).

Paul is by no means saying that our faith pushes or pulls
God to give us the Spirit. The Spirit precedes faith; he pricks us
when we hear the Word and causes us to hear the voice of the
Shepherd. It's in this sense that Jesus said, "When the Spirit of
truth comes, he will guide you into all the truth"—that is, the
truth of who Jesus is for us (John 16:13). Paul's argument runs like
this: "You can't possibly deny your experience of the Holy Spirit
and the regeneration of your hearts. The life-shaping power of
the Spirit didn't come by works of the law. You experienced the
reality of the Spirit as you heard with faith. It was grace from beginning to end! So what's changed? Why do you now think faith
isn't enough?"

Often we look to our emotions and feelings of holiness, or lack thereof, and feel pride or sorrow over where these place us with God. So we want to add works to cleanse our souls. After all, we've got to work at cleaning the kitchen floor; in the same way, don't we have to work at cleaning up our lives? God surely can't continue to love me if I've failed for the umpteenth time in the same area. There has to be something he needs from me—perhaps a hair shirt or flagellum would do the trick? (If you think this is a bit extreme, you haven't read much church history!) Sometimes we make a community sport of "stoning" sinners. When the gospel loses out, physical and mental flagellation of ourselves and of others are ready to fill the void in a heartbeat.

Like the Galatians, we often fail to interrogate the legalist within us. To break the bewitching spell of legalism, we have to go back to the gospel again and again and again; to see Jesus crucified for us as a finished work. The way of the Christian life is learning to look away from ourselves and to the Lord Jesus. The way of sanctification is learning the art of our justification.

Peter learned this when he stepped out of the boat and started walking on the waves. When did he begin to sink? As soon as his eyes turned away from Jesus' face.

So when your heart is in a dark place, look to Christ. When you feel like a failure, look to Christ. When you feel dirty in your sin, look to Christ. Go again and again to the cross of Christ. The perfectionist within you will tell you that to do so is failure: "Surely I should be beyond this!" But faith speaks otherwise: "The life I now live in the flesh I live [present continuous tense] by faith in the Son of God, who loved me and gave himself for me" (Gal 2:20).

"To progress is always to begin again," said Luther.[5] How did we begin? In faith, at the cross. We never get to a place in this life where we can leave the foot of the cross. We never get past grace, never get to the point where we have fully plumbed the depths of the gospel, fully grasped it, or fully delighted in it. It's God's gracious mercy that he will not let us live without his crucified Son as our constant dwelling place.

> WE NEVER CAN LEAVE THE FOOT OF THE CROSS

GALATIANS 3:5–9

Does he who supplies the Spirit to you and works miracles among you do so by works of the law, or by hearing with faith—just as Abraham "believed God, and it was counted to him as righteousness?"

Know then that it is those of faith who are the sons of Abraham. And the Scripture, foreseeing that God would justify the Gentiles by faith, preached the gospel beforehand to Abraham, saying, "In you shall all the nations be blessed." So then, those who are of faith are blessed along with Abraham, the man of faith.

CHAPTER 8

CHILDREN OF ABRAHAM, CHILDREN OF FAITH

Paul has already made two things very clear: The law can't put us right with God, and the gift of the Spirit comes only by hearing with faith. Both are counterintuitive.

On the one hand, natural human reason relies on the law for righteousness, and on the other, it seems utterly incomprehensible that such an inestimable gift as the Holy Spirit should be received simply through hearing with faith. Surely we have to do something of great worth to gain the Spirit's presence in our lives. We like to think that it might be enough if we deny ourselves pleasure, crawl over broken glass, go to the right meetings, or have our emotions stirred to the critical level—however religious these acts seem, as works of the law, they all ultimately countermand the gospel. They empty Christ's death of its meaning (Gal 2:16). The very fact that Christ died for us—that his death wasn't just an empty tragedy—testifies to the bankruptcy of justification by any other means.

But the agitators marshaled strong arguments; they could cite an unimpeachable historic precedent—namely, Abraham. If circumcision was required for the father of the family, it would

surely be for his children. He's *the* biblical test case. In turning
to the story of Abraham, Paul is out of the trenches, across no
man's land and in hand-to-hand combat with the enemy on their
own ground.

Paul's opponents implied that he had conveniently forgotten to read the fine print to the Gentiles: "Welcome to the family!
Now here are the dance steps: For starters, become fully Jewish
by being circumcised, then we'll go on to step two ... " They would
have no doubt pointed to verses such as Genesis 17:10, 13:

> This is my covenant, which you shall keep, between
> me and you and your offspring after you: every male
> among you shall be circumcised ... both he who is born
> in your house and he who is bought with your money
> shall surely be circumcised. So shall my covenant be in
> your flesh an everlasting covenant.

To this, the agitators might say: See, Paul got it wrong! If you
want to be part of the family, a child of Abraham, you've got to
take the sign of the everlasting covenant. Grace may have a place,
but don't overdo it."

Where Paul says "Grace and grace alone," the others say, "Yes,
but there's more than grace in the picture!" F. F. Bruce summarizes the matter like this:

> The agitators may well have answered that they [i.e.,
> the Gentile believers] were justified by faith while
> they were uncircumcised, as Abraham was; that they
> proposed to accept circumcision after being justified
> by faith, as Abraham did; and that for them, as for
> Abraham, circumcision would be a seal of the justifi-
> cation by faith which they had received in their uncir-
> cumcised state. The Galatian Christians had apparent-
> ly been told by the agitators how necessary it was for
> them to be true sons of Abraham, and therefore to be
> circumcised, as Abraham was.[1]

The term "sons of Abraham" was a critical one. Both Paul and the false teachers would have understood that the Messiah's arrival ushered in the era of Old Testament fulfillment, and that the promise to Abraham (that all nations would be blessed through his offspring) was now being enacted. Logically, then, since the Gentiles are now sons of Abraham, they must conform to the Old Testament laws if they are to inherit Abraham's blessing.

Paul, however, puts the matter of inheritance on a different level. The Gentiles are sons of Abraham by having the same faith as Abraham. Faith, not works righteousness, is the family trait; promise, not law, is the means of their inclusion.

> THE GENTILES ARE SONS OF ABRAHAM. FAITH IS THE FAMILY TRAIT

Paul pushes the argument even further back than Abraham, further even than the covenant sign. He goes back to God's promise and Abraham's response. In Galatians 3:6, Paul quotes from Genesis 15:

> After these things the word of the Lord came to Abram in a vision: "Fear not, Abram, I am your shield; your reward shall be very great." But Abram said, "O Lord God, what will you give me, for I continue childless, and the heir of my house is Eliezer of Damascus?" And Abram said, "Behold, you have given me no offspring, and a member of my household will be my heir." And behold, the word of the LORD came to him: "This man shall not be your heir; your very own son shall be your heir." And he brought him outside and said, "Look towards heaven, and number the stars, if you are able to number them." Then he said to him, "So shall your offspring be." And he believed the LORD, and he counted it to him as righteousness (Gen 15:1–6).

Paul's point is simple: Abraham believed God, and his act of faith was counted to him as righteous.

From the human perspective it was impossible, ridiculous—and yet Abraham cast himself on God's faithfulness. He trusted, and God accepted him as righteous. That acceptance wasn't because of anything in him or anything he did. It was simply that he trusted God's Word. And as Abraham trusted, as he turned away from himself, the relationship lost through Adam's distrust in the garden was restored.

As Paul later says, "There is neither Jew nor Greek, there is neither slave nor free, there is no male or female, for you are all one in Christ Jesus. And if you are Christ's, then you are Abraham's offspring, heirs according to promise" (Gal 3:28-29, emphasis added). These passages are seriously misinterpreted when they're used to remove all distinctions between people. Rather, they're meant to communicate that "it is those of faith who are the sons of Abraham" (3:7) regardless of distinctions of ethnicity, gender, social status, or culture. This means, contra the noisy Jerusalem bandwagon, you don't have to become a free-male-observant Israelite in order to be an heir of the promises to Abraham; you have to believe in the one God has sent (John 6:29). With Jesus, a new era began—and it was newer in more ways than the agitators had ever imagined.

The Gospel's Promise

"Scripture, foreseeing that God would justify the Gentiles by faith, preached the gospel beforehand to Abraham, saying, 'In you shall all the nations be blessed' " (Gal 3:8). Do you see the gospel promise here? It is present in two parts: (1) that God would justify, and (2) that all nations would take part in that blessing.

Abraham was counted as righteous before he was circumcised. Righteousness therefore flourished 430 years before Moses gave the law, before Israel's national identity was formed in the exodus. This fact negates any boasting or bragging about adherence to good works and religion. It calls our attention once more to the truth that salvation is by faith alone; it is not our doing but God's gift (Eph 2:8). God's justifying and adoptive purpose is not about Gentiles becoming Jews or Jews becoming Gentiles; it's about both groups becoming children of God.

So is this all an arcane discussion about an ancient problem? No—because our inner sense of security is typically far more related to our surroundings than we would like to admit. Acceptance, or the lack of it, often drives our decisions, and the sociocultural customs of our community or subculture contribute far more to our sense of self-worth than we realize. There is truth in the expression that "only dead fish float downstream," yet none of us likes to swim against the tide of ostracism, social dislocation, or the inner conflict of cultural upheaval. All of these inhibit change.

The Jewish contingent interacting with the Galatians really believed their cultural identity was at stake; that's why both Peter and Barnabas found it so hard to resist the agitators' arguments. Their words found fertile soil by stirring up deep fears. Believing in Jesus alone seemed to destroy thousands of years of history and culture. If the law was set aside, would the door be opened to ungodliness? Would God's wrath fall? If we accept them without a threshold at the door, won't all the other elements of the unkosher Gentile life be washed in? Such concerns caught Jewish believers in a riptide that carried them out to sea, separating them from true fellowship.

As you might be realizing, this will change everything. Suddenly, faith isn't merely about your set of personal beliefs. If you accept Christ, your culture will change, what you trust in will change, where you look for hope will change. Your sociocultural norms will change. Your friends may no longer count themselves lucky to know you; they may even turn you from their door.

FAITH ISN'T ABOUT YOUR SET OF PERSONAL BELIEFS

Or perhaps you've been a Christian for many years, and as a result you've foolishly convinced yourself that you're not as big a sinner as you used to be, that you're actually better than most of those you meet. It's good for the pastor to evangelize the outsiders, but don't let them come into the church with multicolored hair, multiple piercings, and tattoos without first registering for the discipleship dance class!

What if the gospel threatened to blow both worlds apart—or even better, bring them together? Not as a compromise built on the lowest common denominator, but through a real, heartwarming, emotionally satisfying, and soul-reviving love?

That's what happened in the churches in Antioch, Galatia, and elsewhere as they learned the true gospel. Greeks, Jews, circumcised, uncircumsised, barbarian, Scythian, slave, free—all were in Christ together (Col 3:11), loving, serving, rejoicing, worshiping as a family.

What the Gospel Prescribes

What does the gospel prescribe? What does it direct?

Nothing. This is the amazing thing about the gospel. We do nothing to be justified, nothing to come into the Father's loving embrace. Rather, we are carried by Christ. Faith is merely surrendering to his arms.

Abraham didn't do works of the law; he heard with faith. Some rabbis teach that Abraham passed through 10 trials to earn God's favor (see 1 Macc 2:52). But as we've seen, God accepted Abraham before he did anything; he was justified as a believer, not as a worker (Rom 4:3). The credit and worship went to God, not Abraham. Therefore, the only real way to be children of Abraham and heirs to the promise is to be like him. This is essentially what Jesus said to a crowd:

> They answered him, "Abraham is our father." Jesus said to them, "If you were Abraham's children, you would be doing the works Abraham did, but now you seek to kill me, a man who has told you the truth that I heard from God. This is not what Abraham did. ... Whoever is of God hears the words of God. The reason why you do not hear them is that you are not of God" (John 8:39-40, 47).

Abraham heard and believed. It's a case of "like father, like son": Like Abraham, the children of Abraham should believe and walk by faith. In sharp contrast, those who should have been sons of father Abraham were showing in their deeds that they were of a different father, the devil. Their religious pride was so entrenched, they could justify murder on the basis of obedience. As John Stott described the difference between obeying and believing, "Obeying is to attempt to do the work of salvation ourselves, whereas believing is to let Christ be our savior and to rest in his finished work."[2]

The only prescription of the gospel is faith. The true gospel has not changed from Abraham's day to this, and this is Paul's placard before both the Galatians and us. Paul calls Abraham "the Father of all who believe" (Rom 4:16 NLT) not just because this father believed God's unfathomable promises, but because he believed God himself.

"So does that make faith into slothful passivity?" Surely that's a line that Paul's opponents would have argued. But it certainly belies the Galatians' experience. In Galatia, the Jews and Gentiles together had come out of their bunkers and been united as a unified new community in Jesus. An entirely new vista of life had opened for them. Faith led to all manner of bold action; still today, it conquers kingdoms, overthrows forces of darkness, and suffers the loss of all things for the sake of Christ.

And despite the law's promises of self-sufficiency, life without the Father takes its toll on our ability to act boldly. Among the college-aged, for instance, surveys have shown anxiety to be the basic reaction to life. Anxiety reflects a fear of death, expressed as a fear of life: "In place of guilt and judgment we may now speak of anxiety and destiny," says Helmut Thielicke. "Anxiety is the secret wound of modern man."[3]

Anxiety is the fear of the uncertain—and without faith in our acceptance by the Father, the soul has plenty of fuel for that fire. If we believe ourselves to be alone, abandoned, and rejected, if we believe we must establish our own security, that life has to be lived out of the wisdom we can cobble together, and then, on top of all that, if we try to construct meaning out of it—it's no wonder anxiety has such a hold on us. But breaking out from our sociocultural confines to embrace another in utter freedom requires the boldness of faith. What pushes out anxiety is not fortitude, courage, or heroism, but resting in the astounding freedom of God's love.

UTTER FREEDOM REQUIRES THE BOLDNESS OF FAITH

Noel's old Bible college principal was a prisoner of the Japanese in Singapore during WWII. He spent three and a half years in the notorious Changi POW camp, where he and other prisoners experienced a revival of the gospel. When the camp was liberated, only a handful of the emaciated and shell-shocked soldiers immediately embraced their freedom. Most who had been conditioned by fear, acculturated into permanent anxiety, found it unimaginably hard to cross the threshold. The first to walk out, without fear, were some of the Christian men. In faith, they walked free.

GALATIANS 3:10–14

For all who rely on works of the law are under a curse; for it is written, "Cursed be everyone who does not abide by all things written in the Book of the Law, and do them." Now it is evident that no one is justified before God by the law, for "The righteous shall live by faith." But the law is not of faith, rather "The one who does them shall live by them." Christ redeemed us from the curse of the law by becoming a curse for us—for it is written, "Cursed is everyone who is hanged on a tree"—so that in Christ Jesus the blessing of Abraham might come to the Gentiles, so that we might receive the promised Spirit through faith.

CHAPTER 9

THE RIGHTEOUS LIVE BY FAITH

Nearly every aspect of our lives involves relating to other people. Even a hermit who lives in the woods is enmeshed in relationships; not only must he interact periodically with others to sustain his life, but he undoubtedly wrestles endlessly with memories. In fact, his very retreat from life is likely an attempt to avoid a personal history of relational pain.

The 19th-century poet Emily Dickinson was a recluse. Her poems often express joy about art, nature, imagination, and human relationships, but they're also permeated with a struggle: to evade, face, and wrest meaning from suffering. In the poem "A Loss of Something Ever Felt I," she recalls a deprivation from her childhood, forgives those who caused her pain, and recognizes, in the last stanza, that her high expectations could only be realized in heaven:

> And a Suspicion, like a Finger
> Touches my Forehead now and then
> That I am looking oppositely
> For the site of the Kingdom of Heaven—

To be human is to be relational. This is our bane and blessing. We all harbor a deep desire for peaceful palaces where we know only the favor and acceptance of our friends, spouses, children, parents, colleagues, or even strangers. We long for the harmony only heaven can bring. And so, we're too often met with disappointment that this world is not yet heaven when we mistake this world for the one it's meant to be.

Our disappointment then provokes a deep perversity in us: When the desire for true relational intimacy is thwarted, we're often so disenchanted that we sabotage what's left. Or we throw ourselves into feverish activity, attempting to secure others' favor, even God's. After all, if we can get it right with him, we can get it right everywhere! Our natural motto is: "By doing right, I can be right." After a domestic spat, we bring home the flowers, bake the favorite pie, and watch good standing reemerge. After a disappointing report card, we knuckle down and resolve to try harder. It's bred into us from childhood, the notion that relational harmony is dependent on doing the right thing and atoning for our actions when we don't. And so we make the logical jump: Being right with God must really be hard.

Don't get us wrong—reparations have their place. Yet Galatians 3:10–14 states unequivocally that it's deadly to relate to God like this. It is so dishonoring to God that any who take this path are accursed. Our passage recalls what Paul has already said in chapter 1: "If anyone is preaching to you a gospel contrary to the one you received, let him be accursed" (1:9).

Notice: Paul isn't cursing those outside the church, he's aiming at those who diminish grace—and cultivate pride—by supposing that it's possible to gain God's favor through God-talk, church attendance, profession of right doctrine, meal-time prayers, regular Bible reading, avoiding gross sins, and the like. The Galatians are running with the ball, trying to score points in helter-skelter frenzy of "doing the right thing," so Paul sounds the penalty buzzer.

Many of us don't see the problem with such a game plan—hence the reason why the book of Galatians has been transformational for many people. It's radically disruptive in its declaration: Blessing isn't for those who live in self-reliance, commit to self-reformation, or adopt some other means of self-atonement. Blessing is for those who confess radical neediness, whose pride has been crucifed, whose lives are dependent upon Christ and his Holy Spirit.

> BLESSING IS
> FOR THOSE
> WHO CONFESS
> RADICAL
> NEEDINESS

Trying to earn God's favor brings a curse, but faith in Christ crucified brings the blessing of Abraham. We admit this is counterintuitive, but it is also freeing.

RELIANCE ON WORKS

Paul quotes from Deuteronomy: "For all who rely on works of the law are under a curse; for it is written, 'Cursed be everyone who does not abide by all things written in the Book of the Law, and do them.'" (Gal 3:10). Breaking God's law—in any way—is to fall under its curse. As this curse is framed in Deuteronomy 27:26, it stands antithetical to the idea of blessing. To be "under" the law is to be bound to keep it for righteousness' sake. If we seek justification by works of the law, then we must keep all of it perfectly. Try telling a police officer when you next run a red light, "But I was doing the speed limit as I passed through. Moreover, I've got my driver's registration and insurance up to date; I've got my seatbelt on. Surely that's worth something!" Sorry, no dice. James says, "For whoever keeps the whole law and yet stumbles at just one point is guilty of breaking all of it" (Jas 2:10 NIV). The broken law doesn't let you off the hook—that's the curse.

Now, there's some really important Old Testament background to this. Deuteronomy 27 recounts 12 curses which were to be pronounced from Mount Ebal as the people entered the land, contrasted with the manifold blessings that were to be pronounced from Mount Gerizim at the same time. The curses are terrifyingly expanded beginning in Deuteronomy 28:15. Read them only if you've had a good breakfast! But long story short, to be under the curse is to be under the inescapable wrath of God. No area of relational harmony is left untouched.

In effect, Paul says to the Galatians, "This is where the false teachers are leading you: back into the penal colony you were rescued from." He's not saying, however, that the law itself is wrong and shouldn't be obeyed. When he says "works of the law," he is speaking about legalism—depending upon morals and religion to gain or keep favor with God. In other words, legalism is a misuse of the law. When Moses received the law, he wasn't being given a ladder to climb to God. So Paul is screaming, "Danger, danger, danger!" Living only by the law isn't gaining merit; it's a death sentence.

Did you know the law itself condemns its use as a means of salvation? The book of Habakkuk contains a dialogue between God and the prophet over a perplexing issue. In chapter 2, Habakkuk condemns the pride and self-confidence of the Babylonians who conquered Jerusalem. They trusted themselves, not God. Habakkuk 2:4 reads, "Behold, his soul is puffed up; it is not upright within him, but the righteous shall live by his faith." This shouldn't surprise us; it's the default position of humanity as a whole and ancient rulers, with their monumentally puffed-up egos, in particular. But the really perplexing part for Habakkuk was this: How could God use a nation even more ungodly than Judah to punish God's own people? In such humiliating defeat, how could they live with hope?

God answers: Habakkuk must trust, as Abraham did, in God's bare word—to live by faith in the promise that God was yet the covenant-keeping, faithful God he had revealed himself to be. In this context, the word

> HABAKKUK MUST TRUST IN GOD'S BARE WORD

"live" must be given full force. Faith gives birth to hope, which was the difference between life and death for the survivors of Babylonian judgment.

In his monastery at Erfurt, Martin Luther fell into a period of darkness and depression in which he felt he was under the wrath of God. Habakkuk's words, "The righteous shall live by faith," spoke to him during this time. The words resonated once more when he journeyed to Rome and visited the Basilica of St. John Lateran. There, certificates for the forgiveness of sins, called indulgences, were issued to all who climbed the steps of the basilica on their knees, pausing to pray and kiss each step. Later, Luther's son recorded what happened:

> As he repeated his prayers on the Lateran staircase, the words of the prophet Habakkuk came suddenly to his mind: "The just shall *live* by faith." Thereupon he ceased his prayers, returned to Wittenberg, and took this as the chief foundation of all his doctrine.[1]

Luther no longer believed his efforts could gain God's favor. He later said, "Before those words broke upon my mind, I hated God and was angry with him ... But when, by the Spirit of God, I understood those words—'the just shall live by faith!' 'The just shall live by faith!'—then I felt born again like a new man; I entered through the open doors into the very Paradise of God."[2]

The law is but verbal form of the holy life of God himself. If we really understood it, we would realize that the life of which it speaks is so far above our meager approximations that it doesn't show us how far we've come, but how far short we've fallen. It slays us, leaving us in despair, crying out to God for mercy like the tax collector who, looking at the dirt, "beat his breast, saying, 'God, be merciful to me, a sinner!' " (Luke 18:13). The function of the law is to condemn, not justify. "No one is justified before God by the law," says Paul (Gal 3:11), because no one keeps it perfectly.

And here's the crux of the matter: Legalistic striving draws us away from God. From beginning to end, it is self-reliance, self-sufficiency, self-effort, and pride. At its heart lies a mindset that relationally separates us from God. It's saying, "I'm doing well on my own. I don't need you to carry me, God. I can do this!"

Why does God justify you when you live by faith? Because faith confesses inadequacy. It doesn't trust in itself. Faith throws itself upon the cross, dying to self-reformation, and lives by union with the "Son of God who loved me and gave himself up for me" (Gal 2:20). Faith, therefore, cleaves to God and lives in intimate fellowship with him. "This is eternal life," says Jesus, for faith is knowing "the only true God, and Jesus Christ whom [he has] sent" (John 17:3). As John Calvin has written:

> The law justifies him who fulfills all of its precepts, while faith justifies those who are destitute of the merit of works, and rely on Christ alone. To be justified by our own merit, and to be justified by the grace of another, are two schemes which cannot be reconciled: one of them must be overturned by the other.[3]

Do you now see why Paul says, "The law is not of faith" (Gal 3:12)? Living by the law cannot lead to reliance on Christ, crying out for his mercy, or casting oneself upon his love.

Redeemed from the Curse

What hope is there for those who have dishonored God by trying to goad him with their virtue? Isaiah announces good news, saying, "All of us, like sheep, have strayed away. We have left God's paths to follow our own. Yet the LORD laid on him the sin of us all" (Isa 53:6 NLT). Paul echoes, "Christ redeemed us from the curse of the law by becoming a curse for us" (Gal 3:13).

What a scandal! God the Son has become accursed. Even further, he has become *the* curse, embodying in his own death the horrendous wrath for our sin. No wonder a crucified Messiah was a bridge too far for many Jews who heard Paul preach.

In the Old Testament, being hung on a tree was evidence of having been cursed by God. Thus if Jesus was hung on a tree (i.e., an executioner's gibbet) he must have become the object of the law's curse. Surely God's chosen servant couldn't suffer this fate. Thus, he couldn't be the Messiah.

The consequences of covenant transgression were terrifying. Jesus' cry of forsakenness is a window into the suffering involved. The physical crucifixion wasn't the real issue, brutal and barbaric though it was. Its mental, emotional, and spiritual dimensions were unfathomable. Jesus entered hell. He experienced in himself the pangs of death, the torment of banishment from God, while still on the cross.[4]

In the one small space of his human frame, in the few short hours of his crucifixion, he faced shocks of unimaginable proportions. In his experience, the curse was unmitigated, irremediably final, and all encompassing. The Old Testament curses touched the deepest abyss of human fears—famine, infanticide, insanity, plagues, dispossession, terrorization, and slavery. Christ experienced all the emotional and mental anguish of these horrors on a cosmic scale, as he became the totality of sin (2 Cor 5:21). The Lamb of God bore the sins of the world.

> JESUS BECAME ALL THAT WE ARE SO THAT WE MIGHT BECOME ALL THAT HE IS

Jesus went to the cross not because he was cursed under the law, but because we were—he became all that we are so that we might become all that he is. Luther calls this the "fortunate exchange," describing it:

> [Christ] took upon Himself our sinful person and granted us His innocent and victorious Person. Clothed and dressed in this, we are freed from the curse of the Law, because Christ Himself voluntarily became a curse for us, saying: "For My own Person of humanity and divinity I am blessed, and I am in need of nothing whatever. But I shall empty Myself (Phil. 2:7); I shall assume your clothing and mask; and in this I shall walk about and suffer death, in order to set you free from death."[5]

The relational intimacy we crave with the Lord isn't found through our doing better, trying harder, or being nicer to him. It's wholly a matter of grace, in which the Father embraces us through the Son's work on our behalf. Faith simply trusts the Father's word that, in Jesus, it is finished. And the Spirit, who prompts our hearts to cry, "Abba, Father!," is given as pledge and seal that it is indeed so.

RECEIPT OF THE SPIRIT

Galatians 3:14 makes one thing crystal clear: to receive the Spirit is to receive the blessing promised to Abraham. This is the inheritance set aside for all the nations of the earth, now made universally available. Intimacy with God through his Spirit is the inheritance we're destined for.

God's wonderful purpose is that his Spirit should be given to all nations. There is no requirement to be Jewish or to conform to the Jewish ceremonial law and customs, nor even to pin hopes on obedience to the Ten Commandments. Everyone may know Abba through the Spirit of Jesus.

The gift of the Holy Spirit brings us full circle, back to Galatians 3:5, that the Spirit is received by faith, not works. Paul has thereby reinforced the point that "those of faith are the sons of Abraham" (3:7, emphasis added). So if the Galatians had received the Spirit they must be children of the promise, no longer under the law's curse. Why, then, should they retreat from freedom to prison? Why should they run from the Father's promise that they will live in liberty?

Take a moment to consider: Are you enslaved to the "be right, by doing right" mentality? Or are you free?

Reliance on works of the law is a blocked highway, a dead end, a spiritual graveyard. All the obedience that you might muster from this day to the day of your death will not make you right with God. Only faith—which abandons self-reformation and striving and receives what God has done—enjoys the promise of his kingdom.

"We must look on the [cross] and take hold of it with a firm faith. He who does this has the innocence and the victory of Christ, no matter how great a sinner he is ... To the extent that you believe this, to that extent you have it."[6] Don't be bewitched; reliance on works of the law leaves you under a curse, relationally distant from God. But "the righteous shall live by faith" (Gal 3:11).

To give a human example, brothers: even with a man-made covenant, no one annuls it or adds to it once it has been ratified. Now the promises were made to Abraham and to his offspring. It does not say, "And to offsprings," referring to many, but referring to one, "And to your offspring," who is Christ. This is what I mean: the law, which came 430 years afterwards, does not annul a covenant previously ratified by God, so as to make the promise void. For if the inheritance comes by the law, it no longer comes by promise; but God gave it to Abraham by a promise.

CHAPTER 10

THE PROMISE IS
FOR KEEPS

S ome years ago a woman willed all her "worldly goods" to a particular college. When her children discovered this after her death, they were livid. They felt the college had manipulated and taken advantage of an old lady. So they contested the will in court, arguing that "worldly goods" applied to their mother's personal effects, but not her real estate.

The children lost the case. They could do nothing to change the terms of the ratified will; it was airtight, irrevocable, unchangeable.

That is exactly what God's promises are like—and the word Paul uses to describe the arrangement is emphatic; it's a testament (*diatheke*)—as in, "last will and testament." It's a bestowal, beyond bickering or legal challenge. God told Abraham what he would do, not what he might do if Abraham showed himself worthy.

Here, Paul encourages us by anchoring us outside of ourselves. You can't stabilize a storm-tossed boat by tying ropes from itself to itself; it needs an anchor down deep, beyond the choppy surface. Paul's argument goes as follows: God's covenant promise to Abraham will be in place forever; it cannot be annulled by the giving of the law (which came later). Therefore, your justification is eternally assured, safeguarded by God Almighty, sworn on the blood of his Son, sealed with the Spirit as the pledge of your inheritance. Your anchor is in heaven, not on earth; it's in the life of the triune God, not the fickle emotions and feeble will of your vacillating heart.

YOUR ANCHOR IS IN THE LIFE OF THE TRIUNE GOD

When life gets difficult, when it all falls apart, where do you look? Christ is still there; the promise is for keeps. That's our anchor.

The Unchangeable Covenant

In chapter 3, Paul triangulates the truth that justification comes by grace alone, received only through faith. He has appealed to our own religious experience, to Abraham's story, and, now, he closes the triangle with an illustration of a man-made covenant.

The illustration removes any objection that the law given to Moses somehow alters the terms of the covenant made with Abraham. That objection might sound like this: "Okay, Paul—if you want to bang on about grace, why would God give 600-plus commandments if it weren't to tell us what we must 'do' to be worthy of the inheritance?" Paul's reply might be paraphrased, "Appeal to law is checkmated by the very fact that the promise was ratified before the law was given; the law can't annul it!" "Brothers," he says (note the change in tone from "fools"), "let's take an example from human law to illustrate: 'Even with a man-made covenant, no one annuls it or adds to it once it has been ratified' " (Gal 3:15).

Today we give our signatures before witnesses. But in the ancient world, it was customary to conduct a ceremony in which animals were sacrificed, cut in two along the backbone, and placed in two parallel rows with a path between. For obvious reasons, this was called "cutting a covenant." Clearly, it was a bit more dramatic than swiping a card through the e-reader or signing on the dotted line! The parties making the agreement would walk between the rows and speak their promises, the shed blood making the oath sacred. As they walked between the slain animals they were in effect saying, "If I break the terms of this agreement, this is what you can do to me!" While it sounds like a scene from *The Godfather*, it was a common practice in the ancient world. But in the case of the covenant with Abraham, and in the face of his anxieties, God put him into a deep sleep to show him this scene:

> "O Lord God, how am I to know that I shall possess it?" He said to him, "Bring me a heifer three years old, a female goat three years old, a ram three years old, a turtledove, and a young pigeon." And he brought him all these, cut them in half, and laid each half over against the other. ... When the sun had gone down and it was dark, behold, a smoking fire pot and a flaming torch passed between these pieces. On that day the Lord made a covenant with Abram (Gen 15:8-10, 17-18).

The ceremony was typical, but did you notice the one significant exception? God alone passed between the sacrifices in a "theophany" (a divine appearing). Abraham was literally out of the picture. He had no lines to learn; he wasn't even an extra on the set. He was the audience.

In nomadic life, the firepot and fire torch belonged together, carrying embers from one encampment to another, ready for the next night's cooking fires. By using this image God was saying two things: "I'll be with you in all your travels. And if this covenant is broken, I will be the one to split myself in two to restore it. That's my guarantee. It's all on me."

The covenant, therefore, was unilateral—airtight, irrevocable, and unchangeable. Don't ever make the mistake of thinking that the later covenant with Moses was either "Plan B" or a replacement "will and testament" to be brought out of the cupboard when the first one went belly up. The covenant God made with Moses, which gave the law, didn't amend, abrogate, or annul the unilateral promise in any way. If it did, if the Israelites were supposed to earn their salvation by keeping the law of the later covenant, God would have been canceling his own promises—making him unfaithful and a liar.

But "God is not a man, so he does not lie. He is not human, so he does not change his mind. Has he ever spoken and failed to act? Has he ever promised and not carried it through?" (Num 23:19 NLT; see also Rom 3:4). In a word: No. There must, therefore, be another reading of the relationship between the Abrahamic and Mosaic covenants—one in line with God's trustworthiness.

We'll come to that in a bit, but for now imagine old, childless, impotent Abraham. Both he and his wife Sarah were as good as dead (Rom 4:19). How could he perform the duties of a husband, and she of a wife? And how could God possibly do anything at all with such a wizened old codger—let alone save the world, which is what he effectively promised?

We understand Abraham's anxiety; trusting God is often really difficult. Christians too get overrun with unemployment that depletes our savings, struggle in unhappy relationships, experience poor health that threatens to take loved ones from us or us from them, and grapple with our children's deeply disturbing decisions. We know in those moments how difficult it is to trust God; we know Abraham's anxiety; we look for surety, as he did.

When life is a mess, it's never helpful to be compared with others' misfortunes—and it's even worse to be told, "Oh, I know just how you feel!" No one else can walk in our shoes and live our own unique story. We need something fixed, beyond the scale that ranks us relative to anyone else—and this is what Paul is pointing us to. His argument ultimately hangs on the fundamental trustworthiness of God. God made the oath with Abraham; he will not break it. "I don't go back on my word," says God. "You will travel rocky roads, but

ROCKY ROADS
DON'T CHANGE
THE PROMISES

they don't change the promises I've made. Nothing changes my promises, not even the law I gave. Trust me with all your heart, soul, strength, and mind. See how I kept my word: I sent my only begotten Son for you."

THE OFFSPRING OF THE COVENANT

We're pulled back to the truth of "promise" in Galatians 3:16: "Now the promises were made to Abraham and to his offspring. It does not say, 'And to offsprings,' referring to many, but referring to one, 'And to your offspring,' who is Christ." Paul's argument is that Jesus embodies the climax of the Abrahamic promise. He's the offspring through whom the fulfillment of the Abrahamic blessings came.

We might, however, be tempted to pull out the red pen and mark Paul's paper, "Wrong. Illegitimate argument! Try again," for his reasoning seems to hang on the interpretation of "offspring" in the singular. And that doesn't work, since "offspring" is a collective noun, something he should have learned in primary school. But give Paul the benefit of the doubt and look deeper. He understood it was a collective word, like "team." He knew his grammar (in at least four languages!), but he's not arguing from syntax as much as from the theological meaning of the Scriptures.

The apostles understood that Christ was the focus of the entire Old Testament (e.g., 1 Pet 1:10-12; Heb 1:1-4; Acts 26:22-23); Jesus himself impressed this on them (e.g., Luke 24:25-27, 44-49; John 5:39). Paul's grammatical point only supports something already taken for granted in the early church, i.e., that in Jesus, all the promises of God are "Yes!" (2 Cor 1:19-22).

The "offspring" (the Jerusalem agitators, biological children of Abraham) weren't the key to the promises; the Offspring was and is! Inheritance doesn't belong to Jews generally—not even the most religious ones—but to the Offspring in particular.

No wonder the agitators were incensed! This is another way of saying that not all those who are born of Abraham are sons of Abraham. To say, "Those of faith are children of Abraham," is equivalent to saying, "Those in Christ (the Offspring) inherit the promises. Abraham's spiritual descendants, not his physical ones, are the true heirs!"

> ABRAHAM'S SPIRITUAL DESCENDANTS ARE THE TRUE HEIRS

Just think how much blood has been spilled over the matter of inheritance. How many kings have lost their thrones (and heads); how many wars and rebellions have begun; and how many families have been torn to shreds over who gets what bits of Dad's stuff when he's gone? Can you imagine the utter dismay that Paul's gospel engendered? That the Gentiles—the pagan, idolatrous, uncircumcised, lawless, ignorant outsiders—should be Abraham's heirs! And they don't even have to stand in line to be circumcised! What is Paul thinking?

But this all matches other examples in the Old Testament. For example, in Genesis 21, where Sarah tells Abraham to send Ishmael away, God tells Abraham, "Whatever Sarah says to you, do as she tells you, for through Isaac shall your offspring be named" (Gen 21:12). Here we see "offspring" is being narrowed down to a single son. The promise to Abraham lies with Isaac, not Ishmael; Jacob, not Esau. That narrowing continues until it lands upon Christ. The promise is fulfilled through the lineage of faith, not the flesh.

Jesus is the "named" Offspring. He blows open the Abrahamic promise to the nations—not through genealogy, but Christology.

Now we see the promise in the proper light. God's intention wasn't simply to give Abraham some kids and a playground. It was to give salvation to the nations through his Son. If blessing came through faith before the law, and if it was through faith that the nations were to be blessed, how could the law given to Moses annul God's promise to Abraham?

It couldn't.

Then how are the Abrahamic and Mosaic covenants related? Or put differently, how are the gospel and the law related?

The Compatible Covenants

Abraham and Moses are compatible. God does not make different rules for different points in history. He has one story to tell, in which both the covenants with Abraham and Moses have a place.

When God says to Moses, "Behold, I am making a covenant. ... And all the people among whom you are shall see the work of the Lord, for it is an awesome thing that I will do with you. Observe what I command you this day" (Exod 34:10–11), he's still setting out what he is going to do; he's not setting up a quid pro quo arrangement. God's promise has no strings attached. That's what makes it grace; that's what makes it good news. If strings were attached, we could claim justice: "Lord, I did this—where is my reward? Give me justice; give me what I've earned!" If God gave us justice, we would be in hell. Hell is justice. Christ is grace.

> HELL IS JUSTICE.
> CHRIST IS GRACE

Moses received God's promise in the same way Abraham did: by faith. The difference between receiving by faith and earning by merit is as clear in the story of Moses and the exodus as it is in the story of Abraham and Isaac.

Nothing in Moses' story lets us think that he had it all together. He was a fugitive murderer; his first attempt at bringing about the exodus as a hotheaded young 40-year-old had ended in disaster. By the time he was 80 and had been following sheep around the back end of the Midianite desert for 40 years, he was almost weak enough to be useful. Yet, even then, he resisted God's call, voiced every excuse under the sun regarding his inadequacy, and to his dying day had a problem with his temper. He and Abraham were both justified by faith. The stories can't be read any other way.

Rather than replacing God's promises to Abraham, the Mosaic covenant portrays faith in a new situation—namely, the growth of Israel from a family into a nation. And it was only given after they were redeemed from Egypt; the giving of the law was only possible after the Passover lamb. John Piper puts it this way:

> The law is a restatement of the Abrahamic covenant applied to a new stage of redemptive history. It is not an alteration. In both covenants the way to obtain blessing from God is to trust him for his grace (life of faith). In both covenants, the faith which saves so taps into the power of God that it obeys.[1]

Obey! The Jerusalem agitators loved that word and waved it like a big switch over the exposed backs of the Galatians. But they had missed Paul's point: Faith is obedience, and it leads to radical dependency on God.

Obedience is faith showing its mettle, being willing to walk a road with an unseen end. It's Abraham responding to God's command, "Go ... to the land that I will show you" (Gen 12:1). It's Moses dying to his own attempts to deliver his people and even to his own expressions of his inadequacy to do so. It's David trusting God for forgiveness in the face of his covetous, death-dealing adultery. It's you and me fleeing to God's mercy in the face of our envious longing for our neighbor's relationship, property, or success. And from this place of faith, we love because he first loved us. That's where the true works of the law come from, for love is what the law is all about.

Because genuine faith unveils itself in love, James says, "Show me your faith apart from your works, and I will show you my faith by my works" (Jas 2:18). True faith turns away from self and self-defined boundaries and walks God's road, even when it's difficult. The point can't be expressed strongly enough: You can't obey God without trusting him, and if you trust him, that faith will be the root and branch of obedience. Anything that doesn't proceed from faith, therefore, is sin (Rom 14:23).

The promise, therefore, is for keeps. The law doesn't annul justification by faith alone. Rather, it promotes it; the Mosaic covenant fits inside the Abrahamic like a hand in a glove. God isn't saying, "Once I taught you to trust me; now I teach you to work for me; once I taught you to rely on grace, now I teach you to earn merit; once I taught you magnify me through childlessness, now I teach you to magnify yourselves through legalism." No![2] Justification is entirely anchored in Jesus Christ, the Son of God.

But what if your faith faints and you stumble in obedience today? The gospel is still there; Christ is still there; and we're still justified before the Father. Christ is still our obedience: "the life [we] now live in the flesh [we] live by faith in the Son of God" (Gal 2:20).

The covenant God made with Abraham is secure; it is not annulled by the law, or by our clumsiness. God's faithfulness exceeds your greatest strength and overcomes your greatest weakness. Cast your life upon his promises. They're all "Yes!" in Jesus.

GALATIANS 3:19–22

Why then the law? It was added because of transgressions, until the offspring should come to whom the promise had been made, and it was put in place through angels by an intermediary. Now an intermediary implies more than one, but God is one.

Is the law then contrary to the promises of God? Certainly not! For if a law had been given that could give life, then righteousness would indeed be by the law. But the Scripture imprisoned everything under sin, so that the promise by faith in Jesus Christ might be given to those who believe.

CHAPTER 11

WHY THEN THE LAW?

If you don't know what something is for, you can't make the best use of it. Dan learned this vividly as a young man learning to whittle. Scouring his father's shed for scrap wood and tools, a flathead screwdriver seemed like it would do the trick. When it didn't work well, it seemed an easy matter to use the grinding wheel to put a nice sharp point on it.

In short, if you don't know what a screwdriver is for, you might come to know the wrath of Dad. If you don't know what a red light is for, you could smash into someone at an intersection. And if you don't know what God's law is for, you can kill yourself with it.

This is exactly what was happening in the congregation Walter Marshall pastored in the mid-17th century. His congregation practiced self-mutilation, deprivation, and inflicted all kinds of pain on themselves in efforts to please God and be pure. But for all their efforts, they were no more pure and no more loving. They were miserable! So their response was to double their efforts, until Marshall stepped in, praying, "May God bless my discovery of the powerful means of holiness so far as to save some from killing themselves."[1]

In Galatians 3:19–22, we meet the most marked contrast between the gospel and everything else: In the New Testament, "moral effort can be a mortal sin."[2] Universally, natural human reason—especially when applied to religion—puts the law to the wrong use, and out of it we kill ourselves and one another. That was Paul's story, but it's also ours.

WHAT IS THE PURPOSE OF THE LAW?

Put simply, the law wasn't given to make you better, but to make you worse. Martin Luther explained it thus:

> The Law cannot do anything except that with its light it illumines the conscience for sin, death, judgment, and the hate and wrath of God. Before Law comes, I am smug and do not worry about sin; when the Law comes it shows me sin, death and hell. Surely this is not being justified; it is being sentenced, being made an enemy of God, being condemned to death and hell. Therefore the principal purpose of the Law in theology is to make men not better but worse; that is, it shows them their sin, so that by the recognition of sin they may be humbled, frightened, and worn down and so may long for grace and for the Blessed Offspring.[3]

Luther is giving voice not just to Paul's theology, but to the depths of his own experience. Guilt, shame, judgment, fear, anxiety, wrath, the sense of impending doom and the indescribable wickedness of the heart, all of which he experienced, are products of the law. And Luther isn't the only one to have had a guilty conscience; all cultures have religious systems by which they seek to deal with ritual transgressions, shame, loss of face, and fear-filled superstitions. Either that, or we turn to substance abuse or psychology to do the job for us. And the law is unanimously put to the wrong use, trying to whittle smooth consciences with the wrong tools.

Against natural reason and in contradiction of his own life as a zealous Pharisee, Paul says the law "was added because of transgressions, until the offspring should come to whom the promise had been made" (Gal 3:19). Two things stand out: the function of the law, and the duration of its particular role.

The Function of the Law

Paul's vocabulary in Galatians 3:22 is telling; he's not speaking about "sin" in a general sense, but "transgression" in a legal sense. He's saying the law was given for the sake of defining transgression. It came to identify sin not as a vague sense of wrongdoing, but as specific transgressions from which no one can hide (see Rom 3:20; 4:15; 7:7–12).

THE LAW CAME TO IDENTIFY SIN

In a similar way, the police may arrest you for one thing, but pretty soon you're charged with a raft of offenses. It wasn't just that you robbed a bank; you also carried an unregistered firearm, broke the speed limit, ran a red light, and resisted arrest. You're not just a felon, but a felon facing multiple charges. The law comes from behind, places its vice-like grip on your shoulder, and says, "Accompany me to the station!" As a Pharisee, Paul had thought he was serving exactly this role in the name of God's glory. He was the long arm of God's law, heaven's gift to make the world conform to God's decrees. Confronting sinful, misguided, and heretical individuals with their failure was righteousness in action.

What a change had taken place! When he was a Pharisee, Paul sang one song, while as an apostle, he worshiped in the Spirit. As an apostle, he saw that the law delineates the true nature of sin: It isn't a power against sin, it's a power used in the hands of sin (1 Cor 15:56) because of the opportunity sin takes in the commandment (Rom 7:8, 11).

In opposing our sinful desires, the law stirs up greater fury. That's why you see finger marks under "Wet Paint, Do Not Touch!" signs. It's why the more you tell yourself not to think about that cream cake, the attractive neighbor, the better work conditions of your colleague, or the deficiencies of your spouse, the more it eats you. Out of this maelstrom arise murder, adultery, jealousy, envy, self-harm, and all manner of evils. "Thou shalt not" causes sin to "live"—and us to die (Rom 7:9). The law increases wrath, contention, and strife (Rom 4:15; see also Gal 5:18–26). It reckons sin to my account and holds me in prison as a debtor (Rom 5:13; 11:32). While the law may be our guardian, it can never be our savior.

> THE LAW CAN NEVER BE OUR SAVIOR

But there's also this. The law increases sin in still another way: "Satan would have us to prove ourselves holy by that which God gave to prove us sinners," noted Andrews Jukes.[4] The flesh uses the law as a step ladder to climb above others, and from this exalted position of moral worth we cuff the heads of passersby—for their own good, naturally. Someone has to teach them a lesson! The law hardens the self-aggrandizement we feel over our progress in law-keeping, thereby inflating our comparative righteousness.

Some of us in the church have been working in that field so long that the sun has baked the mud on really well. If we ever think kindly of a sinner, it's more by way of pity than mercy. Certainly it's not love.

Screwdrivers weren't the only tools in Dad's garage. He also had many other tools that would have been ridiculous for whittling, including a large variety of hammers: ball-peen hammers, sledgehammers, claw hammers, magnetic tack hammers (a 10-year-old's dream).

The law is God's sledgehammer. It shatters the rock of self-righteousness of your heart; it pulverizes the pride of our moralistic endeavors. It's too big to be wielded by even the biggest Pharisee, but in the Spirit the smallest child can bring down kingdoms. Paul makes it clear that we can't do without it, but it's not ours to do with as we will: "If it had not been for the law, I would not have known sin. For I would not have known what it is to covet if the law had not said, 'You shall not covet'" (Rom 7:7).

Yet, once it's done its work, producing in you coveting of every kind (7:8) and then condemning you for it, you'll bless God for having it in his toolbox.

The Duration of the Law

This function of the law is of limited duration. Paul's going to have a lot to say about that soon, but he runs a signal up the flagpole here to let us know that this purpose of the law is not endless. Its unfailing word of condemnation isn't God's last word; Christ is.

Once the law has caused us to long for Christ by exposing us as sinners and expanding our sins on all fronts, it has done its proper job. It doesn't give life, but kills so that we turn to Christ for life each and every day. Through the law, we die to the law as a means of life, so that we may be crucified with Christ.

This is what the law does "until the offspring should come to whom the promise had been made, and it was put in place through angels by an intermediary. Now an intermediary implies more than one, but God is one" (Gal 3:19-20). What in the world is Paul after, with all this angelic-intermediary talk? He's saying the same thing we've just been talking about, albeit in another way. He's pointing to the temporary and supportive function the law plays and, in so doing, keeping it from upstaging the gospel. He says that the law was given by God to the angels, to Moses, to Israel. The New Testament picks up on the obscure language in Deuteronomy 33:2. Before being stoned to death, Stephen says, "Moses was with our ancestors, the assembly of God's people in the wilderness, when the angel spoke to him at Mount Sinai. And there Moses received life-giving words to pass on to us" (Acts 7:38 NLT).

The point lies in the contrast. Where God gave the promise of the gospel firsthand to Abraham, the law was passed on third-hand to Abraham's offspring. The law is, then, subservient to the gospel; it supports its ministry. Its job is not to save; its job is to slay. It's God's sledgehammer to shatter our hard hearts. And that's not irreconcilable with the gospel.

Is the Law Contrary to the Promises of God?

Galatians 3:21 rhetorically takes up a critically important question: "Is the law then contrary to the promises of God? Certainly not!" says Paul. "For if a law had been given that could give life, then righteousness would indeed be by the law."

No one has ever kept the law except Jesus. Scripture consigns all things to sin. We aren't as bad as we could be, but we're as bad off as we can be. Every aspect of us is tainted: Mind, emotions, will, conscience, and even the cells of our body are all damaged by sin. This is so for the whole race: "They have all turned aside; together they have become corrupt; there is no one who does good, not even one" (Psa 14:3). This is total depravity. The law condemns all humanity, not just godless Gentiles or self-righteous Pharisees.

Some might draw from Paul's teaching that, since the law is inferior to the gospel and opposite to grace, it is therefore evil. Paul counters such an abhorrent thought with his second question: "Is the law then contrary to the promises of God?" (Gal 3:21). The law doesn't give life, precisely because it is pointing to life elsewhere. The law "imprisoned everything under sin, so that the promise by faith in Jesus Christ might be given to those who believe" (3:22).

In other words, the law makes us ready for the gospel; it prepares us to dance with the Trinity. It kept people in sin because the life-giving Holy Spirit, who enables faith, was not given with the law. Moses knew only too well that the Israelites didn't receive the Spirit. Notice what he said to the people: "To this day the Lord has not given you a heart to understand or eyes to see or ears to hear" (Deut 29:4). He saw that the law stood constantly as a jailer locking them in a prison. In fact, he said, "Take this Book of the Law and put it by the side of the ark of the covenant of the Lord your God, that it may be therefore a witness against you" (Deut 31:26).

Yet the law is not evil but holy, and as such, it does reflect the character of God. But its goodness lies in a different purpose than we expect. Romans 7 rings out:

> The very commandment that promised life proved to be death to me. For sin, seizing an opportunity through the commandment, deceived me and through it killed me. So the law is holy, and the commandment is holy and righteous and good (Rom 7:10–12).

It is good not because it gives life, but because it kills.

Chemotherapy doesn't give life. Rather, it is actually an instrument of death: the chemicals are toxic, and they destroy healthy cells. The patient feels worse during the treatment, not better. But this kind of death—and it is death—is necessary for the patient's long-term health. In the same way, the law kills so Christ may heal.

THE LAW KILLS SO CHRIST MAY HEAL

Owning the truth that our sin is more than skin deep opens up hope, but not a moment before. Sadly, many Americans think they're good enough to go to heaven. There will always be someone who is more moral and more religious reminding us of that fact. But in resting in their own morality, they don't truly see their need for Jesus. Perhaps one day, they'll discover they don't live up to their own standards, let alone God's. Then they'll be ripe for the harvest.

Dietrich Bonhoeffer once said, "It is only when one submits to the law that one can speak of grace."[5] By this, he meant that we should submit to what the law is telling us: Our sin goes all the way through, and we really aren't getting any better. When we can agree with God on this, then we'll truly hunger and thirst for righteousness that is not our own (see Matt 5:6). As Luther said:

> Only when a person's sin is disclosed and increased through the law does he begin to see the wickedness of the human heart and its hostility towards both the law and its author, who is God. Only then does that person realize that not only does he not love, but that he hates and blasphemes God, and as a result he is forced to confess that there is nothing good in him at all. When

the law forces us to acknowledge and confess our sins in this way it has fulfilled its function and is no longer needed, because the moment of grace has come.[6]

This is why Paul can confess freely what he once would have thrown himself into prison for:

Even though the Gentiles were not trying to follow God's standards, they were made right with God. And it was by faith that this took place. But the people of Israel, who tried so hard to get right with God by keeping the law, never succeeded. Why not? Because they were trying to get right with God by keeping the law instead of by trusting in him (Rom 9:30–32 NLT).

When God confirmed his promises to Abraham, he took him outside in the dead of night. There were no street lights, and in the darkness of the desert night—where you can't see your hand in front of your face—the stars shone with unsurpassed brilliance. We, on the other hand, live in a world of artificial light, not merely from the street lights, marquees, and glitz of the city, but also within our own souls. We fill our lives with the sparkle of entertainment, distraction, and noise and the bling that goes with ambition, wealth, and power.

But God cuts the power cord. In the darkness, we loathe ourselves and God for making us. He turns the lights off, draws us away from the bling and the tinsel, and gives us a glimpse of the darkness: our selfish ambition, our pettiness, our greed, our self-righteousness, our continual proclivity to build a reputation for ourselves.

Then he takes us to the desert, to stand with Abraham, there alone to see the brilliance of the promise. The stars shine. The light of Christ pierces the darkness: His beauty, stability, and glory raise us to heaven.

GALATIANS 3:23–29

Now before faith came, we were held captive under the law, imprisoned until the coming faith would be revealed. So then, the law was our guardian until Christ came, in order that we might be justified by faith. But now that faith has come, we are no longer under a guardian, for in Christ Jesus you are all sons of God, through faith. For as many of you as were baptized into Christ have put on Christ. There is neither Jew nor Greek, there is neither slave nor free, there is no male and female, for you are all one in Christ Jesus. And if you are Christ's, then you are Abraham's offspring, heirs according to promise.

CHAPTER 12

EVERY CHRISTIAN'S BIOGRAPHY

"My intention is to produce a large-scale, one-volume, cradle-to-grave narrative that will be both dramatic and authoritative," noted Ron Chernow about writing and researching his masterpiece, a biography of George Washington. "The upshot, I hope, will be that readers, instead of having a frosty respect for Washington, will experience a visceral appreciation of this foremost American."[1]

Paul is doing the same thing in Galatians 3:23–29: He's giving a cradle-to-grave biography of every Christian, not only setting our place in redemptive history, but, more important, giving us a visceral appreciation of our identity in Christ. Where Chernow tells Washington's story in 67 chapters, Paul tells ours in 2: captives under law, and sons in Christ. So important is this biography that he says it twice—here at the close of chapter 3 and again at the beginning of chapter 4.

Captives under Law

The law is a guardian, not a liberator. Paul writes, "Before faith came, we were held captive under the law, imprisoned until the coming faith would be revealed. So then, the law was our guardian until Christ came, in order that we might be justified by faith" (Gal 3:23–24).

We've seen previously how the law is a stern friend who will not let us escape to phantom, false, futile freedom, but holds us under lock and key until the right time. It exposes and expands sin, tempting us to gain the Lord's acceptance by law-keeping. Therefore, as long as we remain captive to law, sin reigns. The words are conclusive—"captive, imprisoned" (Gal 3:22–23). No light-hearted spiritual gaiety here, no deluded sense of autonomy to "choose for God" as we like. The law is an unforgiving jailer, who hums only one tune: "Bad to the bone!" Paul calls the law our "custodian," "guardian," "schoolmaster," or "tutor" (translations vary). It's perhaps better expressed, "So the Law was serving as a slave to look after us, to lead us to Christ, so that we could be justified by faith" (Gal 3:24 NJB).

> THE LAW IS
> AN
> UNFORGIVING
> JAILER

The actual Greek word is *paidagogos*, from which we get the English word "pedagogue." Therefore, it's natural to turn to educational vocabulary, e.g., "tutor" or "schoolmaster." It doesn't normally mean "slave," yet this translation is helpful in unpacking the cultural assumptions. In well-to-do households, the *paidagogos* was a slave assigned to a boy from the age of 6–16. While he had some oversight of the basic education of the child, the *paidagogos* was essentially the child's guardian. He would feed, dress, and chaperone the youth to school. He would carry his supplies, wait for him, bring him home, and have him recite his lessons. But he was also the boy's disciplinarian, ruling over every aspect of his life—chiding and scolding as needed, keeping him within strict limits. All the while, the child was virtually a slave to the slave.

The defining feature of life under the *paidagogos* was regimentation, which created an understandable thirst for freedom— when you're 16 you don't want a minder, you want a motorcycle! So also in the ancient world: The *paidagogos* was in charge of the child's life until he could take the reins of the chariot (and the management of his inheritance) into his own hands. The Greek historian and philosopher Xenophon wrote, "When a boy ceases to be a child, and begins to be a lad, others release him from his 'pedagogue' and from his teacher; he is then no longer under them, but is allowed to go his own way."[2] This is what the gospel has brought—freedom from the *paidagogos*, so that we can be truly free sons and daughters of God.

But often, that's not how we live. One crosscultural missionary couple, for instance, was so burdened by homesickness and the fatigue of cultural immersion that they took radical steps: They shipped some peanut butter to themselves. When they received it, others on their team judged them as being materialistic and unspiritual. The others' judgment was so intense that shortly afterward, this couple left the mission field. The illustration seems petty, but it's near to us: Do we whip ourselves for our imperfections and then, feeling judged, bludgeon our neighbors for their inadequacies? Are we so blind that we "strain out a gnat" of peanut butter while "swallowing a camel" of judgmentalism (Matt 23:24)?

How, then, can we avoid becoming closet Pharisees? What law do we apply to ourselves to stop it from happening? How can we perfect our discipleship so that we're never part of the peanut-butter police?

These are absolutely the wrong questions to ask. To see why, we need to explore a puzzling paradox; let's use Paul himself as the illustration. When did he discover that he was under a *paidagogos*? When did his strict regimentation unravel? When did he realize he wasn't free? His personal testimony (e.g., in Gal 1 or Phil 3) tells us he was cruising. His life as a Pharisee wasn't marked by angst and all things dark and gloomy. He was right; others were wrong. It was as simple as that. He brought light, fought darkness, and knew that God was grateful to have him on his side. He was the prequel to the Inquisition: powerful, authorized, and free.

We get a hint of a troubled conscience, but not in the way we might expect. Paul reports it this way. Speaking of the events on the Damascus road, he says, "When we had all fallen to the ground, I heard a voice saying to me in the Hebrew language, 'Saul, Saul, why are you persecuting me? It is hard for you to kick against the goads'" (Acts 26:14). It's as though Christ is saying, "Paul, what you're doing is not merely against my people, but against me, and it's hurting you. It's hard for you to keep going against what you're seeing and feeling. So why do it?"

Something was pricking Paul (as the word "goad" may be translated), stinging his conscience even as he sought to overcome it by ever-increasing zeal. But that something wasn't his failure before the law—in his mind, he was the model of success which he expected others to follow. Rather, it was his failure to believe in Jesus as God's gift of grace.

Here's the picture: Paul was a driven, type-A personality, a bulldozer of religious passion. But in his pursuit of the foolish, disobedient, deceived followers of Jesus, he was getting grit in his fuel tank. As he tortured and imprisoned the disciples of the Way, he heard their testimonies. In trying to get them to recant, he must have had a good grasp of what they believed and why they believed it; otherwise he wouldn't have known if they'd recanted or not! All the while, however, there was something else in operation: In the face of all this brutality and violence, he saw love like he'd never known. This was to become a force majeure even he couldn't resist.

Perhaps Stephen put one of the biggest chinks in his dozer blade. In Acts 7:58 we read that the vigilante group about to stone Stephen placed their cloaks at Paul's feet, probably meaning that he was regarded as the leading authority on site. We can barely imagine the viciousness of an ancient stoning. The victim was tossed into a ditch or sometimes partly buried so that the head and torso were exposed. Rocks big enough to cause severe injury, but not so big as to kill outright, were chosen—pebbles weren't an option. The death was painful, protracted, and extremely messy. And all of this happened under the semijudicial oversight of the leader of the stoning party. A stoning is one thing, but a righteous stoning really gets the blood pumping! Yet as Paul watched Stephen being stoned to death, saw his face and heard his words of love, he was confronted with something he didn't have: peace and surety in the face of death—and a terribly unjust death at that.

Arguably, this experience so impacted Paul that he, too, longed to be so filled with grace that he might be conformed to such a death should the time come (Phil 3:10). He would have known the story of Jesus' crucifixion and heard of his prayer: "Father forgive them, for they know not what they do" (Luke 23:34). The parallels between Stephen's last moments and Jesus' are inescapable. What enables a man to die at peace in such circumstances? What empowers him to pray for his enemies? How can a persecuted, powerless minority not seek revenge? As the grand inquisitor, Paul heard the gospel from the lips of every tortured and imprisoned Christian. No matter how much zeal he fired up, the stings and pricks of a thousand words started to eat into his armor plating.

So the curious paradox is this: Until the Damascus road, Paul had been under the law, enforcing the law, and glorifying the law in his life, but he seemed to have no conviction of sin. That is, until he met Christ; then everything came crashing down. Because Jesus loved Paul, treasured the Christians he was killing, and wanted him to be rescued from the terrible blindness of his self-righteousness, he unknotted Paul with a simple question, "Why do you persecute me?"

The love of it all heaped burning coals on Paul's head. It confronted him, convicting him of sin, because love so undeserved warrants love in return, not hatred.

LOVE SO UNDESERVED WARRANTS LOVE IN RETURN

Many chemical reactions need a catalyst. Christ catalyzes the law in our experience, crystalizing all our failures, transgressions, and sins under the impact of his presence. The Spirit causes us to see ourselves as we really are, as Christ shines the light of his glory into our hearts (2 Cor 4:4–6). But the law—without that living Word or the life-giving Spirit—remains merely a dead letter "until" a catalytic encounter with Christ (Gal 3:19; 4:2). As hymn writer John Newton once put it, "...'twas grace that taught my heart to fear, and grace those fears relieved." The goodness and kindness of God leads to repentance (Rom 2:4).

THE LAW REMAINS A DEAD LETTER "UNTIL" A CATALYTIC ENCOUNTER WITH CHRIST

What a ground-shifting experience, both for Paul and for us! Paul had come to see he didn't get God's will done by preaching the law and reinforcing it with stern punishments, but by preaching Christ crucified. As the gospel is preached, the law's dreadful work is brought to full completion, terrifyingly revealing to us that we've been slaves under a slave until the date set by our Father.

This is where the first chapter of our biography ends, and the second chapter begins.

Sons in Christ

When faith comes, "we are no longer under a guardian, for in Christ Jesus you are all sons of God, through faith. For as many of you as were baptized into Christ have put on Christ" (Gal 3:25–27). Paul will say more about this through the rest of the letter, but here the point is plain: If your faith is set on Jesus, you're no longer "under the law." It no longer condemns and imprisons. You have a radically new relationship to God, one which can be observed in the difference between duty and desire.

It's similar to a conversation Dan once had with their family domestic helper in the Philippines. When asked if they could deposit money in her bank account, she replied that she had never had one; she gave her pay away each week to her immediate and extended family. When further asked if she did this out of duty or love, she admitted, after an introspective pause, "Out of duty; I'd be shamed if I held any back for myself." She worked tirelessly, but doing her duty left her penniless. Many experience the Bible this way; it's oppressive, duty upon duty, making one feel miserable, exhausted, shamed, and depressed. Such an experience leads to one of two responses: rebellion or self-assertion. "Alright," we tell ourselves, "I'll work again today to get the moral job done, even though I'll have nothing to show for it." The law kills; we feel it!

The gospel, however, releases us into a deep passion for God, a desire to trust him more than ourselves. Our love becomes a reflection of his (1 John 4:19); this is the experience of genuine sonship. As we experience his mercy, mercy flows from us. As we know his blessing, blessing also flows from us. We're sensitized to our failures in a way we weren't before, but only because we're truly children of the Father and have his Spirit in us. The awareness of our continuing sins is met also by the awareness of the grace of God in the gospel.

We're often so acutely aware of our pains and failures that we feel depressed. Their weight is crushing; we long for freedom (in reality, for God himself). But what if reality was the reverse; what if we were truly free now? Our greatest sin is not the failure to confess all our sins, but the failure to confess Christ in the face of them.

Paul will have much to say about living the Christian life later on, but here it is in a nutshell: The gospel keeps us free. Hearing with faith keeps us filled with the Spirit, and only thereby is duty translated to glorious, freely-willed, love-filled obedience. None of this is naïveté or foolishness, but a radical trust that surrenders to a loving Lord. When such trust is present, the *paidagogos* isn't needed.

THE CHRISTIAN LIFE IN A NUTSHELL: THE GOSPEL KEEPS US FREE

So full is the Father's work on our behalf that our whole identity is bound up in Jesus— no more with ourselves! "For as many of you as were baptized into Christ have put on Christ" (Gal 3:27). In the New Testament, baptism stands for an inseparable complex of events. The outward act of baptism expresses many things at one time: faith (trust); incorporation into Christ; sharing in his death and resurrection; washing and renewal; a new allegiance; membership of the new covenant community, and anointing with the Spirit. But all of this is merely testimony to God's grace. Baptism isn't a work which we do, but a participation in what God has already done.

What has he done? It's really better to ask: What has he not done?

Sons are free from condemnation, and therefore free from the need to condemn. Paul knew God was his creator and judge; he ran to do his duty by rallying to his law. But then he knew him as he really is: the Father who freely forgives and justifies. Fear is removed as we are transformed from the mastery of the *paidagogos* to the freedom of our inheritance.

Hate is turned to love. And this opens up a new world of relational power. Believing sons are one with each other, sons of the same Father. Notice we didn't say "sons and daughters" this time; that's because Paul doesn't say it. He's not being insensitive. Rather, he's making a sensitive theological point. In the ancient world, women were thought of as less than a person; they couldn't give legal testimony or inherit property, for example. But Paul is blowing access to God's inheritance wide open by saying, "There is neither Jew nor Greek, there is neither slave nor free, there is no male and female, for you are all one in Christ Jesus" (Gal 3:28).

Distinctions of race, rank, and gender are torn down in God's family. Sure, differences remain—especially functional ones—but all are equal heirs of the Father's inheritance. In terms of status, everyone in Christ is a son! There's no fillip in being a free Jewish male, nor lesser honor in being female or a slave. Because believing sons are also "Abraham's offspring, heirs according to promise" (3:29), we are blessed with every spiritual blessing that belongs to Christ (Eph 1:3). The Son and the sons are as one in the Father's household. Jesus has become everything that we are so that we might share in all that he is!

We aren't yet the sons we will be. Yet, as sons in Christ, we are in the perfect place. Jesus' inheritance is unassailably ours, and in due course we will be conformed to his very image. This is the blessing God promised to the nations through Abraham. We simply receive it—not by works of the law, but by hearing with faith. This is every Christian's biography.

GALATIANS 4:1–7

I mean that the heir, as long as he is a child, is no different from a slave, though he is the owner of everything, but he is under guardians and managers until the date set by his father. In the same way we also, when we were children, were enslaved to the elementary principles of the world. But when the fullness of time had come, God sent forth his Son, born of woman, born under the law, to redeem those who were under the law, so that we might receive adoption as sons. And because you are sons, God has sent the Spirit of his Son into our hearts, crying, "Abba! Father!" So you are no longer a slave, but a son, and if a son, then an heir through God.

CHAPTER 13

FULLY ADOPTED

The young Abraham Lincoln reputedly purchased a slave girl from a New Orleans auction yard. The slave was perplexed by his first words to her: "You are free!" She didn't know what he meant, so Lincoln instructed her: She was owned by no one; she could go where she liked, when she liked; she needn't fear beating or incarceration again; she was nobody's property or play thing; and though he had bought her, he had done so only to free her. "Then," she supposedly said, "If I can go anywhere, I'll go with you!"

It's a tale worthy of Lincoln's stature, but one that's sadly untrue. Lincoln did visit such a slave auction in New Orleans, watching until he could stomach no more, and the event strengthened his resolve to deal with the issue decisively. To free all, not just one, had to be the aim. Against the tide of political popularity and the advice of some of his closest allies, he was determined to see the 13th Amendment ratified, for he knew his wartime Emancipation Proclamation would be legally tenuous in peace time. Only the 13th Amendment would truly guarantee the emancipated their freedom.

The fanciful and factual in this story help carry us into the realm of Galatians 4, but they still pale in comparison: In Galatians, the difference isn't between slavery and freedom, but slavery and sonship. It's not just that we're purchased to be freed, nor even that that freedom is irreversible, but that we're both redeemed and adopted. J. I. Packer once responded to the question "What is a Christian?" thus:

> The richest answer I know is that *a Christian is one who has God as Father.* ... Our understanding of Christianity cannot be better than our grasp of adoption. ... The truth of our adoption gives us the deepest insights the New Testament affords into the greatness of God's love.[1]

IT'S ADOPTION, BUT NOT AS WE KNOW IT

"The heir, as long as he is a child, is no different from a slave, though he is the owner of everything, but he is under guardians and managers until the date set by his father" (Gal 4:1-2).

In the Roman world, a father could set the date in which his son came of age, an event marked by exchanging one toga for another. The toga of a child was taken off and that of an adult son put on, with all the rights and responsibilities the exchange implied. But here's the thing: Generally we take adoption as creating a parent–child relationship where none exists; it's not an organic connection, but a legal one. While this periodically happened in the ancient world, Paul deliberately uses Roman intrafamiliar adoption—where there's an existing, biological relationship between the son and his father—to explain his point. This better represents the teaching of the New Testament, because we're adopted by the Father who has also created us. There is a legal connection ("justification" is legal vocabulary), but the connection is not only legal.

GOD RUNS
TOWARD US
TO REDEEM US

Erstwhile children we may be, but everyone lives and moves and has their being in God, irrespective of their belief in him (Acts 17:27-29). That's the hell of it. We prodigals can't escape the Father's presence no matter how far we run. Yet, while we run from him, God doesn't run from us. He runs toward us, sending his Son in the fullness of time to redeem us. Why? So that, through the gift of forgiveness, we would exchange our destructive, surrogate spiritual fathers (our idols) for the one true Father and thereby be free (1 Thess 1:9; Acts 17:30).

Adoption, then, is both redemption and reinstatement. Our rebellion consigned us to slave status. Grace brings our "coming of age" party, so-to-speak. Through grace we exchange the toga of our childish idolatry for the garment of a son of God. Yet there's more to Paul's teaching: We're adopted in and

> WE'RE LOVED WITH THE SAME LOVE THE FATHER HAS FOR THE ETERNAL SON

through a person. We know the Father through union with Jesus, his only begotten Son (John 14:7).

We're loved with the same love the Father has for the eternal Son. We're not freed to be let loose on the streets, fending for ourselves as homeless orphans. We're brought into the innermost sanctum of God's family. The reign of the *paidagogos* has truly ended. He had his place, but only "until Christ came, in order that we might be justified by faith" (Gal 3:24).

"In the same way," says Paul, "we also, when we were children, were enslaved to the elemental principles of the world" (4:3). There's no neutral ground. Our consciences are shaped by the laws of culture, custom, and religion. The conscience—together with issues of shame, saving and losing face, rules of taboo and the like—spins a web which holds us captive. This is so for the Hell's Angels or the Mafia as much as for any religion. There's an inescapable slavery, with death, literally, the only way out.

Being mainly pagans, the Galatians hadn't been under the custody of the Jewish law, but they did lie in bondage to their own law nonetheless. The "elemental principles" are always related to the law's way of living, the old way: Do A to get B. The ancient world was awash with fear and superstition. The gods of the elements (earth, wind, fire, water) as well as the elements of the heavenly bodies (sun, moon, and planets) all had to be appeased to obtain blessing. Just a little later, Paul says, "Formerly, when you did not know God, you were enslaved to those that by nature are not gods" (Gal 4:8; see also 4:9-10). Everyone worships (serves) someone or something. In adoption we're turned to God from idols (whatever shape they come in) and grow to desire the Blesser more than the blessing—this is true liberty.

GOD SENT HIS SON: THE GOSPEL IN FLESH AND BLOOD

Charles Spurgeon said, "We moved not towards the Lord, but the Lord towards us! I do not find that the world, in repentance, sought its Maker. No, but the offended God, Himself, in infinite compassion, broke the silence and came forth to bless His enemies!"[2] Spurgeon's talking about us—we're the enemies. "While we were yet sinners"—enemies of God—"Christ died for us" (Rom 5:8; see also 5:10).

Paul lays out the gospel for us in Galatians 4:4-5: "God sent forth his Son." In other words, Christ existed before the manger in Bethlehem. Remember Jesus' words: "Before Abraham was, I am" (John 8:58). God sent his Son, the eternal Son, the divine Word, who became flesh, "born of a woman." He came into our world as we do, through a woman's womb; he was and is fully human. Hebrews says, "Because God's children are human beings—made of flesh and blood—the Son also became flesh and blood" (Heb 2:14 NLT).

Jesus—being born of Mary, a Jew—was also "born under the law." He was circumcised on the eighth day and perfectly kept every element of the law, not out of a punctilious spirit, but because he alone of all humanity loved the Lord his God with all his heart and mind and strength, and his neighbor as himself (Matt 22:37-39).

Had he not been human, Jesus couldn't have redeemed us. Had he not been the righteous Son of God, he couldn't have made atonement for the unrighteous sons and daughters of God. Neither law nor false gods could redeem or adopt us, but Jesus became a curse for us *so that* we might receive adoption as sons" (Gal 4:5, emphasis added). The purpose clause ("so that") is paramount: Knowing God as your Father is what his grace is all about.

Consider another line from J. I. Packer:

> Adoption is a family idea conceived in terms of love and viewing God as Father. In adoption God takes us into his family and fellowship, establishes us as his children and heirs. Closeness, affection, and generosity are at the heart of the relationship. To be right with God the judge is a good thing, but to be loved and cared for by God the Father is greater.[3]

Do closeness, affection, and generosity describe your experience of God? Or are you serving as a slave, like the relationship the elder brother had with his father in Luke 15? He had a pro rata view of his father's affection. So sure that he'd always done the right thing, the elder brother saw his father's love for his wastrel brother as undignified and indulgent. His attitude involved very linear thinking: "I deserve more affection, because I've been the better son." Like so many Christians, the elder brother lived like an accountant in God's house, not a son. He didn't live free, because he didn't live in grace.

None of us, however, is right; all of us are sinners. It was the Father alone who did the right thing. Why, then, do you worry? Why, then, do you fret? Why, then, are you overcome with bitterness and anger? Why, then, does your joy so easily collapse? Do you not have a Father who has given even his only Son in atonement for you? If the Father has gone this far, how can his faithfulness now fail you?

The Good News of the Spirit

If the Son was sent that you might have the status of sonship, the Spirit was sent that you might experience it. The inheritance is for sons, not for slaves! It doesn't come by keeping the law, but by living in the Spirit.[4]

Perhaps you're wondering what the inheritance is; you don't see your life's circumstances getting better, your relationships improving, your health problems resolving, or your bank balance increasing. But the inheritance isn't some material possession. And it isn't, necessarily, freedom from suffering, nor anything which the flesh would call "easy street." Paul suggests that the Spirit is the inheritance (Gal 3:14) because he brings us all the blessings and promises of God by bringing us into communion with the Father and the Son. The inheritance is wholly relational: living in the assurance that God is your trustworthy Father, that you are not a homeless orphan, that you can experience his presence even while your life may be falling apart, that you can be so consumed with who he is—so at peace in the moment of tribulation and trial—that you want to tell others what he is like.

Growth in the Christian life is really settling deeply into the fact that we are loved, wanted, and fully adopted by God. Grace frees us to stop lacerating ourselves over our inabilities and opens our minds and hearts to the reality that we are infinitely loved by God in Christ, with the Holy Spirit interceding even in our weaknesses. Especially there.

WE ARE INFINITELY LOVED BY GOD IN CHRIST

But it's hard for us to surrender our defenses and fully enter the new life opened by God's love. Russell Moore describes his sons' unexpected difficulty after being adopted from the "squalor" of a Russian orphanage:

> We nodded our thanks to the orphanage personnel and walked out into the sunlight, to the terror of the two boys. They'd never seen the sun, and they'd never felt the wind. They had never heard the sound of a car door slamming or had the sensation of being carried along at 100 miles an hour down a Russian road. I noticed that they were shaking, and reaching back to the orphanage in the distance.

I whispered to Sergei, now Timothy, "That place is a pit! If only you knew what's waiting for you: a home with a Mommy and a Daddy who love you, grandparents, and great-grandparents and cousins and playmates ... and McDonald's Happy Meals!" But all they knew was the orphanage. It was squalid, but they had no other reference point, and it was home.

We knew the boys had acclimated to our home, that they trusted us, when they stopped hiding food in their highchairs. They knew there would be another meal coming, and they wouldn't have to fight for the scraps. This was the new normal. ... I still remember, though, those little hands reaching for the orphanage, and I see myself there.[5]

Do you feel you're still in the orphanage? The Holy Spirit came—into the midst of our messy lives—so you would know how greatly the Father loves you. And if you're a Christian, the cry of your heart for God is proof that you've received the inheritance of his Holy Spirit.

The Cry of the Heart

Jesus, uniquely, referred to God by the affectionate Aramaic name "Abba" (Mark 14:36). Abba conveys intimacy, deep affection, respect, love, and security. While toddlers might have used it of their fathers, or students of a much-loved rabbi, it had never been used of God. God was not that familar, surely! Wouldn't any human being claiming such a relationship be guilty of gross presumption?

But this is precisely why the Spirit of the Son has been given to adopted sons and daughters: so they may share in such a relationship with their heavenly Abba (see Rom 8:15). We learn to participate in this cry of the heart for the whole of our lives. Luther says:

Paul ... purposely says "crying" to indicate the trial of
the Christian who is still weak and who believes weak-
ly. ... It is a very great comfort when Paul says here that
the Spirit of Christ, sent by God into our hearts, cries
"Abba, Father!" and when in Romans 8:26 that He helps
us in our weakness and intercedes with sighs too deep
for words ... for in his trial a man feels only the power
of sin, the weakness of the flesh, and his doubt; he feels
the fiery darts of the devil (Ephesians 6:16), the terrors
of death, and the wrath and judgement of God. All these
things issue powerful and horrible cries against us, so
that there appears to be nothing left for us except despair and eternal death. But in the midst of the terrors
of the Law, thunderclaps of sin, tremors of death and
roarings of the devil, Paul says the Holy Spirit begins to
cry in our heart: "Abba, Father!" And His cry vastly exceeds, and breaks through, the powerful and horrible
cries of the Law, sin, death, and the devil. It penetrates
the clouds and heaven, and it reaches all the way to the
ears of God.[6]

The cry of such a heart doesn't originate within ourselves. Rather,
the Spirit of God teaches our souls to cry, and often the lessons
are most acute in the midst of great pain.

In light of this, Christians don't believe themselves to be free
(or, at least, nearly free) of sin. And similarly, Christians aren't
comfortable with their sin. We hate the fact that we don't do
what we desire and that we do what we don't desire to do (see
Rom 7:15-20). We can become frustrated over our lack of progress
and (wrongly) conclude that God is either waiting to crush us or
couldn't care less about us.

But take note. If God didn't love you, you wouldn't cry out to
him for mercy. You would have no interest in him. The cry of your
heart is evidence that the Holy Spirit has touched you and enabled your sonship. As Charles Spurgeon once said, "I once knew
a good woman who was the subject of many doubts, and when

I got to the bottom of her doubt, it was this: she knew she loved Christ, but she was afraid he did not love her. 'Oh!' I said, 'that is a doubt that will never trouble me; never, by any possibility, because I am sure of this, that the heart is so corrupt, naturally, that love to God never did get there without God's putting it there.' "[7] And out of the cry of your heart, you *desire* to do his will. There's a bigger miracle in that than you realize.

Adopted by the will of the Father, in union with the Son, with the Spirit crying out "Abba, Father!" through our hearts: This is the state of every Christian! Such a glorious inheritance won't go uncontested by moments of doubt and attacks by the devil, but you have security better than the 13th Amendment. You have the new covenant, eternally sealed in the blood of Jesus. You are Abba's child forever.

Formerly, when you did not know God, you were enslaved to those that by nature are not gods. But now that you have come to know God, or rather to be known by God, how can you turn back again to the weak and worthless elementary principles of the world, whose slaves you want to be once more? You observe days and months and seasons and years! I am afraid I may have labored over you in vain.

Brothers, I entreat you, become as I am, for I also have become as you are. You did me no wrong. You know it was because of a bodily ailment that I preached the gospel to you at first, and though my condition was a trial to you, you did not scorn or despise me, but received me as an angel of God, as Christ Jesus. What then has become of your blessedness? For I testify to you that, if possible, you would have gouged out your eyes and given them to me. Have I then become your enemy by telling you the truth? They make much of you, but for no good purpose. They want to shut you out, that you may make much of them. It is always good to be made much of for a good purpose, and not only when I am present with you, my little children, for whom I am again in the anguish of childbirth until Christ is formed in you! I wish I could be present with you now and change my tone, for I am perplexed about you.

CHAPTER 14

DON'T SELL
YOUR BIRTHRIGHT

The Christian life had become a gloomy business for the Galatians; joy had left the building. Paul asks them directly: "What has happened to all your joy?" (Gal 4:15 NIV); "What has happened to the utter contentment you had then?" (4:15 NJB). Paul's pastoral method is clear—look back at where you were; then, look at where you are, and ask yourself, "How did we end up here?" Because "here" is a long way from "there," and "here" has neither love nor joy attending it. (This isn't far removed from Jesus' words confronting the church in Ephesus in Revelation 2:4–5.)

Most Christians enter the kingdom on a flood tide of liberty and love. Like Peter on the day of Pentecost (Acts 2:14–15), people get practically drunk with delight as they experience the forgiveness of sins and the Spirit's presence for the first time. Then, bit by bit, the flame is extinguished. Church subcultures, discipleship courses, witnessing methodologies, and other programs shape our consciences to the law instead of the gospel. Strategic plans stultify spontaneity. Nominal religious systems infect our bones with seriousness, churlishness, and cynicism. But, paradoxically, the more we think the Christian life calls us to accept the challenge and muster commitment or radical obedience, the more inflexible and ironfisted we become. Guilt smothers joy, and obedience turns into a caricature of the Spirit-filled life. The fruit of the gospel is pickled in vinegar, and yet we wonder why we've lost our taste for it or why passersby prefer not to taste at all.

In such a state, it's easy to attribute our loss of joy to the circumstances or people around us. Boredom overtakes our monotony, and acedia sets in. We discover we aren't who we thought we were. And, realizing that we're frauds, we recoil in caustic grumpiness at every hint of criticism, fearful of the world in general!

NEITHER PEOPLE NOR PREDICAMENTS ARE RESPONSIBLE FOR OUR MISSING JOY

Does this description seem over the top? The humble heart knows it's merely a step away from a ditch it's visited numerous times.

The truth is, neither people nor predicaments are responsible for our missing joy. When we make them the bricks from which we erect self-esteem and well-being, though, we turn them into idols, forgetting the true source of identity and security. Joy collapses when we tie who we are to people and circumstances rather than to the gospel of Jesus Christ. Thus, we think and live like slaves instead of sons and daughters.

If you're like the Galatians and have forgotten your birthright, what do you do?

Do less; listen more. The forgetful and fretful need to be reminded of this, like a doctor we know sometimes needs to remind the staff in her palliative care ward. In work like theirs, you need to listen to what the patient is saying, not presume that you know what's going on. You need to spend time with them and hear them; their stories, not your busyness, are the most important thing at any given moment. Likewise, for the Christian, God's story is the most important thing. Listen—hear again the love that the Father has for you, be bathed again in his grace, and have your ears filled with the songs of joy he sings over you (Zeph 3:17).

BIRTHRIGHT BLUES

Genesis contains the story of twin brothers, Esau and Jacob. As the elder, Esau could have expected to inherit two-thirds of Isaac's estate. But something else occurred:

> Once when Jacob was cooking stew, Esau came in from the field, and he was exhausted. And Esau said to Jacob, "Let me eat some of that red stew, for I am exhausted!" ... Jacob said, "Sell me your birthright now." Esau said, "I am about to die; of what use is a birthright to me?" Jacob said, "Swear to me now." So he swore to him and sold his birthright to Jacob. Then Jacob gave Esau bread and lentil stew, and he ate and drank and rose and went his way. Thus Esau despised his birthright (Gen 25:29–34).

Did you see what Esau did? He sold his birthright—that's obvious. But he sold it for a mess of pottage—a bowl of slop. He exchanged something infinitely more valuable—although less tangible at the time—for something instantly gratifying.

And aren't our attitudes often just as careless and short-sighted? We can see it in a story told about King Louis XIV, who once walked out of the Palace of Versailles on his way to a gala, down the front stairs with courtiers in tow. At the same time, the carriage that was to transport him drove up and arrived at the bottom of the stairs at the exact moment the king did; without breaking stride, he stepped into it. Annoyed that the carriage was not already at the appointed place before he started walking toward it, King Louis complained angrily, "I almost waited!"

We can also see this attitude in ourselves. We're just as irritable and impatient. Our flesh gravitates to the law, since it's tangible, predictable, and seems to promise quicker rewards. It's entirely quid pro quo: "Lord, give me your blessings; fill me with joy because I've done right, been good, obeyed the rules." Or, if we're not quite on speaking terms with God, we think, "Maybe if I pray longer and attend a church service or two, God will look upon me with a friendly face—and at least I'll feel better about myself." It's all doing, not listening or waiting patiently in faith for God's mysterious timing. For Luther, the most important organ in the body was the ear, because through it we hear the gospel. But when we aren't hearing (because we're absorbed in the Judaizers' message, or because our ears are filled with the wax of our own religious attainment), the quid pro quo life thrives.

About the Christian life, John Stott said:

> What the Christian life is not is bondage to the law, as if our salvation hung in the balance and depended on our meticulous and slavish obedience to the letter of the law. ... [O]ur salvation rests upon the finished work of Christ, on His sin-bearing, curse-bearing death, embraced by faith.[1]

If you're wondering what happened to all *your* joy, Paul's gospel is for you!

KNOWING YOU, KNOWING ME

"When you did not know God, you were enslaved to those that by nature are not gods. But now that you have come to know God, or rather to be known by God, how can you turn back?" (Gal 4:8–9).

Imagine a baby girl in an orphanage. A man comes to visit her, loves her, adopts her, takes her home, raises her, blesses her, and sees her grow to full maturity. She grows up calling him father—he's the only father she's ever known. He's her father because he first knew her and took her as his daughter.

The same thing has happened to us. We know God because he's known us; and because he has known us, we come to know ourselves. As with the woman at the well in John 4, God knows all the sordid details, but he doesn't meet us in the noonday heat to condemn us. He shows us all we've done, but in the light of his grace. At one and the same time, he both brings our sin to the light and his light expels our darkness—setting us free to enjoy

GOD SHOWS US ALL WE'VE DONE, BUT IN THE LIGHT OF HIS GRACE

our birthright. So why would you want to go back to the orphan-age? The thought is as utterly baffling to Paul as it is to us, for returning to life under the law is, literally, a dead end—and our joy shriveling is the first sign.

But it wasn't always that way, and needn't remain that way. Testimony to such was etched into the Galatians' experience. As they looked back, they could say, "Grace did something the law (pagan superstition though it mostly was) could not. Grace freed us to love, flooded us with joy, and furnished us with a home. We welcomed those who were different, embraced our enemies, and lived free from all fears. The elemental spirits lost their grip. We sat tall in the saddle and saw the Spirit stir."

Now, however, they weren't where they had been. They had gotten stuck on that which had marked their previous existence—e.g., observances of days and rituals, as in Galatians 4:9-11—but this time with a Jewish twist. And where once they would have given Paul anything, now they saw him as an enemy (4:16). Their overreliance on the law made them neurotic and paranoid.

BE TRANSFORMED!

It had been a tough mission trip. John Mark quit the team, and Paul got sick and went to the Galatian highlands to recover. Illness had brought him into the Galatians' homeland, and there this pitiful, disease-ridden man had preached to them. Some think Paul may have had malaria, others suggest an eye disease, but whatever his ailment, Paul was a trial to the Galatians. In the ancient world, diseases were often seen as manifestations of a demonic pres-ence or an enemy's curse. Strangers with a disease were a cause for spitting and despising, not rolling out the red carpet. Yet the Galatians received Paul as an angel of God (4:14). Their joy was great, not because of Paul per se, but because of his message. They were so delighted that "if possible, [they] would have gouged out [their] eyes and given them to [him]" (4:15). This may have been because Paul couldn't see, or it may have been a figure of speech, the equivalent of saying that we would give our right arm or the shirt off our back—but they *meant* it.

Transparent and tangible love flowed from transformation in the gospel. Now things had changed. Fear, suspicion, introversion, and hostility had invaded the camp. Why? No sooner had Paul returned to Antioch than the Galatians were allowing themselves to be courted by the Judaizers. Oh, our fickle, foolish hearts! When someone makes much of us, flattering and adulating our steps, our hearts feed on it. Flattery feels good.

The Judaizers were doing just this. "They make much of you, but for no good purpose," says Paul (4:17). They want you to become their converts, not Christ's; they want you to count yourselves as exclusively their followers. They want to put you on the registration list of their school and back under the *paidagogos*.

It may seem that Paul is just jealous. And while that's true, he's not jealous for himself, however, but for Jesus. He's pointing to the one who owns his heart and fills it with grace and love; who has set him free to run with the wind. "Brothers, I entreat you," says Paul, "become as I am, for I also have become as you are" (4:12). In other words, Paul says: "Like Jesus, I entered your world to serve you. I don't want you to mimic my appearance, my interests, my politics. I want you to know my joy, to enjoy the grace and freedom I have. I desire you to delight in Jesus as I do, to be transformed, to join me in saying, 'I have been crucified with Christ. It is no longer I who live, but Christ who lives in me' (Gal 2:20)." Such freedom is what Paul is jealous for.

Not so with the Judaizers. One of the most powerful words in advertising is "exclusive." We're bombarded with exclusive offers and lured by exclusive memberships, be it to the golf club or good ol' boys' club—Dan, for instance, especially pines to be part of the frequent flier Sky Club. Power comes with the ability to define who's "in" and who's "out." While many exclusive clubs are largely benign, religious clubs (sects, cults, and Pharisaic schools) are among the most dangerous. Psychological manipulation is easy:

Create an exclusive inner circle, set some barriers around it, and make sure that it comes with a visible and costly membership fee.

Paul, by definition, was "out." And so, psychologically, the only way the Galatians could justify this was to deliberately forget his love for them and to make him out as an enemy. "Those false teachers are so eager to win your favor, but their intentions are not good. They are trying to shut you off from me so that you will pay attention only to them" (4:17 NLT).

As the bright lights of exclusive club memberships fill your eyes, the light of the gospel seems pale in comparison. Human acceptance is indeed alluring. But before long, guilt—bred by the law, upon which approval is bestowed—blossoms into paranoia; anyone outside is believed to be part of a conspiracy against us. Threatened by the liberty of others who seem to be too free, we fall into slavery once again, shut off from joy found only in Jesus.

> GUILT—BRED BY THE LAW—BLOSSOMS INTO PARANOIA

Paul's attitude to the Galatians is markedly different from their new attitude towards him. He longs for them, like one enduring labor pains. Spiritual friends can ache badly for us, longing for us not to follow them but to be truly transformed and released in Christ. Paul likens his longing for Christ to be formed within them to childbirth, the pains of which are protracted and deep. He had spent much of his life on the path to which the Galatians were turning. He didn't want them to end in the same cul-de-sac of legalism, shut off from the grace of Christ, living in slavery once again.

John Newton was only 7 years old when his mother died; at the age of 11, he went to sea with his father. After numerous voyages, being forced into service in the Royal Navy, and finding himself abused and mistreated with those aboard a slave ship, the 23-year-old Newton was bound for home aboard a merchant ship when it encountered a severe storm and nearly sank. And in that storm, Newton—who'd come to know the depths of human sin and degradation in all he had seen and done in the slave trade—cried out to the Father for mercy. He called on nothing but God's own character. He was truly converted and never forgot God's mercy. He affixed these words from Deuteronomy in bold letters across the mantel in his study: "Thou shalt remember that thou wast a slave in the land of Egypt, and the Lord thy God redeemed thee" (Deut 15:15 KJV). As it was for him, so also for us.

TRUE TEACHERS WANT US TO RETAIN OUR SONSHIP

False teachers want a good showing in the flesh; they push and preach either legalism or license, and proffer exclusive membership benefits in one way or another. But true teachers, like Paul, want us to retain our sonship, to not sell it for a mess of pottage. Painful though it may be, they raise grace before our eyes over and over again, like Newton raised his banner at the very center of his home. We never grow beyond our need of the gospel.

Tell me, you who desire to be under the law, do you not listen to the law? For it is written that Abraham had two sons, one by a slave woman and one by a free woman. But the son of the slave was born according to the flesh, while the son of the free woman was born through promise. Now this may be interpreted allegorically: these women are two covenants. One is from Mount Sinai, bearing children for slavery; she is Hagar. Now Hagar is Mount Sinai in Arabia; she corresponds to the present Jerusalem, for she is in slavery with her children. But the Jerusalem above is free, and she is our mother. For it is written,

> "Rejoice, O barren one who does not bear;
>   break forth and cry aloud, you who are not
> in labor!
>   For the children of the desolate one will be more
>   than those of the one who has a husband."

Now you, brothers, like Isaac, are children of promise. But just as at that time he who was born according to the flesh persecuted him who was born according to the Spirit, so also it is now. But what does the Scripture say? "Cast out the slave woman and her son, for the son of the slave woman shall not inherit with the son of the free woman." So, brothers, we are not children of the slave but of the free woman.

CHAPTER 15

WHO'S YOUR MAMA?

You might be tempted to think that Peter had Galatians 4:21–31 in mind when he said that some of Paul's points were difficult to grasp (2 Pet 3:15–16). But bear with us; Paul is actually making a simple point, and in so doing, echoing Jesus' teaching, "That which is born of the flesh is flesh, and that which is born of the Spirit is spirit" (John 3:6).

Paul's allegory is a word picture, contrasting the irreconcilable difference between mere legal religion and true spiritual life. At its core is an issue of identity: As a person born free by the Spirit, who are you? And what difference does it make?

But why does Paul use allegory—why not express the truth more straightforwardly? He's most likely using the same Old Testament story his opponents relied on, but turning their reading on its head. Their interpretation may have gone like this: "Jews derive their ancestry from Isaac, the son of the free woman (Sarah), and owner of the inheritance. Ishmael was the son of the slave woman (Hagar); he received no inheritance; he was essentially a Gentile. Jews received the liberating knowledge of the law; Gentiles are in bondage to ignorance. Jews are children of the covenant by birth; Gentiles can't enjoy the blessings of the covenant naturally, but they could be adopted into the family by circumcision. By embracing the Mosaic law they can align themselves with the church of the circumcised in Jerusalem, the mother-church of true 'Christ-followers.' "

We need to understand how Paul's allegory turns such thinking on its head and what difference it makes. So be patient and find a comfortable seat—the historical and cultural factors close to Paul are far from us today.

THE HISTORICAL CANVAS

God promised to make Abram into a great nation, but he seemed to be taking his time. Neither Abram nor Sarai (as they were then called) were getting any younger, so, in keeping with ancient practice, "Sarai said to Abram, 'The LORD has prevented me from having children. Go and sleep with my servant. Perhaps I can have children through her.' And Abram agreed with Sarai's proposal" (Gen 16:2 NLT). Abram took Hagar as a concubine, and Ishmael was conceived. It's logical: God's promises don't rule out our cooperation, and we know that God helps those who help themselves, right?

Not at all! Divine promises are never contingent on human cooperation. God hadn't forgotten his promise, despite his timing not being to their liking. Fourteen years after Ishmael, God spoke again to Abraham:

> "Regarding Sarai, your wife—her name will no longer be Sarai. From now on her name will be Sarah. And I will bless her and give you a son from her!" ... Then Abraham bowed down to the ground, but he laughed to himself in disbelief. "How could I become a father at the age of 100?" he thought. "And how can Sarah have a baby when she is ninety years old?" So Abraham said to God, "May Ishmael live under your special blessing!" But God replied, "No—Sarah, your wife, will give birth to a son for you. You will name him Isaac" (Gen 17:15, 17–19 NLT).

Isaac means "laughter," which is understandable. Abraham and Sarah were so old, they were nearly fossils. In a mixture of joyous faith and bewilderment, both Abraham and later Sarah (Gen 18:12) split their sides at what God had said. Sarah's womb had long since given up the ghost, and we can imagine Abraham—looking at his own body, which was as good as dead (Rom 4:19)—thinking, "This is going to be really interesting!"

Isaac was born to Sarah, not of her or Abraham's will or logic, but simply in fulfillment of God's promise. Every time they called Isaac's name, they would have been reminded of how utterly ridiculous the whole thing was—and, simultaneously, would have been reminded to marvel at their God.

> THE STORY'S FOCUS IS ON FAITH, NOT BIOLOGY

These are the basics on two mamas, two sons, and one dad. But here's the critical point: Ishmael was born to the slave woman, Isaac to the free. Despite having the same daddy, only Isaac came according to God's promise. The slave mother gave birth to a son of the flesh; the free mother, to a son of faith (see Heb 11:11). The story's focus is on faith, not biology.

So Paul isn't just reviewing ancient history. The story is our story. "Everyone is a slave by nature, until in the fullness of God's promise he is set free. So everyone is either an Ishmael or an Isaac, either still what he is by nature, a slave, or by the grace of God set free," says John Stott.[1]

THE ALLEGORICAL COMPOSITION

Upon this historical canvas, Paul paints his allegory, using human events to talk about spiritual realities. In this way, he inverts the thinking of his opponents, using the story of Isaac and Ishmael to prove the gospel of free grace and reject legalism. Paul says:

> These women are two covenants. One is from Mount Sinai, bearing children for slavery; she is Hagar. Now Hagar is Mount Sinai in Arabia; she corresponds

to the present Jerusalem, for she is in slavery with her children. But the Jerusalem above is free, and she is our mother (Gal 4:24–26).

Mount Sinai was a covenant of law. Recall Galatians 3:23: "Now before faith came, we were held captive under the law, imprisoned until the coming faith would be revealed." Hagar is another picture of life under the *paidagogos*: Her heirs inhabit the earthly Jerusalem, which Paul uses to denote an entire realm (like Washington being used for America, Beijing for China, or London for England). Hagar stands for the religion of the natural person. She represents what we can do by the flesh: our self-trust, our bondage to legalism and legislation. Sarah, however, stands for grace. She stands for what God has done, for God-trust, for the radical spiritual freedom of unfettered sonship that is ours by faith. Philip Ryken has put this well:

> The New Jerusalem is not just for the future. God has already started to build his eternal city. The "new" Jerusalem has replaced the "now" Jerusalem. The spiritual Jerusalem has superseded the earthly Jerusalem in the plan of God. The promises of the Old Testament were not for the Jews only, but they are fulfilled in the church of Jesus Christ. Anyone who receives Jesus as Savior and Lord is a son or daughter of Sarah, a true child of Abraham. If we belong to God's family in this way, we are free in Christ. We are citizens of the New Jerusalem and enjoy the freedom of that eternal city.[2]

The allegory emphasizes the difference between spiritual slavery and spiritual freedom. It's impossible to overstate how dramatic this would have been for Paul's Jerusalem audience. To a Pharisee, the physical Jerusalem and the temple were sacrosanct, and the potential loss of these were among the motives for Jesus' crucifixion (John 11:47–48). Under the new covenant, on the other hand, all that matters is the spiritual city—a nonethnic, nongeographic entity spanning time, space, and race. No wonder Paul's opponents saw him as a threat—his preaching would lead to the same outcome as Jesus' preaching. He had to be stopped!

Regarding spiritual slavery, Charles Spurgeon once said:

> All those who trust in works never are free, and never can be. ... If I could keep all God's law, I should have no right to favor, for I should have done no more than was my duty, and be a bond-slave still. The law is the most rigorous master in the world, no wise man would love its service; for after all you have done, the law never gives you a "Thank you," for it, but says, "Go on, sir, go on!" The poor sinner trying to be saved by law is like a blind horse going round and round a mill, and never getting a step further, but only being whipped continually; yea, the faster he goes, the more work he does, the more he is tired, so much the worse for him.[3]

So what does spiritual freedom look like? It may seem like a contradiction, but spiritual freedom is not freedom from sin.

You will never, ever, under any circumstances, be free of sin this side of heaven. You will never get out of Romans 7, where Paul decries the fact that the good he would do he does not, and the very thing he would not do he does. But at the very same time, you will never be cut off from Romans 6, where you're told that you have died and been raised with Christ. You will never be excluded from Romans 8, where we're told that there is no condemnation for those in Christ Jesus. You're not a child only of Romans 7 or of Romans 8, but of both, simultaneously!

One of the most potent phrases to come out of the Lutheran reformation was this: *iustus et peccator simul*, often referred to as the *simul* for short. It means "justified and a sinner simultaneously." This *simul* is what we're talking about here and what the perfectionist Pharisee within you hates. But if you can grasp it, the *simul* is the stake in the inner Pharisee's heart. For Luther didn't mean that you've got a split personality, partly sinner and partly saint, nor did he mean you're a sinner only sometimes (when you do bad stuff) and a saint at other times (when you do good stuff). It means you're fully a sinner and fully a justified saint at the same time.

> YOU'RE FULLY A SINNER AND FULLY A JUSTIFIED SAINT

The righteousness you have by faith is Jesus', not yours. Therefore, it can't be spoiled by your arrogance, pride, selfishness, or greed. Jesus made your sin his very own. He wore it on the cross as his only garment, and there it was crucified, died, and was buried. When he rose from the grave, it remained dead. Freedom is found in embracing the *simul*.

Denying that you're a sinner-saint only places you on the same path as the Judaizers. If you merely tolerate it, believing you'll be able to overcome it if only you muster enough commitment, obedience, discipline, or spiritual fortitude, you'll be deceived.

The *simul*, however, is not God's last word on our birthright. We're sinner-saints now, but the sin part will be removed in the hereafter. The Holy Spirit gives us a new will that wants what God wants; a new heart that loves God and hates idolatry; a new purpose, to serve God and others; and a new destiny, hope in the coming kingdom and freedom from trying to build a utopia on earth out of your retirement fund. These are firstfruits of the new covenant blessings being fulfilled in you. Like Isaac, the rest of the inheritance will follow, as surely as dawn follows dusk.

We need to be fed by the gospel over and again, because without it, the truth that we can't do as we desire to do would drive us to natural religion in an instant. The Spirit is the pledge and seal of all that is yet to come.

It's little wonder we ache and groan in the Spirit—along with creation—for the full manifestation of the kingdom of heaven. Don't be surprised that you go through shadows and are sometimes filled with as much fear and doubt as faith and love. This is not yet heaven, nor are you who you shall be when you see your Savior face to face (Psa 17:15; 1 Cor 13:12; 1 John 3:2). You live in the *simul*. Yet because of the sure and finished work of Christ, you live there free. "For the Lord is the Spirit, and wherever the Spirit of the Lord is, there is freedom" (2 Cor 3:17 NLT).

There is no need to pretend to yourself, others, or God that you are not a sinner. There is no need to play the religious obedience card to prove you are justified. You're free to live without pretense, without the enervating navel gazing of examining every minute, thought, motive, action, and intention. There is no need to escape the presence of sin. Your sanctification doesn't lie in escaping the world, but in believing the gospel.

Steve Brown—who has taught the truth about freedom so boldly that he's drawn no little fire from today's Judaizers—writes about freedom this way:

> Almost everything we've been taught to do and think [concerning the Christian life] is not only wrong, it only makes things worse. Trying harder doesn't work. You should know that by now. Becoming more religious will only magnify the problem. Being disciplined and making a commitment will, more often than not, cause you to "hit the rocks of reality"; and your efforts, in the end, will turn to dust. Pretending is stupid. At some point, you will slip up and be shamed. And reading the latest book on making an impact, changing your world, or being driven by a purpose (as good as those things can be) will probably drive you nuts. You will only feel guiltier. Motivational advice, biblical directives, challenges, and resolutions are dogs that simply won't hunt anymore.[4]

Brown summarizes, "What if you had three free sins? Better, what if you had unlimited free sins? Even better yet, what if your sins weren't even the issue? What if the issue were living your life with someone who loved you without condition or condemnation?"[5]

Reflecting on the spiritual freedom of true sonship, Paul breaks into song: "Rejoice, O barren one who does not bear"

(Gal 4:27). He's singing because love has set his feet dancing. He's free to call upon God and to love God; he's so filled with love, he even desires to love his neighbor. And he sees that this freedom is going to fill the new Jerusalem with more souls than the old Jerusalem ever had.

THE PRACTICAL CONSEQUENCES

So Paul looks at the canvas, the allegorical picture, and essentially says, "What are the consequences of these two women, two sons, two cities? And to which do you belong?"

If you insist on living religiously according to the flesh, remember that Abraham had a son according to the flesh, but Ishmael didn't get the inheritance. But if, by faith, you hold on to what Jesus did on the cross, you can bank on two things: the pain of persecution, and the privilege of inheritance.

The Isaacs of this world can expect persecution from Ishmaels. Persecution doesn't come only from outside of the church. Paul speaks of persecution from inside the church when he says that "he who was born according to the flesh persecuted him who was born according to the Spirit" (Gal 4:29). The greatest threat to believers isn't those outside the church, it's those inside—the unbelieving church. Those who want to live by the law are the greatest threat to those who want to live by grace. The unbelieving church wants religion and establishment. It doesn't want the gospel, and, ultimately, it doesn't want God. It lives out a theology of glory and hates theologians of the cross.

> THE UNBELIEVING CHURCH WANTS RELIGION. IT DOESN'T WANT THE GOSPEL

Israel killed her prophets. Jesus' death was orchestrated by the Pharisees. The most persistent and deadly opponents of Paul were fanatical Judaizers, those who had the same background and training as he and who even confessed Jesus. And as Luther once said, "If someone does not want to endure persecution from Ishmael, let him not claim that he is Christian."[6]

Ishmaels need to look down their noses and feel better than others. Admitting guilt and absence of merit is a tightrope too high. Why? Because they don't realize the net of the gospel will catch their fall. We become Ishmaels when we attempt to build our identity instead of receiving it from the one who accepts us, forgives us, and wants to be our loving Father. When Paul says, "Cast out the slave woman and her son, for the son of the slave woman shall not inherit with the son of the free woman" (Gal 4:30), he isn't suggesting we kick our neighbors to the curb. He's saying, "In the attitude of your heart, cast out the tendency to want to get right with God through scruples and rules and law-keeping; they only ever breed pride and self-sufficiency. They bar you from possessing the inheritance that is yours. They rob you of your true identity and steal your joy. Cast them out, and hear once more the gospel from the lips of the Spirit."

The words of Jesus in Matthew apply here: "If you cling to your life, you will lose it; but if you give up your life for me, you will find it" (Matt 10:39 NLT). When you give up trying to walk your way to heaven on the stones of motivational advice, biblical directives, and renewed resolutions—casting off hope in yourself and running to Jesus—it may feel like you're genuinely losing your life. But trust what Paul says—and trust Jesus! Such abandon finds abundant life, a magnificent inheritance in being the Father's legitimate son or daughter. Who's *your* mama?

GALATIANS 5:1–6

For freedom Christ has set us free; stand firm therefore, and do not submit again to a yoke of slavery.

Look: I, Paul, say to you that if you accept circumcision, Christ will be of no advantage to you. I testify again to every man who accepts circumcision that he is obligated to keep the whole law. You are severed from Christ, you who would be justified by the law; you have fallen away from grace. For through the Spirit, by faith, we ourselves eagerly wait for the hope of righteousness. For in Christ Jesus neither circumcision nor uncircumcision counts for anything, but only faith working through love.

CHAPTER 16

CHRIST HAS
SET US FREE

I n Galatians 1–2, Paul defended his apostleship to legitimize the
gospel he preached. In chapters 3–4, he laid out the theological foundation of the gospel. Now, in chapters 5–6, he's taking the
goodness of the gospel and applying it to our workaday lives; he's
going to deal with how we live, not just as individuals but as a true
community. What's ahead should flip our thoughts on Christian
living upside down. Paul will ask us to be radically honest about
what's going on inside and among us. That's not an activity we
run to sign up for; it's starkly unflattering.

Often, one of two things is happening: On the one hand, we
might be convinced that we're performing
our religious and moral "duty" rather well,
or at least better than our neighbor. Such a
comparison comforts us; we rejoice that the
weeds in our garden are less profuse and
exotic than those next door. But such an attitude is a telltale sign that we're in denial.
If you think you're doing better than someone else, then you're
not being honest about what's occurring inside your own heart.

> TRUE SPIRITUAL
> GROWTH
> DOESN'T OCCUR
> BY FLESHLY
> ENERGY

On the other hand, we can live such defeated lives—convinced that things will never change, that we can't change—that we're captive to hopelessness. Living in either denial or hopelessness is to live under the yoke of slavery, because both are under the yoke of the law.

True spiritual growth (personally and corporately) doesn't occur by fleshly energy; that's why Paul says, "Do not submit again to a yoke of slavery" (Gal 5:1). Change isn't a do-it-yourself project. And that's why repeatedly assessing how we're doing by comparison to others fails; security in our own righteousness—or self-pity over the lack of it—diverts us from the promise of Calvary. Change occurs only by faith: remembering who you are in Christ, remembering that God is your Father who calls you into an ever-deepening realization of his grace and mercy. The answer to both denial and hopelessness is not less gospel, but more. Only abundant grace can break the law's choke hold.

The gospel frees your conscience from incessantly checking its own performance as well as from the weight of others' scruples and tut-tutting: "You need to do this, and do it this way." The Westminster Confession expounds it thus: "God alone is Lord of the conscience and has left it free from the doctrines and commandments of men which are—in anything—contrary to his Word, or which—in matters of faith or worship—are in addition to it."[1] The writers of the confession got it: God alone liberates the conscience! Such freedom is "Christian liberty."

Falling from Grace

Imagine it's January 1863, and you're a slave living in the Confederacy. You have just learned of Lincoln's executive order proclaiming your freedom—but you decide not to believe it and continue to live as a slave even though you are legally freed. By living as you were inculcated to live rather than in accord with your new status, you would effectively revoke your emancipation.

In Galatians 5, Paul is concerned that the Galatians' actions amount to rejection of their emancipation, so he says, "Look [essentially, 'Wake up!'] ... if you accept circumcision, Christ will be of no advantage to you. ... you who would be justified by the law; you have fallen away from grace" (5:2, 4). Circumcision and everything like it belong to the rule of the *paidagogos*, not to the dominion of sonship; to return to them is to deny what has been done at the cross.

Paul's attitude toward circumcision likely would have infuriated and confused his opponents. On the one hand, he insisted that Timothy be circumcised, but vehemently guarded Titus from the mohel's blade. Why the disparity? Because circumcision was nothing if it was only a matter of culture. But where it practically represented the law's way of living, it became very dangerous. You can substitute anything you want for circumcision: customs, traditions, ceremonies, moral assets—anything by which you think you might gain God's approval by doing, or increase your piety by refraining. Paul doesn't exchange abstinence or action as a way to bribe God. For him, the entire notion that you can invest anything that would require God to pay out dividends is fundamentally flawed.

> THE DIVIDENDS GOD PAYS AREN'T BASED ON OUR INVESTMENT, BUT HIS

John Piper has said, "Slavery is when you choose to deal with [God] as a banker who needs your investment to produce dividends for his customers."[2] If your aim is to increase dividends, Christ will be a poor fund manager. The dividends God pays aren't based on our investment, but his. The reality is this: There's nothing we can do that will make God love us more than he does already, nor is there anything we can do that will make him love us less. Christ is the surety of that. Denial and hopelessness are remedied only by living in this truth more deeply. Otherwise every force of the world, the flesh, and the devil will conspire to drive us back into ourselves, to redirect our attention onto our performance—filling us with pride when improvement seems at hand or despair when it doesn't—rather than looking at the cross objectively before us.

There was once a fine Christian man, also a successful gardener, who moved into a new home with beastly landscaping and dilapidated flower beds. He soon set to work and found that the soil was hard-baked, rocky, and thin. Yet through constant toil he eventually created a luscious and beautiful flower garden—the envy of the neighborhood. As he removed each rock he thought, "That's the last time I'll have to shift that one!" With every season's tilling and composting he thought, "This will bring fine flowers in the spring." Since his garden worked on the principle of reward for effort, it was only natural for him to think the Christian life worked the same—that, bit by bit, one stone at a time, all would improve until heaven was within reach.

So, again, he set himself to work. He disciplined himself so that he was rather accomplished in his devotional life, church participation, and charitable giving. He was an honored citizen in his community. All seemed as it should be—or so it appeared from the outside. But he had been experiencing relational difficulties for years, and when others had trouble with him, he regarded their own issues of inferiority to be at the root. He was proud of his life—it honored God, so God blessed it—and others were just jealous and lazy.

Then, one day, he was diagnosed with cancer. As he considered all his efforts, he grew frustrated, angry, and bitter with God and others. He had tilled the soil of his life well; certainly he deserved a different outcome—perhaps a big bed of blooming roses, but certainly not cancer! As he sat in the hospital receiving chemotherapy, he opened his Bible to the parable of the Laborers in the Vineyard in Matthew 20. Certainly, this would help him make his case with God. But his heart was opened as he read, "These last men have worked only one hour, and you have made them equal to us who have borne the burden and the scorching heat of the day" (Matt 20:12 NASB). Suddenly he saw himself with radical honesty. Although he'd been a diligent gardener, he had missed the obvious rock of his own pride, which showed up in his life as a lack of patience, empathy, love, and grace.

Sin and the law pay wages, but the kingdom's currency is grace. Most of us are accustomed to applying elbow grease. Like the gardener, we believe that life is governed by a direct proportionality: The more grease we use, the smoother everything goes. In fact, we pride ourselves on our ability to overcome obstacles. A lack of natural gifts can be overcome with hard-won skills; sheer determination, fortitude, and elbow grease are all we need. There is something to be said for that, after all; it seems to work so well in so many ways. And that makes it difficult to imagine such an attitude as toxic when transferred to salvation and spiritual transformation.

The truth is counterintuitive. Merely trying harder doesn't make you holier—although it does make you holier-than-thou—because it doesn't promote faith and dependence upon Jesus. Trying harder doesn't cause you to love God more; it replaces Jesus with your efforts as the object of your faith.

> TRYING HARDER DOESN'T MAKE YOU HOLIER. IT REPLACES JESUS AS THE OBJECT OF YOUR FAITH

The opposite of faith isn't unbelief—we all believe something and live our lives in light of it. The opposite of faith is self-reliance, trying to get dividends from God by self-effort, programs, routines, systems, or rules. Paul's words in Romans 8:1–4 nip the do-it-yourself gardening project in the bud:

> There is therefore now no condemnation for those who are in Christ Jesus. For the law of the Spirit of life has set you free in Christ Jesus from the law of sin and death. For God has done what the law, weakened by the flesh, could not do. By sending his own Son in the likeness of sinful flesh and for sin, he condemned sin in the flesh, in order that the righteous requirement of the law might be fulfilled in us, who walk not according to the flesh but according to the Spirit.

We get the Christian life really wrong when we think "walking according to the Spirit" simply means exchanging immoral actions for godly ones. Paul will say more about this later in Galatians, but simply put, living "according to the Spirit" means "living by faith." The Spirit enables living by faith, not living by fleshly energy.

As Larry Crabb notes: "I don't have much interest in going to a church that values thirst for God less than service for God, and therefore reduces authenticity to confession of surface faults, and inspiring sometimes harshly moralistic accountability."[3] Yoking people to ox carts mistakes moralism for real, grace-filled thirst for God, and to bank on works is to profit nothing from Jesus. If Jesus doesn't do everything for us, he can do nothing for us. "He must be a perfect Savior, or no Savior."[4] Jesus' work can't be mixed with some of our own, not for justification or for sanctification.

It's similar to the story of a man who had an original auto-graphed baseball by Babe Ruth. He wanted to sell it, as it would fetch a great price. But he noticed the signature was a little faint, so he bought a very expensive pen, got out a magnifying glass, and spent hours touching up the signature. Just making it a little bit darker, taking great care to do it—and turning something of great value into a worthless fake.

In just this way, much of what passes for discipleship and spirituality in the church attempts to mix our efforts with Jesus'. Luther said, "We must give up either Christ or the righteousness of the law. If you keep Christ, you are righteous in the sight of God. If you keep the law, Christ is no avail to you; then you are obliged to keep the whole law."[5] And you can't!

Returning to circumcision for the Galatians or to today's equivalent for us is like saying, "Give me the rule book and watch me go! Come back in a few days and give me an exam; I'll show you how well I can do!" Did you know that when we have this attitude it shows up on our faces as a judgmental smirk? It betrays itself in a glance tinged with conceit or perhaps even pity. But people don't want to be around someone who values duty more than relationships—they don't want to be sacrificed on the altar of your religious purity.

Of course there's a place for taking a stand for Jesus, for defending Christian ethics, for speaking prophetically to our culture. But we don't find ourselves in that place as much as we sometimes think.

LIFE IN THE SPIRIT

It's common to think that what counts is my obedience. It's even more common to think what really counts is yours. But look at Galatians 5:6: "For in Christ Jesus neither circumcision nor uncircumcision counts for anything, but only faith working through love."

We might hear this and say, "Hold your horses, Paul; what about what you said in 1 Corinthians: 'For neither circumcision counts for anything nor uncircumcision, but keeping the commandments of God' (1 Cor 7:19)? It sounds like you're talking out of both sides of your mouth."

Not at all! When Jesus is the sole object of your faith, and you're not looking to itemize your virtues and sum up your righteousness, something miraculous and wonderful occurs inside you: You begin to love God. And you discover that you begin to love others too.

This is how the law is fulfilled:

> You shall love the Lord your God with all your heart and with all your soul and with all your mind. This is the great and first commandment. And a second is like it: You shall love your neighbor as yourself. On these two commandments depend all the Law and the Prophets (Matt 22:37–40).

> Love does no wrong to a neighbor; therefore, love is the fulfilling of the law (Rom 13:10).

What matters is faith. Because faith comes before your love, faith is that which enables love. True, the love of God comes even before your faith; he loved you while you were yet his enemy.

But having seen that love by faith—i.e., banking on Calvary alone—the Spirit continues to pour the love of God into your heart (Rom 5:5) as you keep living by faith, not works. If you're having difficulty loving others well, the problem isn't that you haven't tried hard enough. The problem is faith. Energy of the flesh never frees

ENERGY OF
THE FLESH
NEVER FREES
YOU TO LOVE

you to love. Look at your actions, or your abstinence from actions: Do they cause you to love more? No. They fill you with pride and arrogance. So the key to freedom is dependence on grace, not dependence on giving-it-your-best-shot.

The faith that looks away from the self and looks to Jesus comes from the Spirit of God, and it expresses itself in love. That's why James doesn't contradict Paul when he says, "Show me your faith apart from works, and I will show you my faith by my works" (Jas 2:18). His faith emerges in selfless sacrifice. That's the kind of love on which all the law and the prophets depend. That's the kind of love that only faith can produce.

If you opt to be right with God by obedience and duty, you'll be sailing on a tossing sea of "being right" and "reputation building," blown this way and that by every wind of approval or rebuke. You'll be preoccupied with how well you're doing, whether you are acceptable to God, and whether you are approved by others. But you'll be filled with self-consciousness, not God-consciousness. There's no joy in it because it's not freedom! What's more, living like this stops true fellowship from forming; it grieves the Spirit. As Helmut Thielicke said, "The devil ... succeeds in laying his cuckoo eggs in a pious nest. ... The sulfurous stench of hell is as nothing compared with the evil odor emitted by divine grace gone putrid."[6]

In his book *What's So Amazing about Grace?*, Philip Yancey writes of Swiss physician Paul Tournier, who said:

> "I cannot study this very serious problem of guilt ... without raising the very obvious and tragic fact that religion ... can crush instead of liberate." Tournier tells of

patients who come to him: a man harboring guilt over an old sin, a woman who cannot put out of her mind an abortion that took place ten years before. What the patients truly seek, says Tournier, is grace. Yet in some churches they encounter shame, the threat of punishment, and a sense of judgment. In short, when they look to the church for grace, they often find ungrace. A divorced woman recently told me of standing in the sanctuary of her church with her 15-year-old daughter when the pastor's wife approached. "I hear you are divorcing. What I can't understand is that if you love Jesus and he loves Jesus, why are you doing that?" The pastor's wife had never really spoken to my friend before, and her brusque rebuke in the daughter's presence stunned my friend. "The pain of it was that my husband and I both did love Jesus, but the marriage was broken beyond mending. If she had just put her arms around me and said, 'I'm so sorry.' "[7]

Paul's concern in Galatians 5 isn't primarily with our fleshly immoral actions, though he will have something to say about them shortly. Rather, Paul's focus is our fleshly moral actions—our righteous deposits, which delude us into thinking Jesus is pleased with us and which cause us to sneer and snicker at others.

The mark of spirituality and sanctification isn't your growth in virtuousness; it's your growth in love. When faith in the cross is operating at the core of your soul, the Spirit's fruits of love, joy, peace, patience, kindness, goodness, faithfulness, gentleness, and self-control flow out more and more. But the harvest of the Spirit in that way is dependent entirely on its being through faith in the gospel. Remove that message, and the deeds of the flesh become the only alternative—and that's really scary.

GALATIANS 5:7–12

You were running well. Who hindered you from obeying the truth? This persuasion is not from him who calls you. A little leaven leavens the whole lump. I have confidence in the Lord that you will take no other view, and the one who is troubling you will bear the penalty, whoever he is. But if I, brothers, still preach circumcision, why am I still being persecuted? In that case the offense of the cross has been removed. I wish those who unsettle you would emasculate themselves!

CHAPTER 17

RUNNING IN THE PACK

In the 1984 Los Angeles Olympics, Mary Decker was favored to win gold in the women's 3000 meters. On the third lap she was side-by-side with Zola Budd from South Africa, running barefoot and on behalf of Great Britain. Budd decided to overtake. Wanting to keep pressure on Budd, Decker remained close, collided with another runner, fell, and tumbled onto the in-field. Apparently, it's an accepted convention for the lead runner to be a full stride ahead before cutting in—well, on that day, in that race, that didn't happen. But in an interview years later Mary Decker said, "The reason I fell, some people think she tripped me deliberately. I happen to know that wasn't the case at all. The reason I fell is because I am, and was, very inexperienced in running in a pack."[1]

Do you know how to run in a pack? The pack isn't just the church. It's the world, believers and nonbelievers included. And it's the group in which where we're running every day. Sometimes we're cut off from the lead. Sometimes we just stumble. Other times we're in open space. But we're always in the race.

Paul begins, "You were running well. Who hindered you from obeying the truth?" (Gal 5:7). Other translations have "who cut

WE RUN
STRENGTHENED
FOR EVERY
STRIDE
BY GRACE

in on you" or "who deflected you from the course set for truth?" Running well is running for freedom. Recall Paul in Jerusalem: "We did not yield in submission even for a moment, so that the truth of the gospel might be preserved for you" (2:5).

We run as we began: strengthened for every stride by grace, through faith.

REMEMBERING HOW WE BEGAN

God never lures us from grace, or away from faith. If you hear any voice from any preacher doing that—even if they look and sound like an angel from heaven—sniff the air for a waft of sulfur. They haven't come from God. Paul says such "persuasion is not from him who calls you" (Gal 5:8). If law-keeping were the necessary means to continue in the Christian life, God's calling by grace would be contradicted (Gal 1:6). To be called by grace, and then to be told that you must proceed by works, is a bait-and-switch tactic. God called us by grace through Jesus, and he doesn't ask us to proceed by another means. He's no con artist, and the gospel isn't false advertising.

So the first strategy for running in the pack is remembering: We began by faith. We didn't begin when we decided to come to church or to take sacraments as proof of our piety. We came as beggars, and we are beggars still, trusting in God's promises above all else. Moralism—believing God will favor you when you commit yourself to moral improvement—isn't grace, yet grace is the only hope of a truly moral life. Your life didn't change as a precondition of faith; faith changed your life!

How does this go together with a passage like Philippians 2:12, "Work out your own salvation with fear and trembling"? Clearly we've got some work to do—but what does it mean to block elbows and feet and remain on the track? Do we do it by trying harder? By cleaning up our act? By praying more? Or by vowing to make our personal devotional lives more successful? (We've dealt with such thoughts already, haven't we?)

Of course not. Running is learning to focus on the one who said, "I am the way, and the truth, and the life" (John 14:6). It's keeping your eyes on Jesus in the midst of the flying elbows and intruding feet. In his *Lectures on Romans*, Martin Luther said, "To progress is always to begin again."[2] Or, as Tullian Tchividjian has put it, "Sanctification is the daily hard work of getting back to the reality of our justification. It's going back to the certainty of our objectively secured pardon in Christ and hitting the refresh button a thousand times a day."[3] That's how we go forward. We go back to the truth over and over again to understand who we are and find our identity as it is in Jesus, not as the pack tell us. This is the hard work we are to do. "Sanctification is thus simply the art of getting used to justification. It is not something added to justification," says Gerhard Forde.[4] And G. C. Berkouwer has said it's a mistake to ask:

> We know we have imputed righteousness, but now how do we move on to actual righteousness? We do not "move on." Any particular flaw in our actual righteousness stems from a corresponding failure to orient ourselves toward our imputed righteousness. Sanctification happens to the degree that we "feed on" or "orient to" ... the pardon, righteousness, and new status we now have in Christ, imputed through faith.[5]

Progress toward the goal occurs in learning to live the justified life. It's going deeper into the reality of it; living in the truth of it, despite all appearances to the contrary. This is Paul's point when he speaks of "obeying the truth" (Gal 5:7). What truth has he been talking about for five chapters? The gospel! "Obeying the truth" is living in the truth of the gospel. The Judaizers were disobeying the truth in their teaching, and getting the Galatians to follow. To defend the truth of faith in our own hearts, to preach that truth to

PROGRESS OCCURS IN LEARNING TO LIVE THE JUSTIFIED LIFE

the hearts of others, to live in the love that flows from faith: this is obeying the truth.

Remembering Grace

The second strategy is to remember grace—which we need to do often. The devil is crafty; he's a master at the art of distraction. Magicians call it misdirection, drawing your attention to something else so they can deceive you. The devil begins his sleight of hand by convincing us we are doing either rather well or rather poorly, that God must be either pleased or disappointed with us due to any number of reasons. The distraction then leads to the main game, driving us further inward with his accusations and flattery. Then—presto!—we tumble off the track, knocking a few others down as we fall. Why? Because "a little leaven leavens the whole lump" (Gal 5:9). This common proverb pulls us back to when the Hebrews were told to bake the Passover bread without yeast; they'd be ready to run from their Egyptian slavery in haste, unencumbered by still-rising dough (Exod 12:8–11). Run when grace comes calling! Flee to it, hide in it, remember it!

Legalism makes mules of us all. Have you ever seen a mule or a donkey digging its heels in, protesting loudly? If others are around, they join the chorus of dissent. It's infectious. Like a stubborn mule, a legally aligned heart digs its heels in and campaigns for others to do the same. It loves the company of complaint. Grace calls, like wisdom in the streets (Prov 1:20; 8:1), to run into her arms and find shelter. But we stubbornly bray that our legalistically shod hooves know a better place and smoother path. We crucify Wisdom in the name of the law.

What's going on in Galatia? Paul has been accused of not taking the law seriously enough. The Judaizers are saying, "Hey Galatians, Paul was off, we're here to get you back on track. You want to know the delight of God in your life? You want to have peace from that berating conscience of yours? Then something more than faith in Jesus is required." But Paul says, "No—we need nothing but Jesus." Paul takes the law so seriously he knows our only help is to throw ourselves on the mercy of Christ.

British preacher D. Martyn Lloyd-Jones explained the accusation against Paul well:

> There is no better test as to whether a man is really preaching the New Testament gospel of salvation than this, that some people might misunderstand it and misinterpret it to mean ... you can go on sinning as much as you like because it will redound all the more to the glory of grace. ... If a man preaches justification by works, no one would ever raise this question. If a man's preaching is, "If you want to be Christians, and if you want to go to heaven, you must stop committing sins, you must take up good works, and if you do so regularly and constantly, and do not fail to keep on at it, you will make yourselves Christians, you will reconcile yourselves to God and you will go to heaven." Obviously a man who preaches in that strain would never be liable to this misunderstanding. Nobody would say to such a man, "Shall we continue in sin, that grace may abound?", because the man's whole emphasis is just this, that if you go on sinning you are certain to be damned, and only if you stop sinning can you save yourselves. ... Nobody has ever brought this charge against the Church of Rome, but it was brought frequently against Martin Luther. ... It is the charge that formal, dead Christianity ... has always brought against this startling, staggering message, that God "justifies the ungodly."[6]

When Paul is charged with being a lawless antinomian he doesn't answer by saying, "Oh, right, oops! I forgot the law." He answers by giving more gospel. "Antinomians do not believe the gospel too much, but too little! They restrict the power of the gospel to the problem of sin's guilt, while Paul tells us that the gospel is the power for sanctification as well as justification."[7]

Grace is the power for running the Christian life in its entirety, not for merely beginning it. We run well as we continue to remember the grace by which we run.

> GRACE IS POWER FOR RUNNING THE CHRISTIAN LIFE IN ITS ENTIRETY

RELYING ON GOD

Do we fail, do we fall, do we forget? Of course! "But thank God! He has made us his captives and continues to lead us along in Christ's triumphal procession," calling us further into his grace (2 Cor 2:14 NLT). We believe this is what is behind Paul's confidence that the Galatians "will take no other view than [his], and the one who is troubling [them] will bear the penalty, whoever he is" (Gal 5:10). This isn't confidence in logic, persuasive powers, or the Galatians' good sense. Paul confidently trusts God to sort things out.

So often we think we've got to sort things out immediately. So we take onto our shoulders a great burden of anxiety. Ever tried running with a rucksack on? Anxiety, however, will dissipate from our lives almost as fast as it appears—if, that is, we see it as a signal flare alerting us to a misstep. Anxiety is a form of negative meditation, which can only be countered by chewing the cud of the gospel. It's an invitation to put our focus back on Jesus; and it's no accident that there are so very many "do not fear" and "do not be anxious" statements in Scripture. Anxiety is the default position of the flesh. Therefore, as a true and good pastor, Paul places his focus on the one true Shepherd. His confidence is in God. God will keep his flock and deal with the troublemaker in his time. What encouragement! And what a contrast to Paul's days as a Pharisee, when his first impulse was to run to the law to sort things out—even if it meant murder! And that straight-line, right-handed use of power is another default position of the flesh to bring about immediacy.

After the flood, even our all-powerful God "evidently had almost no interest in using direct power to fix up the world"—since, as Robert Capon observes, empowering "loving relationships" sometimes requires *refraining* from exercising power:

> Such a paradoxical exercise of power, please note, is a hundred and eighty degrees away from the straight-line variety. It is, to introduce a phrase from Luther, left-handed power. Unlike the power of the right hand (which ... is governed by the logical, plausibility-loving left hemisphere of the brain), left-handed power is guided by the more intuitive, open, and imaginative right side of the brain. Left-handed power, in other words, is precisely paradoxical power: power that looks for all the world like weakness, intervention that seems indistinguishable from nonintervention. More than that, it is guaranteed to stop no determined evildoers whatsoever. It might, of course, touch and soften their hearts. But then again, it might not. It certainly didn't for Jesus; and if you decide to use it, you should be quite clear that it probably won't for you either. The only thing it does insure is that you will not—even after your chin has been bashed in—have made the mistake of closing any interpersonal doors from your side.
>
> Which may not, at first glance, seem like much of a thing to insure. ... But when you come to think of it, it *is* power—so much power, in fact, that it is the only thing in the world that evil can't touch. God in Christ died forgiving. With the dead body of Jesus, he wedged open the door between himself and the world and said, "There! Just try and get me to take *that* back!"[8]

Things might seem to be messy—or be messy—but God has us in his good hands. Run by relying on God; evil can't touch his plan and purpose.

REMAINING IN THE WORD OF THE CROSS

George Bernard Shaw telegraphed Winston Churchill just prior to the opening of the play *Major Barbara*: "Have reserved two tickets for first night. Come and bring a friend if you have one." Churchill wired back: "Impossible to come to first night. Will come to second night, if you have one."

Sometimes it's appropriate to defend yourself. Paul's defense is not as comical as Churchill's, but it's laser sharp: "'But if I, brothers, still preach circumcision, why am I still being persecuted?' (Gal 5:11). If I were preaching circumcision, the offense of the cross would be dissipated. I wouldn't be drawing all this fire; so why the persecution?" (Need we ask?) It's *because* Paul is preaching precisely Christ crucified and applying the full ramifications of what that means. Persecution calls out the fact that he's honoring God rather than human sensibilities or effort. The cross testifies to our inability to lift ourselves from the muddy infield and put ourselves on the track. It strips away any pretense of spiritual achievement.

During the Protestant Reformation, Martin Luther debated Catholic humanist Desiderius Erasmus on the nature of grace. Erasmus admitted that sin had made humanity sick and said that grace is like one parent helping a wobbly toddler across the room to the other parent, who is crouching down with an enticing apple. The nearby parent watches the little one; if he starts to fall, this parent will hold him for a moment so he can still cross the room under his own power. But Luther, offended by such a weak and pitiful view of grace cried "no!" and countered, "Grace is like a caterpillar in a ring of fire. The only help is from above."

> PERSECUTION CALLS OUT THAT PAUL IS HONORING GOD

Natural reason neither understands nor accepts—and, in fact, hates—this truth (1 Cor 2:14). Why is it so offensive? Because it negates self-sufficiency and bombs to bits the I-can-do-it-myself mentality which is our shelter from grace. Just look at the abundance of self-help books today; we seem hard-wired for "how-to's."

But Paul's answer is never, "How?" but, "Who?" Christian living isn't taking the Bible, shaking its pages until a few principles fall out, and then applying them like a baking recipe. To separate Christ from his benefits is deeply destructive. He lifts us from the ring of fire—he doesn't help us along with principles and tips.

The ministry leader in a preaching rotation once advised Dan, "You need to give them practical things they can do to change their lives. When they see it works, they'll believe in Christianity. They're not ready for this faith stuff." Dan was shocked—the leader was telling me to preach works, not faith, because the idea of works was more popular. The cross "cuts the ground out from under the thought of personal achievement," and that's why it's a stumbling block.[9]

If the gospel brings friction be neither discouraged nor surprised. Just keep running in the Word of the cross, because that's how you began the Christian life, and it's how you'll end it.

ROARING FOR THE GOSPEL

Filled with love for the Galatians, Paul says: "I wish those who unsettle you would emasculate themselves" (Gal 5:12). That's a polite translation of a pretty strong phrase. In effect, Paul's saying, "I wish they'd slip and cut the whole lot off, making themselves eunuchs." According to Deuteronomy 23:1, eunuchs were barred from the temple assembly (emasculation being a pagan practice). "Go ahead," says Paul, "remove yourselves completely from the fellowship— take off, leave the Church alone!"

KEEP RUNNING IN THE WORD OF THE CROSS

Whoa! Is that language we should be hearing from a church leader? In our age of tolerance, we wonder if we could accept such political incorrectness. If you were in Paul's place, would you roar? If not, whom are you trying to impress? Whom do you want to please? And why? Think about it.

There's no need to sugarcoat this: Paul's livid! But he's defending both the gospel and the Galatians themselves. He may roar

loudly, but he's right and true; only love can do this. The caricature of a pastor as a nice man standing in front of nice people telling them to be even nicer is far removed from true apostolic ministry. Apostolic ministry is hand-to-hand combat, with the devil
breathing down your neck and the cross your only sword. There
is no room for self-help-focused, legalistic, moralistic, "nice" cultural religion. The gospel is important; if we're to run free in the
truth unencumbered by elbows and feet, we must clear the way
for freedom by roaring for the gospel: "Get off the track, we're
coming through!"

So roar for the gospel—there's a time and a place for it.
Especially when someone's trying to cut in on you with the law.

GALATIANS 5:13–15

For you were called to freedom, brothers. Only do not use your freedom as an opportunity for the flesh, but through love serve one another. For the whole law is fulfilled in one word: "You shall love your neighbor as yourself." But if you bite and devour one another, watch out that you are not consumed by one another.

CHAPTER 18

LIBERTY IS NOT LICENSE

Paul's main concern so far has been to teach us about the gospel, especially justification by grace alone through faith alone. Chapter after chapter he's been blinding us with its brilliance, showcasing its facets—especially our freedom, as God's adopted children, from the law's curse. But there's more than one way to be a slave. Paul has discussed being enslaved to the law (legalism and moralism) and its curse. That's one type of slavery; now, he names two other types.

Next on Paul's list, one can be a slave to the flesh. To say that you "march to the beat of your own drum," though, to be as enslaved as the legalist trying to merit favor through moralism and religion. In serving the flesh, you're bound to egotism, which destroys true community because it opposes the law of God, which is the law of love.

The final mode of slavery is radically different. It's being a slave to Christ. Paradoxical though it seems, this is true freedom. By way of illustration of these types of slavery, let's contrast two Britons from two different eras: William Wilberforce and Ian Fleming.

At the turn of the 19th century, Wilberforce was the leading abolitionist in the British parliament. For 26 years, he fought the slave trade, finally orchestrating the Act that abolished slavery within the British Empire. The movie *Amazing Grace* shows him growing weary in the three-decades-long struggle against deeply entrenched, vested interests. It also took a toll on his health. Probably suffering from ulcerative colitis, he withdrew to a friend's estate to convalesce; after recasting his methods, his efforts bore fruit. He died in 1833, days after hearing that the Slavery Abolition Act was to be passed by Parliament.

By contrast, Ian Fleming, the author of the James Bond books, was a libertine who shared many characteristics with his fictional hero. Fleming's training at the Royal Military Academy Sandhurst and service in the Admiralty in World War II provided much of the technical background for his novels. He presented his hero as the champion of the good, but his own life was lived virtually without restraint. He had many sexual affairs, was effectively an alcoholic, smoked like a chimney, gambled relentlessly. He lived and played hard. His life was cut short in his mid-50s by a heart attack.

Both Wilberforce and Fleming were free in ways and enslaved in others. Fleming, although he lived as libertine, was a slave to his natural desires; he was shackled to an overmastering love of self. Wilberforce, on the other hand, was yoked to Christ, who constrained him by a greater love so he could give himself freely in the loving service of others. That's the dichotomy of which Paul speaks. Or, phrased differently, "A Christian is the most free lord of all, subject to none; a Christian is the most dutiful servant of all, subject to all."[1]

Called to Freedom

"Rules and regulations are attractive and appealing to a select few who find that their personal style of finding identity, satisfaction, of meeting their needs to feel loved, of feeling good about themselves just happens to be by performance in rule-keeping," notes David Benner.[2] And while it's true that the select few find it appealing, the Christian life isn't like this. Rather, it's a divine

and gracious calling to a freedom deeper and
more profound than we realize. And yet at
the same time, it's anything but a license for
anarchy. To nip the notion of lawlessness in
the bud, Paul says, "You were called to free-

dom, brothers. Only do not use your freedom as an opportunity
for the flesh" (5:13). Here "opportunity" has the sense of a military base camp—he's saying, "Don't let your freedom be a Trojan
Horse which lets the appetites and propensities of the flesh loose
to burn the city."

In most of Paul's writings, the "flesh" is not our body, but our
sinful nature. It's the whole realm of human mind, emotions, will,
and bodily appetites as ruled by sin. It's entirely egoistic and refuses to be subdued. Neither education nor religion can change it.
It's avaricious, ruthless in its drive for self-aggrandizement. And
it loves religion; religion is, after all, the flesh trying to be spiritual. It's the part of our hearts with "the passion for self ('Give me
what I need'), the passion for control ('I'll make it happen'), the
passion to define ('This is life, and this is death'), and the passion
to perform ('I'll try to be good, but can't You just let me do what I
want?')."[3]

In Galatians 5:19, Paul gives the flesh some color, essentially
saying, "When you are operating out of the flesh, this is what occurs; these are the deeds of the flesh." The list contains both appetites (of the body) and attitudes (of the heart). Sexual immorality,
impurity, sensuality, drunkenness, orgies, and the like—all of
these are bodily appetites given over to excess. Idolatry, sorcery,
enmity, strife, jealousy, fits of anger, rivalries, dissensions, divisions, envy, and the like—all of these attitudes and actions flow
from the heart and destroy true community. We'll come back
to this, but note: These characters turn out whenever the flesh
throws the party, even if the party is in the church.

Jesus said, "I tell you the truth, everyone who practices sin is
a slave of sin" (John 8:34 NLT). Christian liberty isn't freedom to
go and sin. In fact, that's the last thing you want to do as a child

of God. You hate your sin; it perplexes you as much as it revolts you. You want to run from it, even if you don't always succeed, because the deepest desire of the transformed heart is for God. That's the miracle: that simultaneously you want the Father to be the strong tower you run to, and that he delights in your running to him in the very moment of temptation or failure. Christian freedom means we're even free to stare into the dark abyss beneath the waterline of our own hearts and to be radically honest with what's there, because Christian freedom means that God meets us in that place with grace—grace which has cleansed all our sins, even today's and tomorrow's!

> THE DEPTH TO WHICH YOU SEE YOUR SIN IS THE DEPTH TO WHICH YOU KNOW GOD'S LOVE

The depth to which you see your sin is also the depth to which you know God's love for you. Paradoxically, only grace can reveal what our hearts are really like. As English Puritan John Owen might have summarized his perspective on the pastorate: There are only two pastoral problems in the world. The first is to convince men in sin that they are in sin; and the second to convince men who are not in sin that they are not in sin.[4] Apart from the light of God, no one naturally assumes they're a slave to sin. But a Christian, having had their sin illuminated and conscience sensitized by the Spirit, constantly needs the gospel to be assured it's not their native soil. That's why we hate it. For, as Paul says elsewhere, "You, however, are not in the flesh but in the Spirit, if in fact the Spirit of God dwells in you" (Rom 8:9).

Christian freedom isn't the freedom from sin's presence—that's heaven. Rather, Christian freedom is freedom from sin's penalty and power. Christian freedom rules in the midst of accusation and fear, and so, in the face of the dark abyss, we can say, "The truth is that Christ was crucified for me. He carried my abysmal condition on his shoulders. So it's not on my shoulders right now! The guilt is taken, the shame is lifted, and he loves me still!" It frees love and longing for Christ to increase. It releases us to be authentic with our brothers and sisters. We don't need to hide behind a mask of victorious piety or sinless perfection; we can freely confess our sins, since the only real community is one which owns the dirt under its fingernails yet links arms to sing songs of grace to each other. "The call to freedom, then, is a call to oneness in Christ and to loving service within the believing community."[5] Love, not libertine licentiousness, is the work of God's Spirit.

CALLED TO SLAVERY

Paul was often accused of being an antinomian (see Rom 3:8; 6:1–14; Phil 3:17–4:1), but in reality his gospel "establishes the law" (Rom 3:31). The gospel message is counterintuitive. The gospel of free grace never leads to lawlessness or anarchy. It leads to love, which is the fulfillment of the law (Rom 13:8–10; Gal 5:14).

> THE GOSPEL OF FREE GRACE NEVER LEADS TO LAWLESSNESS

We might be tempted to regard the law as a temporary measure for our difficult earthly situation, but it's not as if it will be eradicated when the kingdom comes in all its fullness. Heaven isn't the absence of law, but its fulfillment in and among us.

This is what we pray for in the liturgy and in the words of the Lord's Prayer: "Your will be done, on earth as it is in heaven" (Matt 6:10). The Church will stand together, loving God and each other fully—no divisive idols, covetousness, or anything else. Transformation into the image of Christ (the law fulfilled in us) is heaven!

Natural reason can't grasp its powerlessness to fulfill God's law. Natural reason assumes that if a law is established it can be kept—if it can't, then the law can't apply. The flesh, however, is bankrupt; you can't buy bread with an empty purse. So God's law actually calls our very being into question. It says "no" to our natural existence and sends us running to Jesus, in whom our being is changed by love. As Herman Ridderbos says, "Fulfillment [of the law] remains a divine requirement. But since the law, as demanding agent, cannot effectuate the fulfillment, it is not the imperative of the law but the bond of faith in Christ which forms the ground and origin of the fulfillment of the will of God."[6] Or, in other words, the law as command cannot provide the power to fulfill itself. In fact, we've already seen that the law in this way stirs up more sin. So where does that leave us?

Throughout the letter, Paul has used the vocabulary of slavery negatively, but at this point his tone changes. The word "serve" translates the Greek *doulos*, meaning "slave." "Through love serve one another" (Gal 5:13b). The force is, "If you must live under law, live under the law of love—that is, the law of Christ."[7] Why? Because "the whole law is fulfilled in one word: 'You shall love your neighbor as yourself' " (5:14).

Only "the bond of faith" makes love possible. The Galatians were so preoccupied with showing God how much they loved him by keeping the commandments that they failed to notice the deeds of the flesh emerging: Strife, enmity, jealousy, and quarreling prospered because each person thought they were more law-abiding than the next. They totally misunderstood the nature of both law and obedience.

Ironically, the false teachers' emphasis on legal obedience was built on their idea of "holiness." The Judaizers were keen to make the church holy by defending the law. But what does true holiness look like? Biblical holiness is characterized by the fruit of the Spirit—love, joy, peace, patience, kindness, goodness, faithfulness, gentleness, and self-control. Paul was, therefore, more concerned about the law than the Judaizers ever imagined. The fruit of the Spirit, however, isn't harvested by shaking people with rules and regulations. A wholly different power—love—is at work, a power that legalism doesn't understand. As David Benner describes it:

> Growth in love always involves movement beyond the hardened boundaries of the isolated self to the selves-in-relation that make up community. Conversion

always points us towards fellow human beings, not simply towards God. Like the grain of wheat that must fall into the earth and die if it is to flourish (John 12:24), the person who is becoming love leaves behind the broken husk of their isolated self and embraces the new possibilities of life in the human community. ... When love draws me from isolation into community, your life touches mine—your pain touches me, your afflictions touch me, your anxieties touch me.[8]

The community of the Spirit provides the opportunity to serve, not destroy. In this place of mutuality created under divine grace, we respond in love to serve and bless—not bite and devour—each other. But the moment holiness via the gospel is replaced by legal obedience, failures must be concealed and others' condemned—and community is most certainly lost.

The relationship between Joy Davidman and C. S. Lewis pushed both to consider more deeply these many facets of love. At one point in the movie *Shadowlands*, Joy tells Jack (Lewis) about her husband: "He takes the romantic view. If you love someone, you marry them." Good and proper advice—except that for Joy's husband, it meant divorcing her so he could marry another. That's not love, it's selfishness.

Yet Lewis, too, had to reconsider his place in community. To really love this woman who had captured his heart and mind, to marry her and then sit with her until cancer took her, moved him beyond the boundary of his isolated self into a new community—of love, marriage, and the grief of deep loss. His previous self-regard was academic and cloistered, comfortable and bookish. The real world of the Spirit's action was beyond it all.

THE CHARGE TO LOVE ISN'T A CALL TO DUTY; IT'S A CALL TO FREEDOM

And yet, as their story shows, the charge to love each other isn't a call to duty; it's a call to freedom. It's a call to sonship, a call to live in love. It's neither lawlessness nor the deeds of dogged determination but the living water of the Spirit springing up through the gospel. Only this makes you the "most free lord, subject to none, and the most dutiful servant of all, subject to all." This is what it truly means to reign with Christ (1 Cor 6:2; 2 Tim 2:12; Rev 20:6), both in this life and the next.

GALATIANS 5:16–18

But I say, walk by the Spirit, and you will not gratify the desires of the flesh. For the desires of the flesh are against the Spirit, and the desires of the Spirit are against the flesh, for these are opposed to each other, to keep you from doing the things you want to do. But if you are led by the Spirit, you are not under the law.

CHAPTER 19

WALK BY THE SPIRIT

If you're told the Christian life is triumphal, victorious, and easy, don't believe it! If you're told that by the Spirit's power—if only you can find the secret—you'll always be healthy, wealthy, and wise, don't believe it! Rebuke such teaching in the name of Jesus and hit the road. To walk in the Spirit isn't to stroll through the arboretum with butterflies fluttering up from flowers; it's to traverse a battlefield strewn with mines. That battlefield is in your own soul as much as it's in the world, and it rages hot, regardless of how long you've walked with the Lord.

Paul knew this battle well. Even as an apostle he never intimated that he was getting better. In fact, he says the opposite. Around AD 54 he wrote to the Corinthians, saying, "I am the least of the apostles" (1 Cor 15:9)—those were his early days. Then,

> PAUL LIVES
> SOLELY BY
> THE GRACE OF
> CHRIST

around AD 63, he wrote to the Ephesians, "I am the very least of all the saints" (3:8). And then, around AD 65, he wrote to Timothy, "'Christ Jesus came into the world to save sinners'—and I am the worst of them all" (1 Tim 1:15 NLT). His experience is echoed by the people of God throughout the centuries. Over his journey he sees himself ever more clearly, realizing that he lives solely by the grace of Christ.

That's the mark of a truly holy man—dependence. As a wise pastor once said:

> Spiritual maturity isn't the absence of spiritual conflict; it's the awareness of spiritual conflict. The less holy you feel, the better. The less holy you feel—as long as you are seeking to learn to walk by the Spirit—probably the more holy you actually are in your practice of the Christian life ... because of the resulting dependence upon the Spirit. It's not simply being aware of the conflict and where you are weak—a lot of people are aware of their weakness and don't do anything about it, they feel helpless and powerless. But the Word of God doesn't leave us helpless and powerless, so Paul says, "Walk by the Spirit, and you will not gratify the desires of the flesh" (Gal 5:16).[1]

Nothing has changed since John wrote, "If we say we have no sin, we deceive ourselves, and the truth is not in us" (1 John 1:8). So where's the *good* news?

The good news is that walking in the Spirit does something: It changes your desires, so that your deepest desire isn't for the flesh. The New Living Translation puts it this way: "Let the Holy Spirit guide your lives. Then you won't be doing what your sinful nature craves" (Gal 5:16). Note the order: "walk by the Spirit," then "the flesh won't be gratified." It's a promise. Paul doesn't say, "Don't fulfill the desires of the flesh, then you'll be walking by the Spirit." Ascetics—monks and hermits—have tried often enough to retreat from the world so as not to indulge sinful cravings, but the minefield within can't be escaped. The flesh follows them into their solitude and beats them in the darkness.

Therefore, we don't walk by the Spirit by means of the law. We walk by the Spirt by means of remembering, resting, and being quieted by the message of the gospel. It's as simple—and as complex—as that.

WALK BY THE SPIRIT

Can you walk by the Spirit while you're eating your toast? Or only while you're immersed in prayer? "Walking by the Spirit" sounds very spiritual, doesn't it? What does it really mean?

To answer this question we must be clear about who the Holy Spirit is. Some think of the Spirit as a ghost; for example, the sixth-century Gallican version of the Apostles' Creed reads, "I believe in the Holy Ghost." The Holy Spirit, however, is not a specter, but the ever-present Spirit of God, the giver of life. Others read Paul's words "be filled with the Spirit" (Eph 5:18), and the image that comes to mind is gasoline filling a tank. Both of these thoughts view the Spirit as a corporeal property. Another misconception is that the Spirit is a force to be tapped into, like a Jedi knight.

But none of these conceptions is accurate. The Holy Spirit is the personal presence of God. When the Old Testament speaks of God being "with" the people, it speaks of the Third Person of the Trinity, the Spirit. The Spirit empowers, enables, purges, and leads "generation after generation of sinners to face the reality of God," writes J. I. Packer. "And he does it in order that Christ may be known, loved, honored, and praised."[2]

> THE SPIRIT POINTS US TO THE WORD OF GOD INCARNATED IN JESUS

The Spirit focuses on and points us to the Word of God, which is ultimately incarnated in Jesus of Nazareth. The Spirit takes what is his and plants it within us, turning our minds and hearts to Jesus so the Father may be glorified in us.

Note the trinitarian nature of this: The Spirit directs us to the Son that we might love and glorify the Father. As the Third Person of the Trinity, he places us into personal relationship with the Son and Father, uniting our life to the life of the Godhead! It's God in us, us in God (Col 1:27). That's truly dancing with the Trinity.

The Spirit is like a powerful personality who fills the room of your life; he applies pressure to turn desire from the flesh and awakens hunger and longing for God. That is to say, the Spirit works on the affections of the heart. Every Christian "has" the Spirit; he's present to every believer in all his fullness.

But does he have all of you? Are there cupboards and closets in the room of your life that bear "keep out" signs? The New Testament speaks of "grieving the Spirit" (Eph 4:30) and "quenching the Spirit" (1 Thess 5:19), and it's clear from the book of Acts that believers were given fresh experiences of the Spirit's fullness more than once (e.g., Acts 2; 4). Alexander MacLaren explains:

> There was an actual impartation to men of a divine life, to dwell in them and actuate them; to bring all good to victory in them; to illuminate, sustain, direct, and elevate; to cleanse and quicken. The gift was complete. They were "filled." No doubt they had much more to receive, and they received it, as their natures became, by faithful obedience to the indwelling Spirit, capable of more. But up to the measure of their then capacities they were filled; and, since their spirits were expansible, and the gift was infinite, they were in a position to grow steadily in possession of it, till they were "filled with all the fullness of God."[3]

As we are filled, our hearts are expanded, and as they expand we may be filled still more. But in the end, it's all because of the gospel. The pharisaical never attain the fullness of the Spirit. Why? Because they have no gospel to liberate their hearts and minds into God's love.

The Spirit of God isn't unique to the New Testament. In the exodus, Israel walked out of Egypt led by the presence of God as seen in the pillars of smoke and fire; God took his enslaved people into freedom by walking with them. Centuries after the exodus, Isaiah spoke to a wayward Israel, saying:

They rebelled
    and grieved his Holy Spirit;
therefore he turned to be their enemy,
    and himself fought against them.

Then he remembered the days of old,
    of Moses and his people.

Where is he who brought them up out of the sea
    with the shepherds of his flock?
Where is he who put in the midst of them
    his Holy Spirit,
who caused his glorious arm
    to go at the right hand of Moses,
who divided the waters before them
    to make for himself an everlasting name,
    who led them through the depths? (Isa 63:10–13).

God's presence was with them. Reminiscent of the garden of Eden, he walked with them, leading them to freedom by his Holy Spirit. And he still walks his people out of slavery today.

"Walk by the Spirit, and you will not gratify the desires of the flesh," says Paul (Gal 5:16). It's a promise that lays out what will happen; we don't want to take this wonderful promise and turn it into a self-reformation project: "Don't gratify the flesh, and you'll be walking by the Spirit." No. This is a statement about what God does, about the result of faith. If, by faith, the Spirit is guiding your life, you won't be living by the flesh, for you won't be in bondage to desires and affections of the flesh. That's a promise.

WALKING IN THE SPIRIT PLACES US IN THE HEAT OF THE BATTLE

Does that mean the battle is over? Just the opposite! Walking in the Spirit places us in the heat of the battle because the flesh opposes the Spirit and vice versa. In fact, the gospel only makes sense in the light of that battle; it cannot be understood apart from this conflict.

In the days of the Protestant Reformation, John Calvin received a letter from a cardinal concerned that if worship was reduced to matters of faith and repentance and not to the preaching of the law, people would go wild. Calvin's response was essentially, "Your theology and all of this law stuff is a little bit too lazy, which I often find among those who have never had serious pangs of conscience."[4] In other words, if the conscience is alive, faith and repentance become the most difficult things to perform. Martin Luther made the same point when he wrote:

> Even though we are now in faith, the heart is always ready to boast itself before God and say, "After all, I have preached the law, lived so well, and done so much that surely He will take this into account." We even want to haggle with God to make Him regard our life, but it cannot be done. With men you may boast, "I have done the best I could toward everyone. If anything is lacking, I will still try to make recompense," but when you come before God, leave all that boasting at home. Remember to appeal from justice into grace. But let anybody try this; and he will see and experience how exceedingly hard and bitter a thing it is for a man who, all his life, has been marred and has worked righteousness to pull himself out of it and with all his heart would rise up through faith in the one mediator. I myself have been preaching and cultivating it through reading and writing for almost twenty years and still feel the old clinging dirt of wanting to deal so with God that I may contribute something so that He will have to give me his grace in exchange for my holiness. Still I can not get it into my head that I should surrender myself completely to sheer grace, yet I know that this is what I should and must do.[5]

OPPOSED BY THE SPIRIT

All this goes against our natural reason. Can't we just obey, and do our duty? Why is the Holy Spirit needed?

If you don't have air, you die. We all know this, scuba divers better than anyone. Looking to both Hebrew and Greek, the words for "spirit," "breath," and "wind" (i.e., moving air) are the same. If there's no breath in your lungs, you die. You certainly can't explore the wondrous world of God's watery creation without it. Life-giving breath from above is our most basic need. Similarly, take away the Spirit—who places us in the life of God by applying Christ's work to us and thereby transforms our being—and you drown (John 15:5), overcome by the flesh. The flesh is no more your natural environment than water; but unlike the deep sea you explore while scuba diving, the flesh is never a pretty place to visit. It needs to be overcome, for it is the seat of all our hostility toward God. Indeed, "the desires of the flesh are against the Spirit, and the Spirit is against the flesh, for these are opposed to each other, to keep you from doing the things you want to do" (Gal 5:17).

The Christian finds that that which they want to do—faithfully trust and obey God—is what they find hardest to do. You never reach the point where grace is no longer needed, just as a scuba diver never grows gills.

Why is it so? Because although I'm no longer in the flesh, although it's not my home turf, the flesh is still in me. Bringing Israel out of Egypt took just days, but it took a lifetime before Egypt was out of Israel! They longed for the fish, melons, cucumbers, leeks, garlic, onions, and other exotic delectables of the Nile. That's our battle, too. Day and night, the flesh serenades us with siren songs, seeking to lure our affections away from Christ, tempting us to serve ourselves by our own efforts.

In Galatians, Paul expounds the application of many Old Testament promises linked to the inauguration of the new covenant, promises like that in Ezekiel 36:

> And I will give you a new heart, and a new spirit I will
> put within you. And I will remove the heart of stone
> from your flesh and give you a heart of flesh. And I will
> put my Spirit within you, and cause you to walk in my
> statutes (Ezek 36:26–27a).

That's the story of all believers, whose desire to walk with God
is birthed by the Spirit who gives a new heart (see 1 Sam 10:9).
Heaven is the complete fulfillment of these new desires. But in
this world the flesh opposes the Spirit at every step.

It's similar to the experience of moving, either nationally
or internationally, changing castles, cultures, and customs.
We know what it's like to permanently move overseas, to sell
our homes, say farewell to dear friends, and to—like Cortés—cut
the ropes and burn the boats so we couldn't go back, even if we
wanted to. Even though it was tremendously difficult, God made
it clear that's what we had to do, and he enabled it. Hardships made us yearn and dream
for our old, beloved homes—but they weren't
home anymore. Similarly, the flesh isn't your
home anymore. Your key no longer fits the
lock. But sometimes we want to go back and
peek in the windows, don't we? It's familiar and comfortable.
Those words, thoughts, actions, and attitudes are like a warm
blanket; they're patterns of thinking and relating laid down
from childhood.

THE FLESH
ISN'T YOUR HOME
ANY MORE

But we no longer live there—not because we don't desire it,
but because grace has given us a new home that we desire much
more. That's why we can't do what pleases us; our hearts have
been changed, and it wouldn't actually please us in the least.
It's merely a siren song.

LED BY THE SPIRIT

How do we "walk by the Spirit?" The answer is embedded in
Galatians 5:18: "But if you are led by the Spirit, you are not under

law." The flesh seeks to bind you under the yoke of the law (if necessary, dressing it up as piety and true commitment). The Spirit, however, leads deeper into the sonship that's been granted through the gospel. In other words, the Spirit implants within us a longing for the Father; it's why we're sometimes overcome with a profound feeling of homesickness. Paul says in Colossians:

> If then you have been raised with Christ, seek the things
> that are above, where Christ is, seated at the right hand
> of God. Set your minds on things that are above, not on
> things that are on earth. For you have died, and your
> life is hidden with Christ in God (Col 3:1–3).

How does one walk? Reduced to a simple axiom, recall your sonship. Remember the gospel; remember that you are no longer an orphan. You belong in Abba's family. Remember, against all the devil's accusations, which will drive you to justify yourself in the flesh, that you're justified and sanctified by faith. If the waters of doubt overwhelm you, look at the cross, and the outstretched arms of the horizontal beam—the embrace of Jesus is where the Spirit is leading (Heb 12:2). He is a strong tower and living water (Prov 18:10; 1 Cor 10:4). And his yoke is easy and his burden is light (Matt 11:30). There is rest in remembering the promises of God's fatherhood.

REMEMBER THE GOSPEL; YOU ARE NO LONGER AN ORPHAN

How does one recall the promises? The same way you began in the faith: by hearing the gospel! Remembering is such a burden for us. So God has gifted us the means of grace (not to grace) as helpful signposts, the efficacy of which is the word of the gospel they proclaim: the Word and the sacraments. They immerse us in Christ.

The gospel overcomes all obstacles posed by the flesh—as shown in a story told about Hudson Taylor, a missionary to inland China:

Mr. George Nichol was with [Taylor] on one occasion when some letters were handed in to his office, bringing news of serious rioting in two of the older stations of the Mission. Thinking that Mr. Taylor might wish to be alone, the younger man was about to withdraw when, to his surprise, someone began to whistle. It was the soft refrain of the same well-loved hymn:

"Jesus, I am resting, resting, in the joy of what Thou art..."

Turning back, Mr. Nichol could not help exclaiming, "How *can* you whistle, when our friends are in so much danger!"

"Would you have me anxious and troubled?" was the quiet reply. "That would not help them, and would certainly incapacitate me for my work. I have just to roll the burden on the Lord."[6]

Only the gospel lets you do that. The flesh hates it—but that's what it means to walk by the Spirit.

GALATIANS 5:19–23

Now the works of the flesh are evident: sexual immorality, impurity, sensuality, idolatry, sorcery, enmity, strife, jealousy, fits of anger, rivalries, dissensions, divisions, envy, drunkenness, orgies, and things like these. I warn you, as I warned you before, that those who do such things will not inherit the kingdom of God. But the fruit of the Spirit is love, joy, peace, patience, kindness, goodness, faithfulness, gentleness, self-control; against such things there is no law.

CHAPTER 20

WHAT CONTROLS YOU?

O vert or covert, we all love control. It's everywhere in our culture, from advertisements to TV shows. None of us is all that different from French fashion designer Coco Chanel, who reputedly said, "My life didn't please me, so I created my life."

The Judaizers' so-called gospel springs from the flesh, which, like the ad, "loves being in control." The drive to legalism and moralism both arise from the desire to control God and other people, to work out the "secret" to get them to do what we want. On the one hand, it's about insecurity born of an edgy conscience marred by shame; the flesh loves any way of making you feel like you're more holy or more acceptable to God, others, or yourself. On the other hand, it's about monitoring the lives of others; control means nothing if you can't get others to dance to your tune, thereby serving your desires!

> THE FLESH LOVES A MARIONETTE GOD

But the only thing the flesh loves more than controlling others is having a marionette God who's moved by the strings of piety or passion. The flesh abhors the Spirit, who's as free as the breeze and outside the control of religiosity. "And so it is with everyone born of the Spirit," John goes on to say (John 3:8). This is why if you are a child of the promise you'll be persecuted; your freedom is hated. Just ask Paul—he had been both the persecutor and persecuted!

The problem with legalism is not only that it denies the all-sufficency of Christ; it also becomes a force to break love and fellowship, rather than making us more holy like it promises. Law and piety have been used to cover all manner of sins and shameful secrets; we're hypercritical of the very thing of which we're most (covertly) guilty. Then we make a "Things that Must Be Done" list, topped by what we're good at. It's a two-for-one deal: a handy ruler with which to measure the shortcomings of others, and a scale already calibrated to our own success.

Paul will show the results of this hidden life in the next chapter: "It is those who want to make a good showing in the flesh who would force you to be circumcised. ... For even those who are circumcised do not themselves keep the law, but they desire to have you circumcised that they may boast in your flesh" (Gal 6:12-13), a trove of bloodied trophies to testify to their success. Their reputation and boasting were built on the pain-filled "obedience" wrung from others. Yet these were nothing more than a detour from their own failure to keep the law, ending in broken fellowship and exclusivism.

Christian discipleship, however, isn't about striving to gain control. It's about continually relinquishing control. The law relies on my effort; discipleship trusts God as my Father. Jesus was getting at this when he said: "If anyone would come after me, let him deny himself and take up his cross daily and follow me. For whoever would save his life will lose it, but whoever loses his life for my sake will save it" (Luke 9:23-24). Paul has learned the delight of that journey and doesn't want us to derailed from it, so he gives two contrasting vignettes of life: the way of the flesh, and the way of the Spirit.

The Way of the Flesh

In Mark 7:21-22, Jesus says it's not what goes into us that defiles, but what comes out. In other words, it's out of the heart that the works of the flesh flow; so the deeds of the flesh Paul speaks of in Galatians 5:19-21 come from our very being. Our actions aren't just wrong; we are wrong. Paul's list is merely describing the types of deeds of the flesh.

First on his list are the sensual deeds: sexual immorality (sex outside of marriage), impurity (unnatural vices), and sensuality (recklessly seeking the pleasure of the senses); these show our insatiable appetite for bodily pleasure. Why are we so hungry in these ways? What will satisfying this hunger provide? Love is communicated through the senses, and we want to be loved. We want connection with another person that's deeper than mere ideas. We want our loneliness relieved, our isolation ended. We want security. Satisfying the hunger gives us, in all our physicality, a sense of belonging, acceptance, and security—at least for the moment. The problem is, we see these things as ends in themselves. We think we have the power to define how we use them, and this makes them destructive. Warming by the fire is wonderful, but outside the fireplace, the flames will reduce your cabin to cinders. Using things and other people for our ends leaves us standing in a heap of ashes.

> WE SEE THESE THINGS AS ENDS IN THEMSELVES, AND THIS MAKES THEM DESTRUCTIVE

Second, being in the flesh can lead to religious deeds: idolatry (finding our identity and security in anything other than God himself) and sorcery (tampering with the powers of evil). What's behind these? The issue is power. Both idolatry and sorcery attempt to garner blessing through our works, replacing trust in God with self-reliance. To what end? Namely, to call down ourselves the blessings we crave—it's faith gone astray. Martin Luther put it this way:

What does it mean to have a god? or, what is God? Answer: A god means that from which we are to expect all good and to which we are to take refuge in all distress, so that to have a God is nothing else than to trust and believe Him from the whole heart; as I have often said that the confidence and faith of the heart alone make both God and an idol. If your faith and trust be right, then is your god also true; and, on the other hand, if your trust be false and wrong, then you have not the true God; for these two belong together faith and God. That now, I say, upon which you set your heart and put your trust is properly your god.[1]

> ALL OF THESE ATTITUDES VIOLATE BROTHERLY LOVE,

Third, being in the flesh may bear deeds of social malevolence: enmity (hatred of others), strife (quarrelsome spirit), jealousy (wrong or misdirected zeal), fits of anger (outbursts of rage), rivalries (getting ahead at someone else's expense), dissensions, divisions (party intrigue), envy (unhappiness when someone else succeeds). All of these are attitudes that violate brotherly love; all cause division. Where do they come from? They all attest to a preoccupation with ourselves at another's expense: You, your group (ethnic, religious, social, or political), and your agenda are all that matter. They rip community apart because they aren't other-centered and, thus, deny the nature of God, who is love.

Fourth, the deeds of the flesh are self-indulgent: drunkenness (or "getting wasted") and orgies. In Paul's day the latter was often associated with pagan worship and exstasis (from which "ecstasy" is derived), in which the worshipers worked themselves into a trance-like state as a "sign" of the "presence" of their gods. Orgies were marked by frenzied sexual activity, drunkenness, powerful rhythmic music, and hallucinogenically fueled visions. The same behavior is still with us today simply as a means of casting off all restraint. This self-indulgent conduct isn't just casually looking for fun; it's giving the flesh free rein, flat-out railing against God's created order.

"The list is a mirror to reveal the corruption of our own hearts," noted Puritan William Perkins. We recoil from these deeds of the flesh. Yet if we knew ourselves, "we would not need this [catalog]," said John Calvin, "but such is our innate hypocrisy that we never perceive our foulness until the tree has been made known by its fruits."[2]

Ancient philosophers and rabbis were making lots of lists like Paul's, long before Paul came on the scene. The reason? Like many today, they imagined it was possible to get beyond wrong behavior by education and effort: "If you just understand what sin is, and what the problems are, you can fix it." We hear such tidy lists and think, "Great! By reading those lists and being prodded a few times, I'll know what not to do! That gives me more power to not do them!" The Judaizers were pushing that cart, but its wheels were broken. They still are.

GRACE TRANSFORMS, NOT WILLPOWER

Why doesn't education and effort release us and set our hearts free? Because redoubling our efforts returns us to the flesh, moving back toward our selves rather than toward faith!

Paul's having none of it. He's saying, "The problem isn't education because the flesh can't be instructed to behave, except for outward conformity. It has to be destroyed. It's opposed to the Spirit, not merely misinformed. We're born of the flesh and remain in the flesh until we're born of the Spirit. Only then can things change." In Paul's theology, being justified, sanctified, and glorified are inseparable from being in Christ. Grace transforms, not willpower.

The Way of the Spirit

Children of God aren't born of blood and the will of man, but of God. That's grace (John 1:12–13). The "yes" of grace is also a "no" to all human strength and definitions of power. Growing in the fruit of the Spirit is relinquishing control—the mark of the flesh—to walk by faith, trusting God—the mark of the Spirit.

Paul had been a peacock on parade, bearing the sword to destroy willful blasphemers who followed their false Messiah. His strength was in the flesh. But grace rendered him weak so God's power could be made perfect in him (2 Cor 12:9). And consider Peter's experience of grace:

> Getting into one of the boats, which was Simon's, [Jesus] asked him to put out a little from the land. And he sat down and taught the people from the boat. And when he had finished speaking, he said to Simon, "Put out into the deep and let down your nets for a catch." And Simon answered, "Master, we toiled all night and took nothing! But at your word I will let down the nets." And when they had done this, they enclosed a large number of fish, and their nets were breaking. ... But when Simon Peter saw it, he fell down at Jesus' knees, saying, "Depart from me, for I am a sinful man, O Lord." ... And Jesus said to Simon, "Do not be afraid; from now on you will be catching men" (Luke 5:3-10).

Do you ever wonder how this simple fisherman could become a fisher of men? It's not because he polished up on his studies and got fired up with enthusiasm. It's because, falling at Jesus' knees, he essentially said, "In my very being I'm wrong, and I can't fix it. Have mercy, Lord!" It's at this point that Peter is connected to the vine, moving with the Spirit of God. Only then could the Spirit's fruit grow on the branch that Peter became. Grace had weakened him so that he could bear the weight of being one of the foundation stones of the church. When he drew strength from himself, he was too brittle to be useful.

ONE IS A LIST OF DEEDS; THE OTHER A DESCRIPTION OF FRUIT

Here's the central difference between the list of fleshly works and the description of the Spirit's fruit: One is a list of deeds (i.e., works, arising from actions that we will); the other is a description of fruit (i.e., a harvest arising from what the Spirit does). It's not the flesh trying to be spiritual, but the Spirit reproducing his life in us.

Because the fruit comes from one source, it's more like a cluster of grapes on a vine than a variety of fruits grouped in a basket. Although Paul's description falls into three sections, they're all one "fruit" of the Spirit's gracious presence. Old Testament professor Samuel Hooke put it this way:

> A vine does not produce grapes by Act of Parliament; they are the fruit of the vine's own life; so the conduct which conforms to the standard of the kingdom is not produced by any command, not even God's, but it is the fruit of the divine nature which God gives as a result of what he has done in and by Christ.[3]

Before we address the fruit, a warning: Don't read what follows as a checklist. It will drive you to either pride or despair and would overlook the fruits' real purpose. Rather, they're descriptions of the inevitable outcome of life in the Spirit. As you walk by the Spirit you won't carry out the desires of the flesh (Gal 5:16). Why? Because the Spirit changes your taste buds! You'll increasingly long for his fruit and disdain your fleshly works. The Spirit awakens you to the vintage wine of the Father's cellar.

The first cluster of three fruits, then, is love, joy, and peace. The mark of a true Christian is that his or her chief love is God himself—Christians' greatest joy (which is also their strength) is found in God himself, and their deepest peace (security because all hostilities are over) is with God himself. Love, joy, and peace are orientated first and foremost toward God.

The second cluster of fruits is patience, kindness, and goodness—or, being longsuffering toward those who aggravate and persecute; a disposition to bless; and good words, actions, and attitudes. Clearly these three fruits have a social orientation. They belong to true community and only are enabled as we find our love, joy, and peace in God. When our inner self is at peace in God, then patience, kindness, and goodness may flow through us to others.

The final cluster of fruits is faithfulness, gentleness, and self-control. These look like reliability; humble meekness like Christ's; and not being driven by the impulses of the flesh. All of these are aspects of self-mastery; a snapshot of a Christian man or woman rescued from drivenness and resting in Christ.

Together, the fruit contain God-ward, man-ward, and self-ward dimensions—quite like the great commandment, "You shall love the Lord your God with all your heart and with all your soul and with all your mind. This is the great and first commandment. And a second is like it: You shall love your neighbor as yourself" (Matt 22:37–39, emphasis added). Such is the life of God reproduced in us—that's why it's good!

Gloriously, Paul says there's no law against this surrendered life. As you yield to the Spirit, being led as a child of God, God does something you can't. He makes his likeness grow in you. It's all a matter of faith in God's grace. "It is no longer I who live, but Christ who lives in me. And the life I now live in the flesh I live by faith in the Son of God, who loved me and gave himself up for me" (Gal 2:20).

> THE FLESH TRUSTS ONLY ITSELF. THE SPIRIT DECLARES ALL THINGS DONE.

Day by day—even against the pressure of the flesh—you trust in the faithful love of the Son of God. The flesh trusts only itself. It leaves you to carry the load and finish the work. But the Spirit declares all things done and enables you to roll all your cares over onto Christ, who cares for you. As David Benner says:

> God does not ask for resignation based on acquiescence in the absence of a better option. Nor does God ask for reluctant, grudging submission. What God wants is surrender based on love and trust. ... God invites us to abandon our neurotic displays of self-sufficiency. He invites us to surrender our stolen independence

and exchange it for a willingly accepted dependence. God takes our humble offering of powerlessness and turns it into a voluntary subordination—a freely chosen laying down our life that leads to our transformation and fulfillment.[4]

Life in the Spirit is a life of slow and silent transformation. When God ripens apples he isn't in a hurry, and he doesn't make a lot of noise about it. Such will be your experience as you live in the gospel.

Resting in the work of Christ cuts the root of our self-sufficiency. The flesh sees this humble trust as powerlessness. But it's where the grace of God proves all-sufficient—his power made perfect in weakness (2 Cor 12:9). We're not in control, the Spirit is. This is how we're connected to the vine, and it's the only way the fruit ripens.

GALATIANS 5:24–26

And those who belong to Christ Jesus have crucified the flesh with its passions and desires.

If we live by the Spirit, let us also keep in step with the Spirit. Let us not become conceited, provoking one another, envying one another.

CHAPTER 21

KEEPING IN STEP

The point of these last few chapters is simply this: The fruit of the Spirit is the fruit of faith. People of faith turn away from self-reliance, planting their roots deep into the grace of God, and as they feed on that rich soil the Spirit produces his fruit in their lives.

The faith we're speaking of isn't mere assent to formal doctrine, but faith—wholehearted trust—in the faithfulness of the Son of God. Faith trusts what he has done, what he is doing, and what he will do. It's as much pulled by the future as impelled by the past.

FAITH IS ROOTED
IN HISTORY

Such faith is rooted in history; it looks back to the cross, where the flesh was crucified. There, the deadly enemy lost its foothold and was cast down. Why? Because there sin was forgiven, the broken law atoned for, shame removed, and guilt washed away. And where there is no guilt, the flesh and the devil lose their power.

This is the doctrinal truth of the matter, but we're not yet singing on the summit of Mount Zion, free from all strife. The intensity of battle between the flesh and the Spirit cannot be overstated, nor can it be reduced to a phase of life. It's a lifelong engagement in which final victory is delayed, though never in doubt. We daily begin again in faith, rejecting the strength of the flesh. In the present, it's the way of the cross, not glory.

While Paul's gospel isn't a "positive thinking" program, it does change our thinking. It asks us to think—hard—on the real situation, on who we are in Christ. Hence, it calls us to live by what is, not by what seems to be. It demands that we turn from our assessment of ourselves and, even more so, from that of the devil. He will never tell you the truth of who you are in Jesus; he will never get you to dance to the beat of the Spirit's drum. Only the cross keeps you in step.

CRUCIFIED AND CRUCIFYING

When the crowds asked Jesus, "What must we do, to be doing the works of God?," he could have answered in a myriad of ways; he could have given them a big book of self-help rules. But he didn't; he answered them, "This is the work of God, that you believe [i.e., trust] in him whom he has sent" (John 6:28–29).

Nothing could be clearer or more direct: Christian living is always concerned with the outworking of faith. This isn't just the first step of the Christian life, but every step along the way. Jesus is the Alpha and the Omega, the door, the direction, and the destination.

CHRISTIAN LIVING IS ALWAYS CONCERNED WITH THE OUTWORKING OF FAITH

But how does all this square with Paul's announcement? "Those who belong to Christ Jesus have crucified the flesh with its passions and desires" (Gal 5:24). The verb "have crucified" is active, not passive. It's also past tense. In other words, Paul's not giving a command; he's stating the case. Belonging to Christ means that we have crucified the flesh.

How do you square that circle, an active verb in the past tense, especially in light of what we've been saying about the battle being a lifelong one? How can you crucify the flesh? Doesn't it contradict what Paul's been saying about our utter dependence on the grace of God and what he has done? And how can the flesh, crucified in the past, still seem so alive?

An imperfect illustration: When you're on the highway the road behind you is behind you, yet in most instances the scenery through the windscreen looks much the same as that in the rear-view mirror. In one sense, the road you've left behind is present to your vision, but in another sense you'll never pass that way again.

By faith we know the flesh has been crucified in the cross; we see it in the rearview mirror of the gospel, preached orally and in the holy sacraments. We've left it behind, but we're also still leaving it behind. The old Adam struggles against yielding to the Word of grace, as Karl Barth has noted:

> If it is not to yield, as it certainly will not, it must come out of its den and take action. And the simplest and most obvious thing to do consists simply in acting as if it had not heard the Word, as if it had not been spoken, as if that which it says has happened had not happened. In other words, it sets one fact against another: against the fact of accomplished reconciliation, of the fulfilled covenant, the fact of indifference to what this Word proclaims, to the divine Giver and His divine giving and gift; against the fact of grace the fact of the calm but all the more effective continuation of pride; against the fact of man's liberation from his old being for a new the fact that he can obviously continue to exist in his old and usurped freedom and make no use of the new freedom which he is given; against the fact of the drowning of the old Adam the fact that the rogue is an expert swimmer; against the fact of the new birth of man in the mystery of Christmas the fact that the old game of self-reconciliation and anxiety and indifference still goes on, so that the news of the irruption of the new aeon with its peace and joy and fellowship is easily given the lie by this very continuation.[1]

This is why Paul says in Romans, "So you also must consider yourselves dead to sin and alive to God in Christ Jesus" (Rom 6:11), and in Colossians, "Put to death therefore what is earthly in you: sexual immorality, impurity, passion, evil desire, and covetousness, which is idolatry" (Col 3:5). The "therefore" is there because of what precedes it: We've been crucified, buried, and raised with Christ, and our lives are hidden with Jesus in the very life of God. *Therefore*, put to death in your life things that don't belong with your true position. Put the flesh out of action in your life—it's already out of action through the cross.

Jesus didn't come merely to give an example for us to emulate, nor is he a spectator to our faltering efforts to follow his steps. He came to enable true participation in his life, death, and resurrection. To understand this, we need to look to what the Old Testament sacrificial system teaches about the meaning of faith. A person would bring the sacrificial lamb, lay a hand on its head—symbolically laying their sin on the lamb—and then slaughter it. Its death was, symbolically, their death; its sacrifice in the flames, their symbolic passing under the flaming sword of God's wrath (see Gen 3:24). The blessing pronounced by the priest after the ceremony signified that they lived by the death of another. It was a participatory system, gifted by grace.

FAITH TURNS AWAY FROM OUR RIGHTEOUSNESS AND LIVES ON THE BASIS OF HIS

Faith in Christ accepts his substitutionary death in the same way. Faith turns away from each of us and our righteousness and lives on the basis of his. As Charles Spurgeon said:

> You have not really grasped what faith means unless you have grasped this. With him you suffered the wrath of God, for he suffered in your stead: you are now in him—crucified with him, dead with him, buried with him, risen with him, and gone to glory with him—because he represents you, and your faith has accepted the representation.[2]

To turn from myself and rely upon another is to turn my back on the flesh, to crucify it. The crucified always have cried out in agony; the flesh will do no less.

We might imagine the flesh—that old ego with the mentality of merit, reputation, self-reliance, and power—as a dragon in some cave of your soul. Jesus comes in the gospel, saying, "I'll make you mine, take possession of the cave, and slay the dragon. Will you yield to my possession? It will mean a whole new way of thinking, feeling, and acting."

You reply, "But that dragon is me. I'll die."

"You will—and you'll rise to new life too. I will make my mind, will, and heart your own."

"What must I do?" you ask.

"Trust me. Just trust me—believe."

Ruthless crucifixion of the flesh is absolutely necessary for spiritual growth. New life only comes by death and resurrection. But it's all by participation, by union with Christ through faith, not through fleshly law-keeping. Wrestling yourself to the mat by the strength of your will, in some self-chosen "spiritual" work, is not what crucifies the flesh. If you've tried that, you're aware that 9 times out of 10 it fails, leading to self-pity and despair. The one time you succeed in the flesh, the dragon of your pride awakens from the deep to destroy you by glory instead of despair.

It's painful to say "no" to my flesh. It hurts to watch a loved one starve to death. It hurts to not feed the dragon, let alone pound nails in and abandon it. Every impulse is to insert the feeding tubes and help it down from the cross. Yet the cross is where Christ has taken it; it's where it is and where it must stay, for it has no part in Christ, in whom you now live.

By what means can we crucify the flesh, if not by willpower? How can it be overcome if not by the strict discipline of the law? Only by "the expulsive power of a new affection," as 19th-century Scottish minister and theologian Thomas Chalmers noted:

> It is seldom that any of our tastes are made to disappear
> by a mere process of natural extinction. At least, it is

very seldom, that this is done through the instrumentality of reasoning. It may be done by excessive pampering—but it is almost never done by the mere force of mental determination. But what cannot be thus destroyed, may be dispossessed—and one taste may be made to give way to [another], and to lose its power entirely as the reigning affection of the mind. ... There is not one of these transformations in which the heart is left without an object. Its desire for one particular object may be conquered; but as to its desire for having some one object or other, this is unconquerable. ... It is when released from the spirit of bondage with which love cannot dwell, and when admitted into the number of God's children through the faith that is in Jesus Christ, the Spirit of adoption is poured upon us—it is then that the heart, brought under the mastery of one great and predominate affection, is delivered from the tyranny of its former desires in the only way in which deliverance is possible.[3]

But what does this actually look like in our lives? You might be at work when a coworker, supervisor, or a customer causes everything to flare up. In the emotional chaos and frustration, you're debating whether to give the person a verbal thrashing or take to the hills—both are psychological techniques that resonate with us. But the true power isn't the law, but a gospel-centered mindset. You don't need to give the person a thrashing or take to the hills, for Christ has borne the sins of you both. He will be sufficient for you in the moment. You don't even need to defend yourself, for Jesus is your reputation. Cling to him—the flesh is crucified in running to Jesus and trusting in his finished work. Affection for the old way is pushed out by a new affection for and reliance upon him. And this new way is radically different from moralistic law-keeping.

> JESUS IS YOUR
> REPUTATION.
> CLING TO HIM

But what if you blew it, lashed out at the other person or ran away from the situation? Well, the flesh, which wanted to hold a self-atonement party, is crucified the same way—namely, by running to Jesus. In him, your righteousness is secure. And we have good news: God isn't mad at you. Whether you run to Jesus before or after you sin, the dragon is nailed to the cross through faith. Leave it there!

KEEPING IN STEP WITH THE SPIRIT

The pattern we've just seen repeats in Galatians 5:25: "If we live by the Spirit, let us also keep in step with the Spirit." This isn't "if" in the sense of wishful thinking. Rather, the "if" means "since" or "in view of the fact that" we live by the Spirit. Again, our starting point is the finished work of Christ. It's true of us because of Christ, not because of us. So, says Paul, keep in step with the Spirit. Don't strain against him. Let him take you where he wants. "The death of the flesh is the life of the Spirit. If God's Spirit lives in us, let Him govern all our actions," in the words of John Calvin.[4]

Paul is talking to a community of believers—the pronouns "we" and "us" are plural. The community might be in a mess theologically; the preaching they have received might be leading them to bite and devour one another (a diet of law has that effect), but they're sheep, not goats, confused though they may be. The flip side of this—and it might come as a shock—is that it's not our job to tell a dishonest businessman to be honest or to tell a philanderer to be faithful. The New Testament has one message for the unbeliever: Repent and believe in the Lord Jesus (see Mark 1:15; Acts 2:38), because they're yet in bondage to the evil age. A Christian community isn't about sin management in the lives of others, certainly not the lives of unbelievers. It's about the gospel, which is, by the way, the only power against the deeds of the flesh. Keeping in step with the Spirit, then, isn't a program of sin mitigation, but gospel maximization. As Michael Mangis has written:

When we abandon the idea of sin as failure to manage external behavior and look at sin as a failure of our soul to be fully attuned to God's soul, we can let go of the compulsive practice of speck spotting. Jesus asked, "Why do you look at the speck of sawdust in your brother's eye and pay no attention to the plank in your own eye?" (Mt 7:3). Not only must I give up the guilty pleasure of comparing the quality of my sin management to that of others, but I must begin to face up to my responsibility for my own sin.[5]

What does keeping in step with the Spirit look like? To walk with the Spirit means to be in harmony with him. When we walk with someone, we draw near, match our cadence to theirs, and as we walk we begin to talk and relate to one another. The Spirit is intensely interested in us and the community in which he's placed us. He never goes on about his own things. Rather, the Spirit walks us over to Jesus; he prompts our souls

> TO WALK WITH THE SPIRIT MEANS TO BE IN HARMONY WITH HIM

to cry, "Abba, Father"; he teaches us who we are in relationship to the Father—his children, not orphans, but coheirs with Christ; and he makes us aware of the family we're walking with.

Yet, the walk isn't a stroll through the arboretum. As we walk, the Spirit attunes our senses to the sounds of battle, shows us the camouflage and strongholds of the dragon, and gives us the desire to fight. He teaches us how to live by repentant faith, turning from the flesh with decreasing confidence in ourselves and increasing our confidence in Christ.

We can get so depressed over our sin and its lingering presence that we question if we really belong to God. But do you think someone without the Spirit even mourns its breath, even contemplates crucifying the flesh? Never. The one who is in the Spirit is sensitized to the true nature of things. As Paul says, "The spiritual person judges all things, but is himself to be judged by no one" (1 Cor 2:15). Seeing both themselves and Christ rightly, they let go of their idols so their hands are free to cling to him alone. From this flows the freedom to forgive and serve the family in love. This is what it means to "set your minds on things that are above" (Col 3:2). It's not dreaming of heaven or holy living; it's clinging to the one whose abode is heaven, delighting in the Father's face turned toward me, living in his Spirit who walks with me as he leads me to the one who is living water.

Serve One Another in Love

Galatians 5:26—"Let us not become conceited, provoking one another, envying one another"—could be paraphrased, "Let us serve one another in love" (compare Gal 5:13). The sins listed here are the socially malevolent modes of fleshly living. Wrestling with theological confusion and wanting to control their progress in holiness, the Galatians were biting and devouring each other (5:15).

When we break fellowship over issues of piety, scruples, preferences, or even doctrinal issues, we're really full of ourselves, not holiness. The flesh loves to muddy the water and cloud our vision. The Lord calls us to a different walk: "You were called to freedom, brothers. Only do not use your freedom as an opportunity for the flesh, but through love serve one another. For the whole law is fulfilled in one word: 'You shall love your neighbor as yourself'" (Gal 5:13–14). It's a walk of freedom characterized by love and service. Hence it's not a freedom marked by doing, being, and saying whatever we want, regardless of our connection with a larger community. It's not freedom from constraint, but freedom from self-preference. This love is freedom; as the English poet Robert Browning once said, "Not where I breathe, but where I love, I live." The impulse and opportunity to serve others—to really engage in heartfelt care, concern and charity (1 Cor 10:23-24)—this is what we're redeemed for:

> Truly Christian relationships are governed not by rivalry but by service. The correct attitude to other people is

not, "I'm better than you and I'll prove it," nor, "You're better than I and I resent it," but "You are a person of importance in your own right (because God made you in His own image and Christ died for you) and it is my joy and privilege to serve you."[6]

Freedom is not a simple expression of unchecked, unthinking self-interest; it's the capacity to crucify the flesh by turning to Jesus in a step of faith. This is keeping in step with the Spirit, moving with the Spirit, hearing the voice of the Spirit leading into a lifestyle of repentance, deepening reliance, and real love.

When Paul encouraged the Corinthians to follow through with the famine relief offering they'd pledged for the stricken Jerusalem church, he said, "For you know the grace of our Lord Jesus Christ, that though he was rich, yet for your sake he became poor, so that you by his poverty might become rich" (2 Cor 8:9). Keeping in step with the Spirit doesn't mean grasping for power and position, but giving up such to raise another, without care for merit or the lack thereof.

> FREEDOM IS THE CAPACITY TO CRUCIFY THE FLESH BY TURNING TO JESUS

The flesh always looks for its investment to be returned with interest; it's capable of nothing but self-enhancement. Serving without reference to return is beyond its conceptual framework. Therefore, loving others well only comes through the Spirit's leading us to trust in the faithfulness of God for our needs, so we're free to be his tools in the lives of others.

It's that simple. I'm not free to serve you if I'm worried my needs won't be met—I'm bound to serve myself. But the way of the Spirit is always toward greater faith that is willing to wait on God's time, willing to walk his way no matter the depth of suffering that love and hands-on service plunges us into. Loving service is a step of faith. My well-being surrendered into the Father's hands, not into yours or fastened in mine.

Understand: Paul is issuing no orders. Rather, his desire is that we would grow deeper in grace, deeper in the knowledge of God. In keeping in step with the Spirit, in serving one another in love, we're directed again and again back to Jesus and away from ourselves and our resources. It's all by participation in the life of Christ, who loved us and gave himself for us. Such union means the community is built up and served in the love of God himself—and keeping us in step with the community through the Spirit is something the flesh can never do.

GALATIANS 6:1–5

Brothers, if anyone is caught in any transgression, you who are spiritual should restore him in a spirit of gentleness. Keep watch on yourself, lest you too be tempted. Bear one another's burdens, and so fulfill the law of Christ. For if anyone thinks he is something, when he is nothing, he deceives himself. But let each one test his own work, and then his reason to boast will be in himself alone and not in his neighbor. For each will have to bear his own load.

CHAPTER 22

THE TRULY SPIRITUAL LIFE

We're drawing near the end of Paul's letter, but just as the foundation isn't the completed building, the end of the letter doesn't contain the sum total of the Christian life. Mostly, Paul's been re-laying foundations—hot, hard, sweaty work, without which the superstructure would be twisted and dangerous. But here in the sixth chapter we glimpse the spiritual life those foundations give rise to—and it's a beautiful building.

True spirituality arises out of a grace-based relationship with God. It is, therefore, defined by him and flows from his Spirit. To the flesh, the Spirit's way is weak and ineffective. Where the law's way deals harshly—condemning those who stumble and distancing others out of a sense of superiority—the Spirit's way is marked by gentleness, understanding, and grace.

One of the chief criticisms leveled at Paul's gospel, both then and now, is that grace makes for lazy living. The logic is simple: Holiness advances by hard labor, so the horses need a whip to keep them running. Fear seems a far better motivator than grace. Changing the metaphor, Robert Capon says:

We slip into the stupor of imagining there are things we have to do—some additive of religious works we have to put into the gasoline of grace—if the gift of God is to get its work done in us. And the sad thing about it is that we'll scour the New Testament (especially the Epistles, and in particular the Pastoral Epistles) for every moral "requirement" and religious "condition" we can find in order to slap a behavioral surcharge on our free acceptance in the Beloved.[1]

It was inconceivable to Paul's opponents that grace could be truly sufficient, not only for the beginning of the Christian life, but for every step. But why? It's helpful to quote Capon again, who says of the "grim pills" of religion, spirituality, and morality:

They're nothing more than three packagings of the same pain-killer. Or, better said, religion is the generic version of the drug, while spirituality and morality are higher-priced name brands. Moreover, the pain we take them to kill is the agony of not having *control* over our lives. The ostensible purpose of religion is to give us the power to make things happen the way they "should," but all it gives us is the *illusion* of such control. We swallow it in the same hope with which Adam and Eve ate the fruit of the Tree of the Knowledge of Good and Evil: to convince ourselves that when all is said and done, *we're* the ones in charge of the management of creation. That never works. We may think that we're practicing our religion because God told us to. But the side effect of the drug is always and invariably the depressing feeling that if we don't practice it, God either won't be able to help us, or he'll get mad and decide not to (which amounts to the same thing).[2]

Grace means that Jesus closed the metaphorical drug store. The spiritual life has to do with trusting that the sacrifice and oblation of the Good Physician was sufficient, that we should pack up our plastic doctor kits and end the game. We aren't in control!

Good works may be an indication of the grace of God, but they're not the fuel. If the fuel isn't grace itself, then "works" are inevitably dead—"grim pills" that load the patient up with guilt and other toxins and kill their relationship with God. If we get it into our heads that religion and morality are what God desires, then we have the gospel upside-down and backwards. God desires communion; he looks to the one "who is humble and contrite in spirit and trembles at [his] word" (Isa 66:2). Works, then, flow from a good conscience; they don't fuel it. Free grace alone cleanses the conscience. Think about it like this:

FREE GRACE ALONE CLEANSES THE CONSCIENCE

> When we know God has been gracious to us, when we know we are miserable, rat-bag sinners who don't deserve a thing from God and never will; when we know our righteousness is Christ's righteousness and that it's the only righteousness we'll ever have and it's all the righteousness we'll ever need; when we know deep down we can rest in the grace of God; when we know this deeply in our souls so that it affects our whole sense of identity and well-being and composure; when we know that God sees us in Christ, then we become gracious.
>
> The dynamic is that if we start living a legalistic life because we think it's what God wants us to do, we become legalistic with one another. What we are before God because of how we think that he views us, we end up being before one another because of the way we view them. If we think God wants us to jump through hoops or he won't have anything to do with us, then we'll start doing that with other people. If we think we have to qualify for mercy, then we'll cease to show mercy. This is the simple dynamic of the Christian life: What you

are before God because of how you think he views you, you will become before others because of the way you view them.[3]

Getting this backwards makes us not only legalists but also idolaters, as Martin Luther explains:

> All those who do not at all times trust God and do not in all their works or sufferings, life and death, trust in His favor, grace and good-will, but seek His favor in other things or in themselves, do not keep this [First] Commandment, and practice real idolatry, even if they were to do the works of all the other Commandments, and in addition had all the prayers, fasting, obedience, patience, and chastity of all the saints combined. ... If we doubt or do not believe that God is gracious to us and is pleased with us, or if we presumptuously expect to please Him only through and after our works, then it is all pure deception, outwardly honoring God, but inwardly setting up self as a false [savior].[4]

If we do good works to justify ourselves, we're actually trashing the first commandment, "You shall have no other gods before me" (Exod 20:3). That's what it comes down to. Seeking to justify ourselves by religion, spirituality, or morality is defining ourselves as our own saviors and, therefore, our own gods.

HEALING IN THE SPIRIT

Galatians 6:1 gives a central trademark of the truly spiritual life: "If anyone is caught in any transgression, you who are spiritual should restore him in a spirit of gentleness. Keep watch on yourself, lest you too be tempted." The emphasis here is on the "who" and "how" of correction: The "who" is our brothers and sisters in Christ—it's an in-house deal. The "how" is beautiful: The key action is "to restore," which is different from "rebuke," "ridicule," "humiliate," "chastise," or "dominate." In other words, when a family member has been caught with their hand in the cookie jar, we're to restore, not penalize, them.

How we treat one another testifies to our spiritual wellspring. If we have pharisaical tendencies, then, those attitudes will still come across, even if we go to one another individually. Why? Because the legalistic mindset of the flesh taints the water at its source.

> HOW WE TREAT ONE ANOTHER TESTIFIES TO OUR SPIRITUAL WELLSPRING

We've seen the effects. Those who feel ridiculed typically disappear from fellowship; they don't dare darken the church's doors—it's an unsafe place, full of disapproval and rejection. In reality, the "spiritual" are those who know they're constantly walking the trail with their shoes untied, yet they're aware that their insurance has been paid in full. As Paul reminds us in 1 Corinthians, "Let anyone who thinks that he stands take heed lest he fall" (1 Cor 10:12). Luther advises:

> Love is gentle, kind and patient, not in receiving but in doing, for it has to overlook many things and bear with them. In the church faithful pastors see many errors and sins that they are obliged to bear. If we can put up with our own sins, then let us learn to put up with those of others as well.[5]

Luther was talking to pastors, but his advice applies to us all. "A Christian must have broad shoulders and husky bones to carry the flesh, that is, the weakness, of the brethren," he notes elsewhere.[6] In so doing we join Christ in the burdens he bore—a unique form of communion.

Correction has its place, but there's also a place for forgiveness, for overlooking opportunities for redress. Paul reserves his most rigorous language for the various false teachers who perverted the gospel (e.g., Gal 1:7–9; 4:29–31; 5:10–12; see also Acts 20:29–30; 2 Cor 11:13–15; Phil 1:15; 2:21). Of course there is love in correcting a brother or sister under the guidance of the Spirit; that's why Proverbs warns, "Do not reprove a scoffer, or he will hate you; reprove a wise man, and he will love you" (9:8). When the Holy Spirit is guiding and controlling, correction leads to fruitfulness rather than one-upmanship. Those led by the Spirit know just how much they themselves are in need of grace, that they're simply fellow pilgrims on the journey.

Remember the woman who was caught in adultery and was tossed in the dirt before Jesus by the scribes and Pharisees? They had stones at the ready, and just paused long enough to solicit Jesus' opinion. But what did he say? "Let the one who has never sinned throw the first stone" (John 8:7 NLT). And her accusers left.

Jesus stands in the vicious circle of our accusers to free us from their deadly threats. "Neither do I condemn you," he says. "Go, and from now on sin no more" (John 8:11). His words are restorative, releasing the heart from asphyxiating guilt and fostering a yearning for the oxygen of divine grace.

MUTUALITY IN THE SPIRIT

The second trademark of the truly spiritual life is found in Galatians 6:2-3: "Bear one another's burdens, and so fulfill the law of Christ. For if anyone thinks he is something, when he is nothing, he deceives himself." Here Paul says, "These are the burdens I'd have you bear—not the vexations of the law, but your neighbor's errors and weaknesses, his sorrows and sufferings." Restoring with grace is one way of bearing a burden; another way is taking practical responsibility for each other. Look no further than Genesis 4: "Then the LORD said to Cain, 'Where is Abel your brother?' He said, 'I do not know; am I my brother's keeper?' " (Gen 4:9). He tries to wriggle out of any responsibility for Abel's welfare, but the truly spiritual life is intensely practical. It includes caring enough to be a listening ear, a strong shoulder, a helping hand. But there's also more: Spiritual friendship follows the rhythm of the Holy Spirit, moving and speaking with spiritual wisdom, rendering soul care through the gospel.[7]

SPIRITUAL FRIENDSHIP FOLLOWS THE RHYTHM OF THE HOLY SPIRIT

Loneliness, illness, relational pain, sorrow, anxieties, fears, disabilities, and depression will stalk us all at some point. When they come after your friend, walk with him or her; soon, they'll have to walk with you.

"If you must needs impose burdens on yourselves, let them be the burdens of mutual sympathy," wrote J. B. Lightfoot, a bishop and New Testament scholar. "If you must needs observe a law, let it be the law of Christ."[8] Psalm 55:22 reminds us, "Cast your burden on the Lord, and he will sustain you"—but at times it is supremely difficult to do this. Sometimes we need a friend to draw near, to take our hands, and to place our grip on the cross when we're too tired and too exhausted to even lift our arms and to hold them there, with their hand over ours, until we can hang on ourselves. True indeed is Dietrich Bonhoeffer's statement:

> God has willed that we should seek and find His living Word in the witness of a brother, in the mouth of man. Therefore, the Christian needs another Christian who speaks God's Word to him. He needs him again and again when he becomes uncertain and discouraged, for by himself he cannot help himself without belying the truth. He needs his brother man as a bearer and proclaimer of the divine word of salvation. He needs his brother solely because of Jesus Christ. The Christ in his own heart is weaker than the Christ in the word of his brother; his own heart is uncertain, his brother's is sure. We need the word of grace to come to us, through the lips of a fellow Christian. We can't do it alone.[9]

If pride fills our hearts, though, we won't want to carry one another's baggage; self-centeredness will keep us from self-giving. To bear for another and to allow another to bear for us requires us to have the mind of Christ—*kenosis*, "self-emptying." Paul writes of Jesus in Philippians that "though he was in the form of God, did not count equality with God a thing to be grasped, but emptied himself, by taking the form of a servant" (2:6–7). Being like God is giving, not grasping.

As the gospel embraces us ever tighter we begin to find rest in the Father's acceptance of us and, thus, rest from the urge to continually compare ourselves to others. This transforms our actions; rather than think, "I'm better than you, so it's beneath me to help you with your baggage, and I don't need your help with mine!," grace moves differently. We bear burdens not because it's the right thing to do, but because we have the mind of Christ, who bears us all and regards us more important than himself.

Awareness in the Spirit

The last trademark of the truly spiritual life is found in Galatians 6:4–5: "Let each one test his own work, and then his reason to boast will be in himself alone and not in his neighbor. For each will have to bear his own load." Admittedly, this is a bit confusing. How can we be told to boast and carry our own loads, after just being told in Galatians 6:2–3 to carry one another's and not be boastful?

Paul isn't contradicting himself; he's making a point about awareness and responsibility. The way of the Spirit is to check one's own actions and motivations, rather than comparing and judging those of others. Let's compare the wording in another translation: "Pay careful attention to your own works, for then you will get the satisfaction of a job well done, and you won't need to compare yourself to anyone else. For we are each responsible for our own conduct" (Gal 6:4–5 NLT). In other words, each of us stands before an audience of one; all that really matters is what he thinks of us and what he's doing in and with us.

Peter learned this lesson on the beach. After Jesus' resurrection, when he was throwing fish on the fire with the other lads, Peter took great interest in what Jesus was saying about John's ministry. When he tried to poke his nose into that conversation, Jesus simply answered, "If it is my will that he remain until I come, what is that to you? You follow me!" (John 21:22). In other words, "Peter, I'm John's Shepherd as well as yours. So let me lead both of you as I will." We don't have to pry into what Jesus is doing with someone else. His attention is fully devoted to us, and that's all we need.

Before we move on, notice the future tense: "For each will have to bear his own load." That is to say, on the last day, all will be unveiled and shown for what it is. What we do is important, not because it saves, but because it accentuates the One in whom we have trusted. Having sown to the Spirit, we "will from the Spirit reap eternal life" (Gal 6:8). All else will be worthless. In its essence, Paul is asking us to test our own work to see if we truly are walking by the Spirit before an audience of One.

When a carpenter builds a series of frames, he doesn't build each one by taking measurements from the previous one. His work soon wouldn't be square. Instead, he measures from the original. Similarly, comparing ourselves to others always gives us skewed results. We can end up judging ourselves harshly, either thinking we should be better than we are or that we're something when we're really nothing. Either way, we will lock ourselves or others into a prison of shame, guilt, and impossible expectations, even while we idolize some image of a super-Christian. But there are no super-Christians! Thank goodness Christ's "power is made perfect in weakness"—we're weak in him (2 Cor 12:9; 13:4).

When you look at Jesus, you'll discover two things: that you don't measure up, and that you are, nevertheless, deeply loved. And knowing your own wretchedness not only keeps you near the cross; it also changes your attitude toward the inadequacy of others. Looking at Jesus frees us from the terrible burden of comparison: No one measures up, so our only recourse is to stop striving against irresistible grace.

> LOOKING AT JESUS FREES US FROM THE BURDEN OF COMPARISON

Resting in Jesus' love frees us to love. The more we gaze on him as our only help and salvation, the more grace characterizes our relational life. Why? Because we have no direct relationship with another; Jesus is the one in whom we all meet. This is what Bonhoeffer was getting at when he wrote:

> One is a brother to another only through Jesus Christ. I am a brother to another person through what Jesus Christ did for me and to me; the other person has become a brother to me through what Jesus Christ did for him.[10]

This is the essence of the truly spiritual life. It's animated and sustained by the Word and Spirit. The fruit of the Spirit is never ours to boast over, only to delight in, since it comes from him, not us.

GALATIANS 6:6–10

Let the one who is taught the word share all good things with the one who teaches. Do not be deceived: God is not mocked, for whatever one sows, that will he also reap. For the one who sows to his own flesh will from the flesh reap corruption, but the one who sows to the Spirit will from the Spirit reap eternal life. And let us not grow weary of doing good, for in due season we will reap, if we do not give up. So then, as we have opportunity, let us do good to everyone, and especially to those who are of the household of faith.

CHAPTER 23

SOWING TO THE SPIRIT

In Galatians 4, Paul asks, "What has happened to all your joy?" (4:15 NIV). The Christian life had become a business to the Galatians, and a gloomy one at that. We don't have much trouble accepting the principle that "whatever one sows, that will he also reap" (6:7); there's an easy logic to it. It's the default position of natural wisdom, and plenty of people believe in karma—what goes around comes around. If you work hard, you'll make the grade; if you slack off, you deserve failure. Finally, Paul's speaking our language!

But Paul is merely voicing a well-attested biblical principle. The Old Testament also speaks about sowing and reaping. Hosea says, "For they sow the wind, and they shall reap the whirlwind" (8:7), and Job says something similar: "As I have seen, those who plow iniquity and sow trouble reap the same" (4:8).

That doesn't, however, mean that either Paul or the Old Testament are buying into karma, or pop wisdom. Pop wisdom presupposes the sower is in a neutral position—we're free to do good or bad deeds, and such will return to us by way of reward or punishment. Larry Crabb has aptly called this the "Law of Linearity."[1] According to this law, the sower remains sovereign. The seed is in his or her hand, not simply to disperse but to create.

Good seed equates to good deeds. Surely we can do those, can't we? Let's spread some about and wait for the harvest. After all, it's a law as natural and predictable as gravity, right? It's still a linear equation, just with spiritual variables.

At this point we're no longer in the realm of biblical Christianity. In fact, we've joined the chorus of Job's friends, whose "comfort" provided more pain than Job's multiplied losses. We've moved off base for three reasons: (1) the starting point isn't what we think it is; (2) the seed isn't what we think it is; and (3) the harvest isn't gathered by the means we think it is.

We've already seen that the flesh and the Spirit are two opposing modes of existence. Paul hasn't left the flesh versus Spirit battle of chapter 5 behind. Instead, he's picturing the flesh and Spirit as two fields. Winning the battle by faith is sowing in the field of faith: running to Christ and holding fast, trusting, watering our souls with who he is for us. Such dependence marks our sowing to the Spirit. As Puritan William Perkins said of this principle:

> WINNING THE
> BATTLE
> BY FAITH
> IS SOWING
> IN THE FIELD
> OF FAITH

> There are two sorts of seeds which men sow in this life, good and evil. Two kinds of sowers, spiritual men, and carnal men. Two sorts of ground, in which this seed is sown; the flesh and the Spirit. Two sorts of harvests, which men are to reap according to the seed; corruption and life.[2]

Notice that the sower isn't in a neutral position; he or she belongs already to the flesh or the Spirit. The seed isn't ours to create; it is an expression of a preexisting situation. And the harvest isn't ours to gather; it's brought in by the Spirit (or the flesh). Therefore, it's not a question of moral versus immoral; such is the crop, not the seed. The principal question is: What field are you sowing in? Or, in other words, what are you oriented to: the flesh or the Spirit?

Before Paul met Christ he was an expert at sowing and reaping. He'd been fixated on producing a visible harvest. He had won respect and adulation: "There goes a truly zealous man! As to righteousness, impeccable; as to holiness, unsullied! God be praised he's on the 'right' side!"

God isn't fooled by display crops. He knew, though Paul didn't, that in spite of the impressive religious husk, the seed sown was rotten; it was all a work of the flesh. The flesh loves to masquerade in spiritual costumes. "Don't be deceived: God is not mocked, for whatever one sows, that will he also reap" (Gal 6:7). Fruit is the proof of the seed—good root, good fruit (Matt 3:10; 7:18). The crop will be consistent with the seed sown. If a farmer sows corn, he won't harvest watermelons. Good seed will produce corn useful for nourishment and sellable at the market. But if the seed has been sitting in a warehouse, cooked by the sun, or rotting in a mildew-infested sack, it's not worth the dirt it's tossed on. If we desire a bumper crop, good seed must be sown liberally; thus 2 Corinthians 9:6: "Whoever sows sparingly will also reap sparingly, and whoever sows bountifully will also reap bountifully."

This is the principle Paul means and of which he gives two helpful illustrations: sharing all good things with those who teach the gospel; and persisting in doing good, even if it seems like nothing's coming back. It's not about what you get back, after all.

Sharing All Good Things

In Galatians 6:6 Paul says, "Let the one who is taught the word share all good things with the one who teaches." There's nothing difficult to grasp here, and yet the directive is prickly, poking us because it asks us what we're doing with our stuff, which is ultimately an arresting question about where our hearts are (Matt 6:21).

Paul didn't ordinarily take an honorarium for his ministry. He could have—others did, and one way wasn't more godly than another. He received gifts thankfully when given but provided for himself and his team largely by his own hand. His circumstances provided a framework for such decisions. As an ex-Pharisee, Paul knew one of the markers of his religious flesh was greed (which often hid behind a mask of piety); Pharisees were a rapacious bunch whose greediness was legendary (Luke 16:14; 20:47). Yet in contrast, Paul's saying, "Share your stuff with the gospel preachers who serve you, not just for their sake, but for yours. Break out of the cycle of self-referential greed that legalism induces; sow generously according to the one to whom you truly belong."

If we move from his mission field to a situation where churches have a settled pastoral ministry, there's a temptation to greet his appeal with a chorus of "buts": But what if our pastor's a lazy bum? But what if he doesn't do what we want him to do? But what if we don't like his preaching? But if we're providing for him, don't we get to write the job description? But doesn't the idiom apply: He who pays the piper calls the tune?

This conversation, however, is literally unhinged, *non compos mentis*. Christian ministry isn't a fee for service situation! It's not about performance and productivity driven by accountability. It is about sharing based on trust and grace. Paul nowhere speaks of "payment." When he does occasionally mention his authentic right for subsistence support, he also surrenders it, driven by the internal necessity laid upon him for the sake of the gospel (see 1 Cor 9:1–18). From his side, he is a servant who *must* share the gospel, and yet this fact doesn't relieve others of what they must share. So the key word is "sharing" because it captures the richness of the gospel's fruit, couching the entire conversation within the fellowship of the Holy Spirit. The flesh pays wages, the Spirit shares fruit. This isn't semantics!

THE FLESH PAYS WAGES, THE SPIRIT SHARES FRUIT

John Stott has recognized the strong temptation on the side of a congregation to want to engage in control, "positive tyranny and blackmail," to make the minister preach what they want to hear and do what they want. Many ministers are more than tempted to give in to this pressure to keep their families fed and to stay in the good graces of the congregation. This is the temptation on the side of the congregation, and from the pastor's side the temptation is real to be lazy unless there is a fire in the belly.[3]

What's clear is that the "fire in the belly" is expressed in preaching. It was for Paul. "Woe to me if I do not preach the gospel," he wrote to the church in Corinth (1 Cor 9:16). Pastoral ministry doesn't neglect the Lord's Supper and other means of grace, but without the preached Word, these become mere formalism. The New Testament portrait of ministry vitally relies on preaching; it's impossible to remove it and have anything remotely resembling Christian ministry left.

When there's no fire in the belly to preach, ministers overexert themselves in other areas, from surfing the Internet and playing solitaire to writing strategic plans, typing minutes, and leading so many community-based programs that there's no time to actually study the Scriptures they claim to follow. True preaching—the agony and the ecstasy of it—is pushed to the sidelines; messages are simply plagiarized. The devil smiles as the Spirit is quenched and the fire in the congregation is extinguished.

The apostles were so serious about preaching they resisted the temptation to get involved in other types of work in order to devote themselves "to prayer and to the ministry of the Word" (Acts 6:4). Luther said, "It is impossible that one man should be devoted to household duties day and night for his support and at the same time pay attention to the study of Sacred Scripture, as the teaching ministry requires."[4] That's why pastors first received stipends—to free them to study so they could preach.

Richard Baxter once said about the centrality of preaching, "Our work requireth greater skill, and especially greater life and zeal than any of us can bring to it. It is no small matter to stand up in the face of a congregation, and to deliver a message of salvation or damnation, as from the living God, in the name of the Redeemer."[5] The message of the living God has the ability to tip our nicely ordered church communities upside down. So where preaching wanes in the church, the church becomes sick and dies. Where the Word of God isn't rending and binding hearts, the church becomes just another community organization.

WHERE PREACHING WANES, THE CHURCH BECOMES SICK AND DIES

In this particular case, therefore, sowing to the Spirit means loving one another well. It means that the pastor shares the gospel with the congregation, time and again, publicly and from house to house, in prayer and the ministry of the word. It means that the congregation also shares with him, giving to and receiving from him as he gives to and receives from them. We could read Paul as saying, "Let the gospel break up your fixation on self; live by faith and be free of self-concern; let giving be the proof of it. Live before God, not before each other. Don't raise a display crop, but sow good seed in the Spirit by providing for gospel ministry among you."

Persisting in Doing Good

Sowing to the Spirit is more than sharing all that is good with the pastor, but it's not less. What else might it include? What might it look like in other areas? Philip Ryken gives some examples:

> A young couple sows to the Spirit when they pursue purity of the marriage bed; a man sows to the Spirit when he dies to his own ambitions in order to serve others; a woman sows to the Spirit when she is reconciled to her sisters in Christ; a husband and wife sow to the Spirit when they repent of their selfishness and begin to work together in true spiritual partnership.[6]

The common thread in these is a life that is other-centered. It's responding to the promise of Christ, held out through Isaiah:

> He gives power to the faint, and to him who has no might he increases strength. Even youths shall faint and be weary, and young men shall fall exhausted; but

they who wait for the LORD shall renew their strength;
they shall mount up with wings like eagles; they shall
run and not be weary; they shall walk and not faint
(Isa 40:29–31).

Sowing to the Spirit comes down to persisting in the strength
that he supplies, rather than our own. It's doing good, under-
pinned by hope.

But how should you persevere when something you hope will
happen just doesn't? If you're really spiritual you may be able to
be patient for months or years—truly growing in realizing that
God is enough for you. But the reality is that we might find the
work demanding and grow exhausted. We may look for accolades
or simple appreciation and not find them; our work may not produce payback we can see. Alternatives may look more and more
attractive, tempting us to think, "Why keep
on with this relationship, employer, church,
those people?"

When we stop sowing to the Spirit, issues of self-concern become the bottom line.
The question, "What am I getting out of this?,"
dominates the field of the flesh. It's born out
of a heart that mistrusts God in the moment;

> "WHAT AM
> I GETTING
> OUT OF THIS?"
> DOMINATES
> THE FIELD OF
> THE FLESH

hope gets replaced by hype, as we attune everything to our measure of success. If we're looking merely to gather stuff for ourselves, to please the sinful nature—not debauchery or lust, but
simply life lived with ourselves on the throne—then we quickly
become weary of doing good things. It happens when we're looking for a goal other than Jesus.

We all have our favorite forms of self-indulgence; none of us
is above slipping back into misplaced confidence in someone or
something other than God, trusting what we might be able to accomplish, receive, or control in our own time and space. Only the
gospel can break us out of this cycle and bring forth a harvest of
the Spirit. That which is extrinsic to us and beyond what we can

accomplish in the flesh must be gathered by the Spirit himself, in his time.

Let's take William Carey as an example. A shoemaker by trade, Carey was the first modern missionary to India. He arrived in 1793, and as soon as he had mastered the language, he began preaching to anyone who would listen. He continued to do this for the next seven years without a single convert. Not surprisingly, Carey sometimes got discouraged. On one occasion he wrote to his family in England:

> I feel as a farmer does about his crop: sometimes I think the seed is springing, and thus I hope; a little time blasts all, and my hopes are gone like a cloud. They were only weeds which appeared; or if a little corn sprang up, it quickly died, being either choked with weeds, or parched up by the sun of persecution. Yet I still hope in God, and will go forth in his strength.[7]

In 1800, he finally saw the beginning of the Spirit's harvest, baptizing his first Hindu convert in the Ganges River. It was the firstfruit of a great harvest among the Indian people that transformed many aspects of the society for good.[8] Carey and his team—Joshua Marshman and William Ward chief among them—left an astounding legacy. His translation of the Scriptures into various Indian languages was groundbreaking; his evangelistic, church-planting, and pastoral oversight tireless; his efforts in bettering the lot of the common people exemplary. Among the long-term fruits of his ministry were the establishment of the printed word in India; pioneering approaches to the care of leprosy patients; clinics for general medical care; breakthroughs in agriculture, education, and community banking; the foundations of legislation to outlaw widow burning; and many other contributions that laid the groundwork for the modernization of India. Understandably, he has had an abiding impact on Western theology of mission.

Until the harvest comes, we must keep sowing. The harvest will come at its proper time—according to God's timing. Our place is to be aware of the seed we sow and into which field—the flesh or the Spirit—we sow it. The field of the Spirit is the one in which the gospel is sown to the glory of the Father alone through faith in the Son alone. And although evaluating ourselves in regard to the other-centered field of the Spirit is often excruciatingly difficult and humbling, nevertheless, remember: You sow in the Spirit. Let God worry about the rest.

See with what large letters I am writing to you with my own hand. It is those who want to make a good showing in the flesh who would force you to be circumcised, and only in order that they may not be persecuted for the cross of Christ. For even those who are circumcised do not themselves keep the law, but they desire to have you circumcised that they may boast in your flesh. But far be it from me to boast except in the cross of our Lord Jesus Christ, by which the world has been crucified to me, and I to the world. For neither circumcision counts for anything, nor uncircumcision, but a new creation. And as for all who walk by this rule, peace and mercy be upon them, and upon the Israel of God.

From now on let no one cause me trouble, for I bear on my body the marks of Jesus.

The grace of our Lord Jesus Christ be with your spirit, brothers. Amen.

CHAPTER 24

BOASTING IN THE GOSPEL

When a fire broke out at Christina Simoes' apartment complex in Haverhill, Massachusetts, she cared only about saving her son. With a brave leap, the mother of 18-month-old Cameron did just that: After noticing smoke and realizing they were trapped in the apartment, she ran to the window and jumped three stories with the toddler, cushioning him from the fall by wrapping herself around him. "I just knew we were either going to die or we were going to get out of there," Simoes told the American Broadcasting Corporation. While Cameron remained unscathed, his mother suffered a serious spinal injury from the jump. Still, she didn't regret the decision: "All I was thinking about was getting him out of there. He mattered way more than I did," she said.[1]

The marks Paul bore on his body were like Christina Simoes'— the consequences of an utterly unselfish love (Gal 6:17). Paul's love for the Galatians was as fiercely maternal as Christina's for Cameron. He had not gilded the lily when speaking to them (3:1), and he has been strident in his criticism of the false teachers (5:12). But Paul hasn't been defending a system of doctrine as a mere set of ideas; he has been fighting to save a living child. The Galatian Christians were as newborn infants in the faith. Paul's love, here and elsewhere (e.g., 1 Thess 2:7, 11), was full of parental passion. He'd seen God launch them into a new world of freedom and love so wonderful they needed a new vocabulary to describe it. But all was at risk; the temple was being set ablaze by religious arsonists. Now, Paul has come to the final paragraph of the letter. How does one end a letter like this so that it continues to do its work long after it has been read?

How about by driving home, one last time, the central principle? Paul concludes with a summary statement and a punch line, and in case such might be overlooked, he writes it in his own hand with large letters. Some scholars suggest Paul used big print because he was going blind, the result of the eye disease possibly alluded to in Galatians 4:15. Most, however, point out that he ends many of his letters in his own hand (instead of using an amanuensis, as he had done thus far) for the purpose of authenticity. He's personally signing off, and in large print.

In a day before printed text, with its typeface changes, italics and underlining, large print added emphasis. Send a text message today in all caps, and it's the equivalent of shouting. Write in big letters to emphasize the point, and your audience just might get it if they haven't already. Paul's saying, "Don't miss this! This is so important I write it in large print! Don't fall asleep here!"

We get his central principle right in the middle of the passage: "Far be it from me to boast except in the cross of our Lord Jesus Christ, by which the world has been crucified to me, and I to the world" (6:14).

That's it. There is no other gospel.

The cross of Christ, through which my relation to the world (and vice versa) has been irrevocably crucified, is effected by grace alone. It's based on God's finished work at the cross, and it goes on impacting us in the present by faith in it. This is Paul's passionate answer to the arsonists.

Throughout the letter Paul has contrasted two mindsets, two ways of actually being in the world. He has been trying to drive human religion out of the church by insisting on real Christianity; his refrain has been "no!" to legalism in all its forms and "yes!" to faith in grace. The message of grace centers your identity, your frame of mind, and your very being in Christ—for that is where you are, no matter the situation, suffering, or sin. Salvation and assurance are entrenched in what's true of Christ, not what you think you must make true of yourself. We're to boast in the cross alone because it alone is what counts.

> GRACE CENTERS YOUR IDENTITY, YOUR FRAME OF MIND, AND YOUR VERY BEING IN CHRIST

BOASTING IN THE FLESH

Our religion tends "to generate a form of devotion, of ceremony, or rituals and rules, but which has no cross, or where it leads; the cross is marginalized and is not the heart of our message and devotion."[2] But why do we drift into cross-less religion time and again? Because the cross is a symbol of death—both death to self-interest, self-promotion, and self-atonement, and death by social or physical persecution. Galatians 6:12 is but one illustration: "It is those who want to make a good showing in the flesh who would force you to be circumcised, and only in order that they may not be persecuted for the cross of Christ."

Perhaps this also nags at us. We too want to look good before others and avoid any kind of persecution. But Paul could testify, from bitter experience, to the worthlessness of trying to live within society's rules.

Those peddling human religion—i.e., the law of circumcision and all it implied about our relationship to God—wanted to make an outward impression not only on other Jews but also on Rome, which had granted Judaism exemption from Roman religious dictates. Gaining a nod from Jerusalem and Rome was a sure way to avoid harassment. So at the end of his letter, Paul, who had received a whip rather than a welcome, is telling the Galatians, "The Judaizers don't care about you. They care about themselves. They aren't just passionate about the law. They are passionate about demonstrating their 'righteousness' so their critics will be silenced." Legalism fosters an incurably self-referential life. But if this is true, why is human religion and legalism so appealing?

The way of the law is enticing because it doesn't make you own a thing about yourself; it even offers the added bonus that if you follow the rules, you won't become a target for stray rocks. Legalism, therefore, offers the opportunity for you to be the architect of your own redemption. It gives you control—or at least the illusion of it. And that's comforting. The cross says, "Come get crucified; it's a great way to live!" Legalism says, "Join the crowd; come be safe." Guess which one is more appealing on the surface?

The very message of the Judaizers was self-contradictory: They themselves couldn't keep the law (Gal 6:13), for the law, as we've said before, isn't a series of discrete commandments but an organic whole. If the third egg broken into a three-egg omelet is rotten, the whole omelet is tainted. And all we bring to the pan stinks, for "we are all infected and impure with sin" (Isa 64:6 NLT). Therefore, boasting in religious accomplishment is a non-starter; no matter how the omelet turns out, it will turn your stomach. There is, however, another reason legalism falls short: It's just not radical enough.

Boasting in the Cross

Do you remember the game Snakes and Ladders? As a child, Noel was hospitalized for an extended period, requiring an even longer recovery—during which long months he was given books and games to relieve the tedium. Snakes and Ladders was a favorite; roll the dice, then go up the ladders or down the snakes as you land. This pattern is similar to how we seem to think life works: If you get the breaks, you can go ever upwards and onwards. Sure, bad luck may bring you down for a while, but just wait to land at the foot of a ladder and climb!

The so-called-gospel of the false teachers was little more than a spiritual version of the old game. It's just that the roll of the dice was replaced with personal effort, and the snakes with getting your just deserts.

By contrast, to be serious about the gospel is to be serious about our dire need for the cross, to know our very beings in themselves are sinful. They cannot be educated, mollified, or re-shaped into a different material. The rotten egg can't make itself fresh. This is the truth behind "total depravity." Corruption affects our minds, consciences, wills, and emotions. To put it differently, every aspect of who we are must be crucified. Hence legalism isn't remotely radical enough to save and sanctify.

Notice the verb tense of Galatians 6:14: Paul says he has been crucified to the world and the world to him. It's both past tense and passive. He's telling us about something already finished on his behalf. That's why it's grace! We need only receive it in faith. Being born in the Spirit means being born crucified—and only because of this can we know the benefits and blessings of the new creation.

> ONLY THE GOSPEL IS RADICAL ENOUGH TO SAVE.

Only the gospel is radical enough to save. It alone says that the old Adam can't be reha-bilitated, but rather must be put to death. A new humanity can't arise from his loins. If there is to be a new humanity, it must be raised up through a new Adam—Christ, the life-giving spirit (1 Cor 15:45).

This has several important consequences. The cross means Jesus isn't here to improve you. The Messiah isn't a psychospiri-tual counselor whose good advice will help you chart a course to paradise. Rather, he's the sole captain of the ship.

The cross implies that you can't improve yourself by your own means—diets, potions, pills, exercise regimes, and surgi-cal options included. You can't generate a new you. That which is born of the flesh is flesh; only the Spirit gives new birth, directing our gaze from ourself to the Son of Man who has been lifted up, like Moses lifted up the serpent in the wilderness (John 3:14). The Son of God didn't leave you a book of rules to follow, a self-help guide for your own redemption.

The cross isn't a gallant action for you to imitate, as if all you needed was motivation to be self-sacrificing. God sent his Son into the world to do something specific: to save us from the penalty of sin. If our problem was something else, the law would have sorted that.

The cross humbles us by telling us that we're the problem. It confronts us not just with our attitudes and actions, but all that lies beneath, all we'd rather not see about ourselves. The cross contradicts us at every turn, negating all human religion and effort.

In opposing us in this way, grace becomes the truly radical means of life and hope. It alone is not of the flesh but is entirely of the Spirit.

When we're exposed and left vulnerable by radical grace, not only do we squirm and shiver, whine and grumble, but, as Paul discovered, we strike out in anger. Toward the end of the passage, Paul says, "I bear on my body the marks of Jesus" (Gal 6:17). He bore the scars of preaching radical grace, having been stoned in Lystra on his first missionary journey (Acts 14:19-23) and subjected to various calamities after that (2 Cor 11:23-28).

BLESSINGS OF THE NEW CREATION

Paul confronts the emptiness of legalism head-on in 6:15: "Neither circumcision counts for anything, nor uncircumcision, but a new creation." In other words, the new creation lies beyond ethnic boundaries or cultural religion. Law, by its very nature, slays and divides. The new creation, therefore, can only be a work of grace.

In Paul, that new creation has two aspects. It's simultaneously both a present reality and a future certainty. The new creation isn't solely futuristic,

WE LIVE IN THE PRESENCE OF THE FUTURE

nor do we live currently in its fullness. Rather, we live in the presence of the future.

The future—in which every tear will be wiped away and death, mourning, crying, and pain will be no more (Rev 21:4)—is yet to come. Yet we're already new creations, raised with Christ and seated with him in the heavenly places through the Spirit of God (Eph 2:6; Col 2:12–13; 3:1–4; 2 Cor 5:17).

This isn't a pie-in-the-sky fantasy; we witness the presence of the future breaking into fellowships that are knit together in the love of Christ despite ethnic and cultural differences. In Ephesians 2, Paul puts it like this:

> For [Jesus] himself is our peace, who has made us both one and has broken down in his flesh the dividing wall of hostility by abolishing the law of commandments expressed in ordinances, that he might create in himself one new man in place of the two, so making peace (2:14–15).

God minted a new humanity in the cross, answering Jesus' prayer in the garden of Gethsemane before his crucifixion, "Holy Father, keep them in your name, which you have given me, that they maybe one, even as we are one" (John 17:11). This one new humanity is the "Israel of God" (Gal 6:16), not the Judaistic theocracy the false teachers wanted to establish.

GOD MINTED
A NEW
HUMANITY IN
THE CROSS

Where we meet in Christ, not in the flesh, there is peace between brothers and sisters. Paul saw that old divisions between Jew and Gentile, slave and free, male and female had been put to death in the cross and that a new humanity was already in operation.

We're not speaking in wishful ideas that may or may not be realized. We're talking about what is and what constant preaching of the gospel reveals. Where the gospel is not preached, law and the flesh rush to fill the void. But as the gospel is preached and received in faith, the barriers to true fellowship—i.e., guilt, shame, and fear—are broken afresh. The gospel reveals the new creation it creates. Nothing else can.

Little wonder, then, that Paul was livid; the Judaizers were working to rebuild what Christ had torn down. If they had won, civil and sectarian warfare would have played out in the church for centuries. If such is happening in your life or in your congregation, more gospel is needed, not less. Only as the church submits anew to the gospel, hearing again the word of Christ's cleansing grace, does transformation of lives occur in the Lord's house.

For when grace is preached, the Spirit's elbow nudges us in the ribs: "Hey, I'm talking to you; you need that!" To receive it, however, we must know our need for it; that is, in humility we must turn from ourselves and our "self-sins." A. W. Tozer writes:

> To be specific, the self-sins are self-righteousness, self-pity, self-confidence, self-sufficiency, self-admiration, self-love and a host of others like them. They dwell too deep within us and are too much a part of our natures to come to our attention till the light of God is focused upon them.[3]

But aren't we supposed to be strong and stable and secure? Isn't turning from self-confidence, self-sufficiency, and the like a bit wimpy? In a word, no. Only when we let Jesus take the basin and towel and wash us do we know his fullness. Only when he washes us do we truly experience "peace and mercy" (Gal 6:16), as Andrew Murray, Scottish missionary and champion of the South African Revival of 1860, noted:

> Brethren, here is the path to the higher life. Down, lower down! ... Just as water ever seeks and fills the lowest place, so the moment God finds the creature abased and empty, His glory and power flow in to exalt and to bless.[4]

This is what Jesus was talking about when he said, "Unless you change and become like little children, you will never enter the kingdom of heaven" (Matt 18:3).

What is child-like humility?

> It's not the lack of intelligence, but the lack of guile. The lack of an agenda. It's that precious fleeting time before we have accumulated enough pride or position to care what other people might think. The same un-self-conscious honesty that enables a three-year-old to splash joyfully in a rain puddle, or tumble laughing in the grass with a puppy, or point out loudly that you have a booger hanging out of your nose, is what is required to enter heaven. It is the opposite of ignorance—it is intellectual honesty: to be willing to accept the reality and to call things what they are even when it is hard.[5]

Through the preaching of grace, the Holy Spirit blows the whistle and stops the game. Only the cross of Jesus relieves the pressure of guilt; only the cross silences the voice that says, "You need to do more. You haven't done enough!" Only the cross removes the shameful skeleton in the closet you're afraid will pop out and bring judgment crashing down on your head. Only the mercy of the cross gives true peace.

ONLY THE MERCY OF THE CROSS GIVES TRUE PEACE

Throughout history, Christ has taken the weak, the fallen, the lame, the morally bent, and the worst of sinners to his heart. He's cleansed addicts, forgiven serial adulterers, washed the feet of social outcasts, cleansed the consciences of cowards, and forgiven the religious pride of Pharisees. He's expelled demons—actual and symbolic—from countless thousands, healed broken relationships, created peace where only war raged, and brought the deranged to their feet, clothed and in their right mind. No treatment program, no amount of medication, no change in political system, no ritual, no worldly power can do that—only forgiveness can.

When the cross defines you, you'll begin to sing with John the Baptist, "He must increase, but I must decrease" (John 3:30). This is what boasting in the cross is all about. It's boasting in the inner work of God upon us; it's going again and again to the cross and finding our life in it. The new creation desires more of Jesus and less of self, but only as it continues to hear the gospel. Hence in hearing by faith the gospel not only justifies, it also sanctifies.

Shall we not then join Paul and boast only in the cross? Shall not our prayer—for ourselves and the church—be that the Spirit might fill us through the gospel? Shall we not receive the gospel for what it is—life from the dead? And shall we not receive Paul's hearty benediction as we come to the letter's end?

The grace of our Lord Jesus Christ be with your spirit, brothers. Amen (Gal 6:18).

STUDY GUIDE

BY LEE BECKHAM

CHAPTER 1: BACK TO THE GOSPEL

1. What does the theme "back to the gospel" make you think of? Do you feel a need to get "back to the gospel" in your own life? What would that look like for you?

_____

_____

_____

2. Where do your good works fit into your salvation? Does God bestow salvation upon you because of the works you have done, or do the works flow out of a changed heart that is overflowing with love and gratitude?

_____

_____

_____

3. Most people like to be recognized for doing good deeds. How does that help you understand the appeal of legalism to the human heart?

_____

_____

_____

4. Can you relate to Martin Luther's experience? What are some ways that you have worn yourself out trying to earn a right status with God? Have you ever felt you had to "clean yourself up" before you could approach God?

_____

_____

_____

5. How would you describe the state of your conscience? Is it quiet before God, or is it struggling to justify you?

_____

_____

_____

6. What does it mean to you that you get the credit for Christ's righteousness as you stand before God? Is this a new idea for you?

_____

_____

_____

7. Which is more appealing to you, a salvation that you have earned based on your works of righteousness or a salvation granted to you because of what God did for you?

_____

_____

_____

8. Do you think of your sin in terms of the wrong things you have done or as a fundamental aspect of your nature? Is your sin more defined by what you do or who you are?

_____

_____

_____

9. Think about Luther's words: "It is the purpose of all Scripture to tear us away from our works and bring us to faith" (*Live in Liberty*, 11). How have your works been a hindrance to your growth in faith and understanding the gospel?

_____

_____

_____

10. Do you feel freedom when you think of submitting to God in Christ? Why?

_____

_____

_____

CHAPTER 2: NO GOSPEL AT ALL

1. Is the idea of Christ speaking through the gospel message new to you? How does that make your salvation seem more personal?

_____

_____

_____

2. Do you have an appreciation for what the doctrines of the Bible teach about God, his character, and his attitude toward you? Do you accept what the Bible teaches you about your own heart?

_____

_____

_____

3. How has your heart been changed by your encounter with Jesus? Do you think salvation is possible without heart change?

_____

_____

_____

4. The law is a useful measuring stick for us. We can easily see where we fail and where we pass. Does knowing the law help you to keep it?

_____

_____

_____

5. Does salvation by grace seem too good to be true? Would it seem more believable, or more attractive even, if you had to do a bit of work for it?

_____

_____

_____

6. What things are you tempted to value more than salvation by grace? Do you have a love for reputation and appearance before others?

_____

_____

_____

7. The desire to earn our way into God's favor is deeply embedded in the heart of fallen man. How do you relate to the feeling expressed by the statement, "My greatest lust is for a life where I don't need grace to be saved"?

_____

_____

_____

8. God's grace is freely available to cover the sin of those who trust in the work of Jesus Christ. How does believing that make it easier to admit and own your sin in all the ways it has separated you from God and the people around you?

_____

_____

_____

9. Do you feel that God loves you more when you don't sin? Why?

_____

_____

_____

10. Have you experienced the trauma of being wrong, realizing that you truly have nothing in yourself to commend you to God, and that your only hope for salvation is his condescending grace to you? Have you reached the place where this is a cause for rejoicing and not despair?

_____

_____

_____

CHAPTER 3: NOT MAN'S GOSPEL

1. Where have you put the most effort in your spiritual life—getting the "dance steps" right, or believing the truth of the gospel?

_____

_____

_____

2. Has the gospel intruded into your life, "radically reorienting [your] worldview" (_Live in Liberty_, 24)? What's the biggest evidence of this in your life?

_____

_____

_____

3. Do you have a favorite "hill" where you like to plant your flag and call attention to what you have done? Where is it?

_____

_____

_____

4. Do you believe in your own powerlessness to change your heart and life? Why?

_____

_____

_____

5. Paul spent many years doing what he was convinced was right, only to discover he had been wrong. What are you aware of in your life that you were completely wrong about?

_____

_____

_____

6. Are you drawn to tradition and law-keeping as ways of gaining approval (either from God or men)? Which traditions and/or laws are most appealing to you?

_____

_____

_____

7. Do you believe that your righteousness comes to you by faith (Phil 3:9)? Would you rather earn it?

_____

_____

_____

8. What has the gospel done in your life that gives you evidence of its truth?

_____

_____

_____

9. Are you willing to let God have all the glory in your life? If yes, how will you do that?

_____

_____

_____

10. How do you keep your heart centered on the gospel? Is the music of the gospel a sweet sound to you?

_____

_____

_____

CHAPTER 4: GOSPEL-SHAPED UNITY

1. Which type of unity have you encountered more frequently—the unity of the gospel or the unity of conformity?

_____

_____

_____

2. Have you ever been in a church where you felt you were "in"? Have you ever felt you were "out"?

_____

_____

_____

3. What's the most important thing to you about your church? Why? Where do you rank the gospel in importance?

_____

_____

_____

4. How has your life been shaped by the gospel?

_____

_____

_____

5. Do you tend to see some sins as "worse" than others? Where do you rank the sins that you are prone to?

_____

_____

_____

6. Do you think that the grace God offers to you is contingent on your performance? Why or why not?

_____

_____

_____

7. Does your spiritual life have the feel of being on a treadmill? Are you ready to get off the treadmill and rest in the gospel?

_____

_____

_____

8. How much do you treasure the gospel? How has it transformed your life? How would your life be different without it?

_____

_____

_____

9. How often do you think about sharing the gospel with those around you?

_____

_____

_____

10. Who do you know that you would like to see taste the sweetness of the gospel?

_____

_____

_____

CHAPTER 5: STAYING IN STEP

1. Do you have any rules that are so comfortable and familiar that you can't imagine breaking them? Are these rules reinforced by your family, church or community?

_____

_____

_____

2. We don't follow the ceremonial laws about food and circumcision, but what other rules do we measure ourselves by today?

_____

_____

_____

3. Do you find it easy to be swayed by devotion to traditions? Which traditions?

_____

_____

_____

4. Peter changed his behavior because of his concern for what the other leaders from Jerusalem thought of him. How easy is it for you to relate to his actions in this instance?

_____

_____

_____

5. Do you value having a reputation or good name? What would have to change for you to find your identity in Christ?

_____

_____

_____

6. How often are you concerned about how you appear before others? Are you more concerned about your sin, or whether anyone sees your sin?

_____

_____

_____

7. "The struggle of the Christian life is the struggle to believe the gospel" (_Live in Liberty_, 47). What struggles in your life make you think this statement is true?

_____

_____

_____

8. How well do you relate to Peter's fear of others' opinions? What helps you resist that temptation?

_____

_____

_____

9. "The struggle of the Christian life is the struggle to believe the gospel" (*Live in Liberty*, 47). How easy is it for you to believe that the gospel has given you righteousness in God's eyes?

_____

_____

_____

10. When you are faced with your own sinfulness, can you still trust in the righteousness that comes by believing the gospel? Do you resort to blame-shifting and excuse-making?

_____

_____

_____

Chapter 6: Justified By Faith

1. The gospel has been described as news of a victory on a faraway battlefield—in other words, the gospel is primarily a message and not a prescription for what you should do. How does that fit with your understanding of the gospel?

_____

_____

_____

2. When you die, do expect God to accept you into eternal life (or heaven)? (This question is the equivalent of asking, "Do you believe you are justified?")

_____

_____

_____

3. If you were to find yourself face-to-face with God today at the gate of heaven, and he asked why you should be admitted, what would you say? (This question is the equivalent of asking, "Why do you believe you are justified?" or "What is the grounds of your justification?")

_____

_____

_____

4. A common but mistaken understanding of the gospel is that our sins are forgiven, but we need to live a good life to be sure we are saved. How does Paul's teaching in Galatians 2:15–21 counter this error?

_____

_____

_____

5. Is having a list of rules by which to judge your behavior attractive to you? Do you also like to judge the behavior of others?

_____

_____

_____

6. How do you feel when someone judges your heart by your behavior?

_____

_____

_____

7. How easy is it for you to accept the free offer of justification through faith? Would it feel better to earn your way? Why is that so ingrained?

_____

_____

_____

8. How has your justification changed you? Do you feel differently about your sin? Could you go back to your old life?

_____

_____

_____

9. How does it make a difference to obey God out of love instead of from a sense of duty ("I have to do this or I won't be righteous")?

_____

_____

_____

10. Do you have a sense that God looks on you with approval, simply because you are his beloved child? How does that make you feel?

_____

_____

_____

Chapter 7: Defeating the Legalist Within

1. How do you react when you are corrected on some point? How important to you is it to be "right"? To be seen as someone who knows and does the right thing? What does this tell you about where your sense of righteousness comes from?

_____

_____

_____

2. Do you have any friends who help you see your own faults and errors? Are you that kind of friend?

_____

_____

_____

3. Do you see any correlation between the amount of joy in your life and your dependence on grace versus self-righteousness? What increases the amount of joy you experience in your life?

_____

_____

_____

4. "Legalism is seeking to achieve forgiveness from God, justification before God, and acceptance by God through obedience to God" (C. J. Mahaney, quoted in _Live in Liberty_, 64). How well does that statement describe your own experience in living the Christian life? Will it be hard to think and live differently?

_____

_____

_____

5. What aspects of legalism are most likely to "bewitch" you? How can you stay focused on the gospel and living by grace?

_____

_____

_____

6. "The law shatters; the gospel dazzles" (George Whitefield). When you have sinned, would you prefer to be shattered (reminded of the law) or dazzled (reminded of grace)? When someone sins against you, do you prefer to shatter them or to dazzle them?

_____

_____

_____

7. What memories do you have of your coming to faith? How has your spiritual life changed (or remained the same) since then?

_____

_____

_____

8. Are there things in your life that make you doubt your justification? What evidence do you see that removes your doubts?

_____

_____

_____

9. How much evidence do you see that your own life has changed since your conversion? Has this resulted more from the work of the Holy Spirit or your own efforts to change?

_____

_____

_____

CHAPTER 8: CHILDREN OF ABRAHAM, CHILDREN OF FAITH

1. Children often learn very early in life that there are "right" ways to do certain things (even folding laundry or eating certain foods). How did you feel the first time you recognized the "rightness" of something you were doing (maybe in contrast to the "wrongness" you saw in someone else)? Can you recall your feelings at that moment?

_____

_____

_____

2. Why do you think our impulse to contribute "something" to our righteousness is so strong?

_____

_____

_____

3. Abraham believed God. Do you believe God makes you righteous because of your faith? Why?

_____

_____

_____

4. Abraham lived four hundred years before God gave Moses the law. He had no Bible of any sort and no community like the church or Israel. Yet God called him righteous because of his faith. How does thinking about Abraham's situation change your thinking about what you "need" to be accepted by God?

_____

_____

_____

5. "The sociocultural customs of our community or subculture contribute far more to our sense of self-worth than we realize" (*Live in Liberty*, 74). Following familiar customs can also make us feel close to God. Do you recognize any customs in your life that you rely on for this?

_____

_____

_____

6. When we come to Christ we must allow the gospel to critique the way we live our lives (i.e., our culture). What things have you found in your culture that are inconsistent with the gospel?

_____

_____

_____

7. Despite God's great promises to them, Abraham and Sarah struggled to trust God (see Genesis 12; 16; 20 for examples). Can you relate to their struggle? How have you struggled to believe God?

_____

_____

_____

8. Why do you think it is easier to work at obedience than to simply believe and trust God?

_____

_____

_____

9. Do you feel anxiety over the state of your Christian life? Do you worry that you haven't done enough? How does the true gospel counter this worry?

_____

_____

_____

10. The picture of prisoners reluctant to be freed from their cells (*Live in Liberty*, 77) is a great reminder to us. Have you stepped out in faith to embrace God's great, free salvation?

_____

_____

_____

Chapter 9: The Righteous Live By Faith

1. How does it strike you to describe what you're seeking for as a "palace" (*Live in Liberty*, 80)? Does that seem like a good description? Do you have "lost palaces" where you long to live?

_____

_____

_____

2. What is your favorite thing to be "right" about? Can you see the folly of using this to be "right" with God?

_____

_____

_____

3. Would you describe your condition apart from Christ as "radical neediness"? Has your pride been crucified?

_____

_____

_____

4. Are you more prone to living by faith or living by the law?

_____

_____

5. Many Christians fall into the trap of keeping the law as a means of getting God's approval. Can you see this pattern in your life? How can you counteract it and learn to live by grace?

_____

_____

_____

6. Do you agree with Calvin's assessment (*Live in Liberty*, 84) that being justified by our own merit (works) and being justified by grace are two schemes which cannot be reconciled? How will this change how you live?

_____

_____

_____

7. Have you considered what it means that Jesus redeemed you by dying in your place? Do you think of yourself as bought by his blood?

_____

_____

_____

8. Can you picture yourself as a joint heir with Christ, a son or daughter of God? How does that change how you see yourself in relation to God?

_____

_____

_____

9. How have you experienced intimacy with God through his Spirit?

_____

_____

_____

10. Do you feel that your faith has enabled you to enjoy the promise of God's kingdom? How does it show in your life?

_____

_____

_____

CHAPTER 10: THE PROMISE IS FOR KEEPS

1. Do you ever think of your salvation as an inheritance you have received? How does that affect the way you view your salvation?

_____

_____

_____

2. The law of God is often embodied in our minds by the Ten Commandments. How do you think of these laws—as rules you need to follow to earn God's approval, or a picture of what the life of faith looks like?

_____

_____

_____

3. The covenant ceremony of Genesis 15 (where Abraham sees the symbols of God passing between the slaughtered animals) is a key passage for understanding God's covenant relationship with his people. What does it mean to you that only God passed between the animals (in other words, that God alone took on obligations in this covenant)?

_____

_____

_____

4. Why is it important that Abraham's children be counted by faith and not by blood?

_____

_____

_____

5. God was very intentional and deliberate in his choice of persons for the lineage of faith (Abraham, Isaac, Jacob, etc.). What does it mean to you that he chose you to be a part of his family?

_____

_____

_____

6. It seems very natural to us to think that we have to earn our approval from God. It feels right on a deep level. Does it seem reasonable to come to God empty-handed, with nothing to commend yourself to him, and trust that he will accept you because of your faith in Christ? How easy is that for you?

_____

_____

_____

7. Why do you think God rescued Israel out of slavery in Egypt before he gave them the law?

_____

_____

_____

8. Do you understand the importance of faith in the context of the Mosaic covenant? Do you think it is possible to obey God apart from faith?

_____

_____

_____

9. Obeying God out of gratitude for what Christ did for you is radically different from obeying God because you desperately want his approval. Serving out of gratitude can be compared to serving out of fullness of heart, while serving to gain approval is like trying to fill an empty heart. Which is the best description of your Christian life?

_____

_____

_____

10. How do you struggle to remember the gospel when you see your own sinfulness? Remember that God's promise does not depend on anything you do.

_____

_____

_____

CHAPTER 11: WHY THEN THE LAW?

1. What do you think the correct use of God's law is? (Background verse: "Now it is evident that no one is justified before God by the law" [Galatians 3:11].)

_____

_____

_____

2. Does the story of Walter Marshall's congregation (_Live in Liberty_, 99) make you think about your own efforts to keep the law? What did your efforts produce?

_____

_____

_____

3. When you find yourself failing to keep the law, what bothers you more—that you have displeased God or that you show that you are fallible? What bothers you more—that you have displeased God or that someone may have seen you failing to keep the law?

_____

_____

_____

4. What has the law taught you about sin? Paul: "For I would not have known what it is to covet if the law had not said, 'You shall not covet'" (Rom 7:7).

_____

_____

_____

5. When you find yourself keeping the law, do you feel satisfaction that you are pleasing God or that you show yourself righteous?

_____

_____

_____

6. What does it cost you to realize that you can't keep the law? Does it cause you shame? If so, let this move you to thank God for the grace by which you are saved.

_____

_____

_____

7. Paul's teaching on the law makes it clear that its purpose is not to enable us to become righteous by obeying it, but to convince us of our sinfulness. How does this change your perspective on the law?

_____

_____

_____

8. Are you ready to believe what the law is telling you (that you can't be saved by keeping it)? Does grace look more appealing when you begin to get a sense of the magnitude of your sin?

_____

_____

_____

9. "But the people of Israel, who tried so hard to get right with God by keeping the law, never succeeded. Why not? Because they were trying to get right with God by keeping the law instead of by trusting in him" (Rom 9:31–32 NLT). As you reflect on Paul's words, how do you see your own efforts to get right with God? Which is more crucial to your efforts—faith or works (keeping the law)?

_____

_____

_____

10. What "artificial lights" keep you from seeing the darkness in your life (*Live in Liberty*, 106)? Do these lights also keep you from seeing the light of Christ?

_____

_____

_____

CHAPTER 12: EVERY CHRISTIAN'S BIOGRAPHY

1. John Stott described the life of every Christian as two volumes: volume I, life before Christ, and volume II, life with Christ (see Boice, *Amazing Grace*, 145). Have you ever thought of your life in this way? How well do you remember when you moved from volume I to volume II? How much of a difference did it make in your life?

_____

_____

_____

2. For how much of your Christian life have you looked at the law as the key to being accepted by God? Do you still see it this way?

_____

_____

_____

3. How does thinking of the law as your guardian (instead of your liberator) change your perception of the role of the law?

_____

_____

_____

4. Do you think "regimentation" is an apt description of life under the law? Why or why not?

_____

_____

_____

5. Do you find yourself more prone to feeling shame over failing to keep the law, or feeling pride about keeping it? How can you avoid these pitfalls?

_____

_____

_____

6. Can you relate to the burden of following the law because you must?

_____

_____

_____

7. How have you experienced the difference in obeying God out of love and obeying God out of duty?

_____

_____

_____

8. Have you learned the peace of confessing Christ in the midst of your sins and failures?

_____

_____

_____

9. Paul experienced a radical transformation when his view of God shifted from "creator and judge" to "Father." Have you experienced a similar transformation?

_____

_____

_____

10. What can you do to embrace the reality of your life as a "new self" in Christ (Col 3:10)?

_____

_____

_____

CHAPTER 13: FULLY ADOPTED

1. Can you imagine what it would be like to be a slave with no hope of freedom—and then to have someone purchase you to set you free? What if that person then adopted you as a son or daughter?

_____

_____

_____

2. Would your friends describe you as a joyful person? Do you think of yourself as joyful? Has your experience of joy changed since you first came to faith in Christ?

_____

_____

_____

3. Some find it easy to accept God's forgiveness of their sins, but struggle to accept the gift of Christ's righteousness. How about you? Do you find yourself approaching your Christian life as if you had to earn what God has already given you?

_____

_____

_____

4. Is your adoption into God's family a new idea for you? Have you considered the parallels between your adoption and real-world adoptions?

_____

_____

_____

5. J. I. Packer's quote (*Live in Liberty*, 119) raises a key issue: seeing God as a judge versus seeing God as our father. Is one of these more natural for you?

_____

_____

_____

6. What evidence do you see in your life that God has made you his child?

_____

_____

_____

7. Is your conscience more informed by the Word of God (the gospel) or by culture and traditions?

_____

_____

_____

8. Do you live like a son in God's house? Or do you live like an accountant (*Live in Liberty*, 122)?

_____

_____

_____

9. Reread the story of the Russian boys in the orphanage (*Live in Liberty*, 123-24). How well does "orphan" describe the way you live?

_____

_____

_____

10. "The cry of your heart is evidence that the Holy Spirit has touched you and enabled your sonship" (*Live in Liberty*, 125). How often do you cry out for God?

_____

_____

_____

CHAPTER 14: DON'T SELL YOUR BIRTHRIGHT

1. Have you experienced a loss of joy since you became a Christian? What do you think caused that?

_____

_____

_____

2. Think about the story of Esau selling his birthright to Jacob. When have you ever acted in a short-sighted manner to satisfy a trivial urgency?

_____

_____

_____

3. "Grace freed us to love, flooded us with joy, and furnished us with a home" (*Live in Liberty*, 132). How does this describe the kind of life you would like to be known for?

_____

_____

_____

4. If you look back over your spiritual life, has it been mostly knowing God or knowing about God?

_____

_____

_____

5. Can you recall a time (or times) where you experienced God's love for you?

_____

_____

_____

6. John Stott said that "our salvation [does not hang] in the balance and [does not depend] on our meticulous and slavish obedience to the letter of the law" (see *Live in Liberty*, 131). Do you agree with that statement? Why?

_____

_____

_____

7. Living by grace often feels strange and unnatural to us (that's probably why the Judaizers were able to lure the Galatians back to the law). Why is it tempting to go back to living by the law instead of trusting in grace?

_____

_____

_____

8. "Thou shalt remember that thou wast a slave in the land of Egypt, and the Lord thy God redeemed thee" (Deut 15:15 KJV; *Live in Liberty,* 135). How often do you remember that God has redeemed you out of your slavery to sin?

_____

_____

_____

9. Do you sometimes find human acceptance or approval to be appealing? Can you see how this undercuts the power of the gospel in your life?

_____

_____

_____

10. "We never grow beyond our need of the gospel" (*Live in Liberty,* 135). Is this a new idea for you? Do you think of the gospel as something only needed to begin your faith journey, or something that will be needed every step of the way?

_____

_____

_____

CHAPTER 15: WHO'S YOUR MAMA?

1. When have you ever had to wait on God's timing for something important to you? What sustained you through that time?

_____

_____

_____

2. Have you ever compared what you have accomplished in your life with what God has accomplished? Whose work do you prefer?

_____

_____

_____

3. Denial (avoiding or refusing to see your sin) and hopelessness (feeling overwhelmed by your sin) are both "religious" responses to sin. Are you prone to either of these?

_____

_____

_____

4. Have you ever felt that you needed to complete some performance of duty (going to church, doing daily Bible reading) before God would bless you? How does this go against the gospel?

_____

_____

_____

5. Seeing our sin exposes our lack of righteousness (guilt). Would you rather trust that God sees you clothed with Christ's righteousness or work to create your own righteousness?

_____

_____

_____

6. Spurgeon compared earning righteousness by obeying the law to a horse going round and round a mill (*Live in Liberty*, 141). How well does that describe your experience?

_____

_____

_____

7. Why is it hard to accept the truth of being justified and a sinner simultaneously? Is that a new idea for you?

_____

_____

_____

8. Does it seem strange to think of moral actions as works of the flesh? What is the difference between obedience that is flesh-based and obedience that is pleasing to God?

_____

_____

_____

9. Do you think your identity is truly based on your relationship to God as a sinner in need of grace, or are you trying to establish your identity by good works? What evidence in your life backs up your answer?

_____

_____

_____

10. Have you ever judged your spiritual life by how well you love the people around you? Does that seem like a good standard to apply? Ask someone close to you how well you love them.

_____

_____

_____

CHAPTER 16: CHRIST HAS SET US FREE

1. How easy is it for you to face up to difficult or unflattering truths about yourself? How does understanding the gospel help ease that pain?

_____

_____

_____

2. Most of us have "favorite" duties that we're good at performing. Do you know what yours are? What do you expect to get for doing them?

_____

_____

_____

3. What do you think is appealing about the idea that we must do something for God before he will do something for us? Do you tend to believe this?

_____

_____

_____

4. Reread the story about the gardener (*Live in Liberty*, 150). Can you relate to the subtle expectation this man had that because he had done so much (in his own thinking) for God, that God "owed" him a "good" life?

_____

_____

_____

5. "The opposite of faith is self-reliance" (*Live in Liberty*, 151). Think about this statement in light of your experiences of trying harder to obey the law. Why does that often feel better to us than trusting the truth of the gospel?

_____

_____

_____

6. The man with the baseball autographed by Babe Ruth ruined its value by trying to improve the appearance of the signature (*Live in Liberty*, 152). How is that a good analogy for what we do with our law-keeping?

_____

_____

_____

7. What do you find more appealing in a friend—a loving heart or their being right?

8. How well do you understand the connection between faith and love (*Live in Liberty*, 153–54)?

9. Do you find yourself preoccupied with how well you are doing, whether you are acceptable to God, or whether others approve of you? What would it be like to be free from these concerns?

10. "The law shatters; the gospel dazzles" (George Whitefield). Are you so in love with being dazzled that you offer it to those around you?

Chapter 17: Running in the Pack

1. When do you feel like you are running in a pack, being jostled and elbowed, trying not to stumble?

_____

_____

_____

2. What role does faith play in your daily spiritual life? Is it a necessity, or could you get along without it?

_____

_____

_____

3. Do you agree that sanctification is not something added to justification? How hard is it to imagine growing in holiness without a list of tasks to do?

_____

_____

_____

4. Luther wrote of Christians obtaining by faith an "alien righteousness"—one that was not originally theirs but from which they benefited through faith in Christ. Has it sunk in deep for you that God justified you when you were ungodly and unrighteous? How often do you remember this?

_____

_____

_____

5. "Thanks be to God, who always leads us in His triumph in Christ" (2 Cor 2:14 NASB). Where have you triumphed in Christ recently? Was it a different kind of triumph than you were expecting?

_____

_____

_____

6. As a child of God, how much do you think your behavior affects his attitude toward you? Do you picture God smiling on you when you obey, but frowning when you fail?

_____

_____

_____

7. Would you agree that "anxiety is the default position of the flesh" (_Live in Liberty_, 162)? How often do you struggle with anxiety?

_____

_____

_____

8. As you grow in faith, do you expect to sin less and feel holier? Or do you expect that you will see more of the depth of your sin and have a growing sense of unworthiness?

_____

_____

_____

9. "Grace is like a caterpillar in a ring of fire. The only help is from above" (Martin Luther, quoted in *Live in Liberty*, 164). How does this statement fit with your view of grace?

_____

_____

_____

10. Is the truth of God precious enough to you that you feel it's worth "roaring" about it? What do want to roar about today?

_____

_____

_____

CHAPTER 18: LIBERTY IS NOT LICENSE

1. Do you think you are more prone to being a slave to rules (the law) or a slave to your appetites (the flesh)?

_____

_____

_____

2. Reflect on Luther's quote: "A Christian is the most free lord of all, subject to none; a Christian is the most dutiful servant of all, subject to all" (*Live in Liberty*, 169). How well does that summarize your life? Do you prefer one part of the quote to the other?

_____

_____

_____

3. What does freedom mean to you? Do you think of freedom more in terms of being free from everything (autonomy) or in terms of fulfilling your calling (identity)?

_____

_____

_____

4. Are you one of the "select few who find that their personal style of finding identity, satisfaction, of meeting their needs to feel loved, of feeling good about themselves just happens to be by performance in rule-keeping" (David Benner, quoted in *Live in Liberty*, 169)? If you are not, do you know someone who is? Does your (their) rule-keeping help you (them) be more loving?

_____

_____

_____

5. Which is harder for you: to be convinced of your sin, or to be convinced of your salvation?

_____

_____

_____

6. How often do you think about your sin? How often do you see its impact in your life and the lives of the people around you?

_____

_____

_____

7. "Conversion always points us towards fellow human beings, not simply towards God" (David Benner, quoted in *Live in Liberty*, 173). Do you see this becoming true in your life?

_____

_____

_____

8. Are you able to enjoy the freedom that Christ has procured for you? Has the truth of the gospel liberated your conscience?

_____

_____

_____

9. Do you feel that you have been set free to love as God intends you to love? Would those around you agree with your answer?

_____

_____

_____

10. How is living by the gospel totally different from living by the flesh (whether legalistic moralism or licentious indulgence)?

_____

_____

_____

CHAPTER 19: WALK BY THE SPIRIT

1. "To walk in the Spirit ... [is] to traverse a battlefield strewn with mines" (*Live in Liberty*, 177). Does that description sound appealing to you? Does it sound realistic?

_____

_____

_____

2. "The less holy you feel, the better" (Tom Holliday, quoted in *Live in Liberty*, 178). What's your first reaction to that statement? If you think about your daily spiritual life, does it change your reaction?

_____

_____

_____

3. "If we say we have no sin, we deceive ourselves, and the truth is not in us" (1 John 1:8). Are you more aware of your sin in things that you do, or in the attitudes of your heart?

_____

_____

_____

4. Is it a new idea for you to think of the Holy Spirit as a person (the Third Person of the Trinity)? How does it change your thinking?

_____

_____

_____

5. How would you rate yourself on "walking by the Spirit"? When you are faced with fleshly desires, is the thought of God's presence a help to you?

_____

_____

_____

6. Living by grace is a huge change for us. Do you find yourself still "wanting to deal so with God that [you] may contribute something so that He will have to give [you] his grace in exchange for [your] holiness" (Martin Luther, quoted in *Live in Liberty*, 182)?

_____

_____

_____

7. "And I will give you a new heart, and a new spirit I will put within you. And I will remove the heart of stone from your flesh and give you a heart of flesh. And I will put my Spirit within you, and cause you to walk in my statutes" (Ezek 36:26–27). This verse describes the heart change that God uses to make his children walk in his ways. When you find yourself needing to change something in your life, do you think about your heart needing to change, or do you think about trying harder to obey?

_____

_____

_____

8. How often do you reflect on the promises of God? Have his promises made a difference in your life?

_____

_____

_____

9. Do you ever find yourself wanting to go back to the familiar ways of fleshly living? How do you overcome that temptation?

_____

_____

_____

10. "When we have received gospel-truths into our minds, we are in danger of letting them slip" (Matthew Henry, _An Exposition of the Old and New Testament_, 703).[1] How important for your spiritual life is remembering the gospel?

_____

_____

_____

CHAPTER 20: WHAT CONTROLS YOU?

1. How much do you like being in control? Here's a test: Do you ever get into conflict with someone you think likes being in control too much?

_____

_____

_____

2. Have you ever hidden your guilty secrets behind piety and obedience to the law?

_____

_____

_____

3. With which of the four categories of the flesh (sensual, religious, social malevolence, self-indulgent) do you struggle most?

_____

_____

_____

4. "A god means that from which we are to expect all good and to which we are to take refuge in all distress" (Martin Luther, quoted in *Live in Liberty*, 191). Based on this definition, what are the idols in your life?

_____

_____

_____

5. "We never perceive our foulness until the tree has been made known by its fruits" (John Calvin, quoted in *Live in Liberty*, 192). Have you ever been surprised by the "fruits" in your life? Which fruits were they?

_____

_____

_____

6. Which of the nine fruits of the Spirit (love, joy, peace, patience, kindness, goodness, faithfulness, gentleness, self-control) would you like to see more of in your life? Do you think you will get it by trying harder?

_____

_____

_____

7. Does the idea of improving your spiritual life through education appeal to you? How effective do you think that will be?

_____

_____

_____

8. Have you reached a place where you say to God (like Peter), "In my very being I'm wrong, and I can't fix it. Have mercy, Lord!" (*Live in Liberty*, 193)? What brought you to this place?

_____

_____

_____

9. "God does not ask for resignation based on acquiescence in the absence of a better option" (David Benner, quoted in *Live in Liberty*, 195–96). Do you believe that God's way is the best way to live? Does your life show it?

_____

_____

_____

10. "He invites us to surrender our stolen independence and exchange it for a willingly accepted dependence. God takes our humble offering of powerlessness and turns it into a voluntary subordination—a freely chosen laying down of our life that leads to our transformation and fulfillment" (David Benner, quoted in *Live in Liberty*, 195-96). Does this laying down of your life in exchange for transformation sound like a good deal to you? Why?

_____

_____

_____

CHAPTER 21: KEEPING IN STEP

1. What does spiritual maturity look like for you? Needing God less? How does the gospel affect your thinking on this?

_____

_____

_____

2. Do you believe that your faith in Christ will produce spiritual fruit in your life without your efforts? How will that work?

_____

_____

_____

3. How do you feel about belief in Jesus being the work of God (*Live in Liberty*, 199-200)?

_____

_____

_____

4. What things in your life have you had to crucify and leave on the cross?

_____

_____

_____

5. What is the most demanding regimen you have ever devised to further your spiritual growth? How well did it work for you?

_____

_____

_____

6. A growing awareness of your sin _and_ a deeper understanding of God's love for you expressed in the gospel. How well does that fit your definition of keeping in step with the Spirit?

_____

_____

_____

7. John Stott says that "truly Christian relationships are governed not by rivalry but by service" (John Stott, quoted in _Live in Liberty_, 206–07). What governs your Christian relationships?

_____

_____

_____

8. Which one of the three steps (crucifying the flesh, keeping in step with the Spirit, serving one another in love) challenges you the most? Commit to praying about that step.

_____

_____

_____

9. How well do you know the affections of your own heart? What things truly move you?

_____

_____

_____

10. Can you remember a time when you were willing to serve someone without thinking about what you would get in return? How were you able to do that?

_____

_____

_____

CHAPTER 22: THE TRULY SPIRITUAL LIFE

1. What do you consider to be the foundation of your spiritual life?

_____

_____

_____

2. "Good works may be an indication of the grace of God, but they're not the fuel. If the fuel isn't grace itself, then 'works' are inevitably dead" (*Live in Liberty*, 212). Do you agree with this statement?

_____

_____

_____

3. Why is it so appealing to think that God requires you to do something to earn his acceptance?

_____

_____

_____

4. Have you ever been "restored in a spirit of gentleness" when you were in the wrong (*Live in Liberty*, 213)? What difference did "the spirit of gentleness" make in how you reacted?

_____

_____

_____

5. "We need the word of grace to come to us, through the lips of a fellow Christian" (Dietrich Bonhoeffer, quoted in *Live in Liberty*, 216). How have you seen this idea play out in your spiritual life?

_____

_____

_____

6. Are you more aware of how much you have to bear with others' sins, or how much others have to bear with your sins?

_____

_____

_____

7. How has your growth in Christ increased your graciousness?

_____

_____

_____

8. How often do you compare yourself to others? Is it more common with regard to your spiritual life or other areas?

_____

_____

_____

9. If you believe God expects good works from you as the basis of your relationship with him, you will expect good works from others. If you believe God accepts you by grace, you will be able to show grace to others. Think about the relationships in your life. What do they show that you believe about that?

_____

_____

_____

10. "Resting in Jesus' love frees us to love" (*Live in Liberty*, 218). Would the people close to you say that you love freely? How do you need to change to love more freely?

_____

_____

_____

Chapter 23: Sowing to the Spirit

1. Has joy increased or decreased in your life since you became a Christian? What influences the amount of joy that you feel?

_____

_____

_____

2. Have you ever thought about your life in terms of what you have sown and what you have reaped?

_____

_____

_____

3. Do you sow more to the Spirit or to the flesh? How can you tell?

_____

_____

_____

4. Does the generosity of God flow through your life to the people around you? Would they agree with your answer?

_____

_____

_____

5. Have you ever felt weariness when you were trying to do good? Why did you feel weary?

_____

_____

_____

6. What do you think it means to "wait for the LORD" (Isa 40:29–31; _Live in Liberty_, 227)?

_____

_____

_____

7. Where in your life do you see a need to be more other-centered?

_____

_____

_____

8. What significance do you place on the preaching of God's Word? What role does it play in your spiritual life?

_____

_____

_____

9. When you listen to a sermon, do you regard it as the Word of God or the word of a man?

_____

_____

_____

10. How easy is it for you to wait patiently for the harvest of what you have sown? How does it test your faith?

_____

_____

_____

Chapter 24: Boasting in the Gospel

1. When have you seen someone do something out of an utterly unselfish love? Have you ever acted out of an utterly unselfish love?

_____

_____

_____

2. What are the things that you like to boast in? What makes you feel good about yourself?

_____

_____

_____

3. Paul expresses his desire to boast only in the cross of Jesus Christ (Gal 6:14). To what extent does that desire characterize your life?

_____

_____

_____

4. "Our religion tends 'to generate a form of devotion, of ceremony, or rituals and rules, but which has no cross ... the cross is marginalized and is not the heart of our message and devotion" (Joshua Moody, quoted in *Live in Liberty*, 233). Have you noticed this tendency in your life? Are you drawn to the outward forms of religion that can take your mind off the cross?

_____

_____

_____

5. "Legalism fosters an incurably self-referential life" (*Live in Liberty*, 234). In what ways has this been true in your life?

_____

_____

_____

6. How many ways you have tried to rehabilitate your sinful self? When did you realize rehabilitation was hopeless and that you needed a savior?

_____

_____

_____

7. Which of the "self-sins" (*Live in Liberty*, 238) do you struggle with the most? Has it been a long battle?

_____

_____

_____

8. "The gospel reveals the new creation it creates. Nothing else can" (*Live in Liberty*, 238). Has the Holy Spirit convinced you that this is true? What reaction do you feel in your heart when you read those words?

_____

_____

_____

9. What barriers has the gospel broken down in your life? Were they barriers between you and others? Barriers keeping you from following after God?

_____

_____

_____

10. What do the people around you see in your life—the outward signs of religion or a life that has been changed by the reality of the cross of Christ? If you're not sure what they see, ask them.

_____

_____

_____

NOTES

FOREWORD
1. Paul F. M. Zahl, *Grace in Practice: A Theology of Everyday Life* (Grand Rapids: Eerdmans, 2007), 1.

PREFACE
1. Martin Luther, *Luther's Works: The American Edition*, ed. Jaroslav Pelikan (St. Louis: Concordia, 1962), 26:307. (Hereafter appearing as *LW*.)
2. Darrell Bock, *Recovering the Real Lost Gospel: Reclaiming the Gospel as Good News* (Nashville: B&H Academic, 2010), 2.
3. Martin Luther, *A Commentary on St. Paul's Epistle to the Galatians*, trans. Theodore Graebner (Grand Rapids: Christian Classics Ethereal Library, n.d.), 3, http://www.ccel.org/ccel/luther/galatians.html.
4. Robert Farrar Capon, *Between Noon and Three: Romance, Law, and the Outrage of Grace* (Grand Rapids: Eerdmans, 1996), 114–15.

CHAPTER 1
1. Philip Ryken, *Galatians*, Reformed Expository Commentary (Phillipsburg, N.J.: P&R, 2005), 3.
2. Bernard Reardon, *Religious Thought in the Reformation* (London: Longman, 1981), 51.
3. Luther, *LW* 26:6.

4. P. W. Barnett, "Apostle," in *The Dictionary of Paul and His Letters*, eds. Gerald F. Hawthorn, Ralph P. Martin, and Daniel G. Reid (Downers Grove: IVP Academic, 1993), 50.
5. C. J. Mahaney, "Only One Gospel," unpublished sermon, Covenant Life Church, Gaithersburg, Md., December 8, 2002.
6. Ibid.

CHAPTER 2
1. Sinclair Ferguson, *The Christian Life: A Doctrinal Introduction* (Carlisle, Pa.: Banner of Truth, 1989), 82–83.
2. Martin Luther, "The Heidelberg Disputation," thesis 26.

CHAPTER 3
1. Thomas Jefferson to William Short, April 13, 1820, in George Seldes, *The Great Thoughts* (New York: Ballantine Books, 1985), 208.
2. Carl Walther, *The Proper Distinction Between Law and Gospel* (St. Louis: Concordia, 1986), First Evening Lecture.
3. Luther, *LW* 26:72.

CHAPTER 4
1. Jeff Purswell, "Entrusted with the Gospel," unpublished sermon, Covenant Life Church, Gaithersburg, Md., January 12, 2003.

CHAPTER 5
1. Joachim Jeremias, *New Testament Theology: Proclamation of Jesus*, vol. 1 (London: SCM-Canterbury Press, 1971), 115.
2. Stanley Voke, *Personal Revival: Living the Christian Life in the Light of the Cross* (1964; repr., Waynesboro, Ga.: OM Literature, n.d.), 43–46.
3. Roland H. Bainton, *Here I Stand: A Life of Martin Luther*, Abingdon Classics (Nashville: Abingdon, 1990), 144.

CHAPTER 6
1. Luther, *LW* 26:9.
2. J. I. Packer, *Revelations of the Cross* (1998; repr., Peabody, Mass.: Hendrickson, 2013), 120.
3. English translates the one Greek word group in two different ways. The *dikaioō* word group stands behind both "justify" and its cognates and "righteousness" and its cognates. We lack a verb to do

the work of "righteous-ify," so to "justify" is to "righteous-ify." To
be justified is to be righteous. To be righteous is to be justified.

4. Luther, *LW* 26:132.

5. Luther, *LW* 31:350–52.

6. F. F. Bruce, *The Epistle to the Galatians*, in The New International
Greek Testament Commentary (1982; repr., Grand Rapids:
Eerdmans, 1998), 142–43.

CHAPTER 7

1. Luther, *LW* 26:187.

2. C. J. Mahaney, "Interrogating the Legalist Within," unpublished
sermon, Covenant Life Church, Gaithersburg, Md., February
8, 2003.

3. Gerhard O. Forde, "The Lutheran View," in *Christian Spirituality:
Five Views of Sanctification*, (Downers Grove: InterVarsity, 1989),
13, 27.

4. John Bunyan, *Grace Abounding to the Chief of Sinners : John Bunyan's
Autobiography*, (1666; repr., Greenville, S.C.: Emerald House,
1998), 74–75.

5. Martin Luther, *Lectures on Romans*, trans. and ed. Wilhelm Pauck,
The Library of Christian Classics, vol. 15 (Philadelphia: Westminster,
1961), 370.

CHAPTER 8

1. Bruce, *The Epistle to the Galatians*, 154–55.

2. John Stott, *The Message to the Galatians*, The Bible Speaks Today
(1968; repr., Downers Grove: IVP Academic, 1984), 75.

3. Helmut Thielicke, *The Silence of God* (1962; repr., Farmington Hills,
Mich.: Oil Lamp Books, 2010), 18.

CHAPTER 9

1. Martin Luther, from a manuscript preserved in the library
of Rudolstadt.

2. F. W. Boreham, *A Bunch of Everlastings* (Valley Forge, Pa.: Judson,
1920), 20, 27.

3. John Calvin, "Galatians," in *Calvin's Commentaries*, vol. 21 (Grand
Rapids: Baker, 1993), 90.

4. Helmut Thielicke, *The Evangelical Faith, Vol. II: The Doctrine of God and of Christ*, trans. and ed. Geoffrey W. Bromiley (1977; repr., Macon, Ga.: Smyth & Helwys, 1997), 418.

5. Luther, *LW* 26:284.

6. Ibid.

Chapter 10

1. John Piper, "The Law Does Not Annul the Promise," unpublished sermon, Bethlehem Baptist Church, Minneapolis, Minn., April 17, 1983.

2. Ibid.

Chapter 11

1. Bryan Chapell, *Holiness by Grace* (Wheaton: Crossway, 2001), 39–40.

2. John Piper, "Why then the Law?" unpublished sermon, Bethlehem Baptist Church, Minneapolis, Minn., April 24, 1983.

3. Luther, *LW* 26:327.

4. Andrew Jukes, quoted in Stott, *The Message to the Galatians*, 90.

5. Dietrich Bonhoeffer, *Letters and Papers from Prison*, ed. Eberhard Bethge, trans. Reginald H. Fuller (London: SCM, 1953), 79.

6. Martin Luther, *Galatians, Ephesians*, Reformation Commentary on Scripture, vol. 10, ed. Gerald L. Bray (Downers Grove: IVP Academic, 2011), 119.

Chapter 12

1. Ron Chernow, *Washington: A Life* (New York: Penguin Books, 2010), p. xxi.

2. Xenophon, *State of Lacedaemonians* 3:1.

Chapter 13

1. J. I. Packer, *Knowing God* (Downers Grove: InterVarsity, 1973), 181–82; emphasis added.

2. Charles H. Spurgeon, "The Great Birthday and Our Coming of Age," unpublished sermon, Metropolitan Tabernacle, London, England, December 21, 1884.

3. J. I. Packer, *Knowing God*, 187–88.

4. Ryken, *Galatians*, 166.

5. Russell Moore, "The Brotherhood of Sons," *Touchstone*, May 2007.

6. Luther, *LW* 26:380–81.
7. Charles H. Spurgeon, "The Relationship of Marriage," unpublished sermon, Metropolitan Tabernacle, London, England, July 1867.

CHAPTER 14
1. Stott, *The Message to the Galatians*, 109.

CHAPTER 15
1. Stott, *The Message to the Galatians*, 124.
2. Ryken, *Galatians*, 187.
3. Charles H. Spurgeon, "The Allegories of Sarah and Hagar," unpublished sermon, Metropolitan Tabernacle, London, England, March 2, 1856.
4. Steve W. Brown, *Three Free Sins* (New York: Howard Books, 2012), 28–29.
5. Ibid., 13–14.
6. Luther, *LW* 26:454.

CHAPTER 16
1. Westminster Confession 20.2, modern English
2. John Piper, "For Freedom Christ Has Set Us Free," unpublished sermon, Bethlehem Baptist Church, Minneapolis, Minn., May 29, 1983.
3. Larry Crabb, Jr., *Real Church: Does It Exist? Can I Find It?* (Nashville: Thomas Nelson, 2009), 47.
4. William Ames, *Galatians, Ephesians,* Reformation Commentary on Scripture, vol. 10, ed. Gerald L. Bray (Downers Grove: IVP Academic, 2011), 329.
5. Luther, *LW* 27:17.
6. Helmut Thielicke, *The Waiting Father*, trans. John W. Doberstein (Cambridge: James Clark, 1964), 133.
7. Philip Yancey, *What's So Amazing about Grace?* (Grand Rapids: Zondervan, 1997), 31.

CHAPTER 17
1. Tara Parker-Pop, "An Olympic Blast from the Past," *New York Times*, 1 August 2008.
2. Luther, *Lectures on Romans*, 128.

3. Tullian Tchividjian, *Jesus + Nothing = Everything* (Wheaton: Crossway, 2011), 95.

4. Gerhard O. Forde, "The Lutheran View," in *Christian Spirituality: Five Views of Sanctification*, (Downers Grove: InterVarsity, 1989), 13.

5. G. C. Berkouwer, quoted in Timothy Keller, "Preaching the Gospel in a Post-Modern World," Reformed Theological Seminary, unpublished lecture, January 2002.

6. D. Martyn Lloyd-Jones, *Romans 6: The New Man* (Edinburgh: Banner of Truth, 1992), 8–9.

7. Michael Horton, "The Fear of Antinomianism," The White Horse Inn Blog, January 27, 2011, accessed September 5, 2012, http://www.whitehorseinn.org/blog/2011/01/27/the-fear-of-antinomianism.

8. Robert Farrar Capon, *Kingdom, Grace, Judgment: Paradox, Outrage, and Vindicaton in the Parables of Jesus* (Grand Rapids: Eerdmans, 2002), 16–19.

9. Bruce, *The Epistle to the Galatians*, 238.

CHAPTER 18

1. Martin Luther, *The Freedom of a Christian*, in William C. Placher, ed., *Readings in the History of Christian Theology*, vol. 2 (Philadelphia: Westminster, 1988), 13.

2. David Benner, *Gift of Being Yourself* (Downers Grove: InterVarsity, 2004), 76.

3. Larry Crabb, Jr., *Becoming a True Spiritual Community* (Nashville: Thomas Nelson, 2007), n.p.

4. John Owen, "A Treatise of the Dominion of Sin and Grace (1688)" in *The Works of John Owen*, ed. William Goold (Edinburgh: Banner of Truth, 2001), 7:517.

5. Bruce, *The Epistle to the Galatians*, 241.

6. James Montgomery Boice, "Galatians," in *Expositor's Bible Commentary*, vol. 10, gen. ed. Frank E. Gaebelein (Grand Rapids: Zondervan, 1976), 493.

7. Bruce, *The Epistle to the Galatians*, 241.

8. David Benner, *Surrender to Love* (Downers Grove: InterVarsity, 2003), 93–94.

CHAPTER 19

1. Tom Holliday, "Living by the Spirit," unpublished sermon, Alexandria Presbyterian Church, Alexandria, Va., September 2, 2001.

2. J. I. Packer, *Keep in Step with the Spirit* (Grand Rapids: Revell, 1984), 47.

3. Alexander MacLaren, "The Abiding Gift and Its Transitory Accompaniments," in *The Acts of the Apostles* (London: Hodder and Stoughton, 1908), 45.

4. See John Calvin, *The Necessity of Reforming the Church*, trans. Henry Beveridge (Philadelphia: Presbyterian Board of Publication, 1844), 53–55.

5. Luther, *LW* 51:284–85.

6. Dr. and Mrs. Howard Taylor, *Hudson Taylor's Spiritual Secret* (Chicago: Moody, 2009), 212–13.

CHAPTER 20

1. Martin Luther, *The Larger Catechism* (Grand Rapids: Christian Classics Ethereal Library), 5, http://www.ccel.org/ccel/luther/largecatechism.html.

2. William Perkins and John Calvin, respectively in, *Galatians, Ephesians*, Reformation Commentary on Scripture, vol. 10, ed. Gerald L. Bray (Downers Grove: IVP Academic, 2011), 194.

3. Samuel Hooke, *The Siege Perilous* (London: SMC Press, 1956), 264.

4. David Benner, *Desiring God's Will* (Downers Grove: InterVarsity, 2005), 43–44.

CHAPTER 21

1. Karl Barth, *Church Dogmatics* IV.3, trans. Geoffrey W. Bromiley and Thomas F. Torrance (New York: T&T Clark, 2004), 253–54. The quote is often attributed in various manners to Martin Luther.

2. Charles H. Spurgeon, "A Vindication of the Doctrine of Justification by Faith," unpublished sermon, Metropolitan Tabernacle, London, England, June 1875.

3. Thomas Chalmers, *The Expulsive Power of a New Affection*, Sermon Chapbook Series (Minneapolis: Curiosmith, 2012), 11–12, 19–20.

4. Calvin, "Galatians," 106.

5. Michael Mangis, *Signature Sins: Taming Our Wayward Hearts* (Downers Grove: InterVarsity, 2008), 15–16.

6. Stott, *The Message to the Galatians*, 157.

CHAPTER 22

1. Robert Farrar Capon, *The Foolishness of Preaching: Proclaiming the Gospel against the Wisdom of the World* (Grand Rapids: Eerdmans, 1988), 32–33.

2. Ibid., 33.

3. Dominic Smart, "Grace, Glory, and Galatians," unpublished sermon, Gilcomston South Church, Aberdeen, Scotland, December 14, 2008.

4. Martin Luther, *A Treatise On Good Works* (Whitefish, Mont.: Kessinger Publishing, 2004), parts X and XI, 18–19.

5. Luther, Reformation Commentary on Scripture, 206.

6. Luther, *LW* 27:113.

7. For more on this concept of "spiritual friendship," see Larry Crabb, Jr., *Becoming a True Spiritual Community: A Profound Vision of What the Church Can Be* (Nashville: Thomas Nelson, 2007).

8. J. B. Lightfoot, *St. Paul's Epistle to the Galatians*, 2d ed. (London: Macmillian: 1866), 212.

9. Dietrich Bonhoeffer, *Life Together: The Classic Exploration of Christian Community*, trans. John W. Doberstein (New York: Harper & Row, 1954), 23.

10. Ibid., 25.

CHAPTER 23

1. Larry Crabb, Jr., *The Pressure's Off: There's a New Way to Live* (Colorado Springs: WaterBrook, 2002), 19.

2. William Perkins, *A Commentary on Galatians*, Pilgrim Classic Commentaries, ed. Gerald T. Sheppard (1617; repr., New York: Pilgrim, 1989), 496.

3. Stott, *The Message to the Galatians*, 168–169.

4. Luther, *LW* 27:126.

5. Richard Baxter, *The Reformed Pastor*, ed. William Brown (1862; repr., Carlisle, Penn.: Banner of Truth, 2001), 117.

6. Ryken, *Galatians*, 26.

7. Eustace Carey, *Memoir of William Carey* (London: Jackson and Walford, 1836), 290.

8. See Vishal and Ruth Mangalwadi, *The Legacy of William Carey, A Model for the Transformation of a Culture* (Wheaton: Crossway, 1999).

CHAPTER 24

1. Mandy Velez, "Heroic Mother Jumps From Burning Building, Saves Her 18-Month-Old's Life," *The Huffington Post*, May 13, 2014.

2. Joshua Moody, "The Gospel of Grace and Peace #32," unpublished sermon, College Church, Wheaton, Ill., December 6, 2009.

3. A. W. Tozer, *The Pursuit of God* (1949; repr., Camp Hill, Penn.: Christian Publications, 1993), 42.

4. Andrew Murray, *Humility: The Beauty of Holiness* (New York: Randolph, 1895), 48–49.

5. Todd Burpo, *Heaven is for Real*, (Nashville: Thomas Nelson, 2010), 74–75.

STUDY GUIDE

1. Matthew Henry, *An Exposition of the Old and New Testament*, vol. 6 (Philadelphia: Haswell, Barrington and Haswell: 1838), 703.

SUBJECT/AUTHOR INDEX

SCRIPTURE INDEX

Old Testament

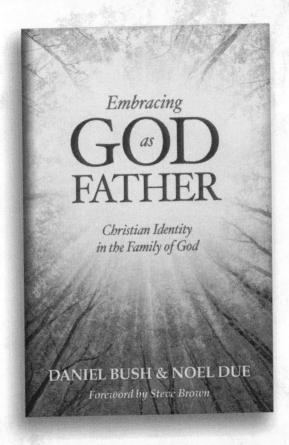